The Traveller's Guide to
Medieval England

The Traveller's Guide to Medieval England

EIGHT TOURS FOR THE WEEKEND
AND THE SHORT BREAK

Colin Platt

SECKER & WARBURG
LONDON

First published in England 1985 by
Martin Secker & Warburg Limited
54 Poland Street, London W1V 3DF

Copyright © Colin Platt 1985

British Library Cataloguing in Publication Data

Platt, Colin
    The traveller's guide to medieval England.
    1. England—Description and travel—1971–
    —Guide-books   2. Historic buildings—
    England—Guide-books
    I. Title
    914.2′04858   DA632

    ISBN 0-436-37559-1
    ISBN 0-436-37560-5 Pbk

Maps by David Charles of The Kirkham Studios

Filmset in 12/13pt Apollo
and printed in Great Britain by
BAS Printers Limited, Over Wallop, Hampshire

Contents

I dedicate this book to my daughter Tabitha
bright and sharp as a spear-point.

List of Illustrations

Preface

The main purpose of this book is very simple. It is to share my pleasure in the surviving buildings of medieval England with anybody who might choose to come along with me. However, I have had a secondary purpose too in blazing a trail back to where we began, to 'the rock whence we were hewn'. England in the Middle Ages was overwhelmingly rural; scarcely five per cent of its population lived in towns. Accordingly, it is in the country that almost all of us will have had our beginnings, and it is to the country that, with reason, we return. In the eight tours of this book, major centres of population (even cathedral cities) have been avoided. Learning to love medieval England will be the easier, I feel, without the hassle and bad temper of the car-park.

Not everybody travels at an identical pace. And why, indeed, should we expect it of them? Each tour has been planned for a break of a few days in which only the active could do everything. But there is just as much profit in taking things slowly, whether by habit or in search of that deeper understanding which a picnic with the guide-book might deliver to us. A simple starring system and suggested itineraries have been provided as a framework for each tour. But far be it from me to dictate your journeys. So much will depend on the weather.

In our climate, of course, there might be a case for reserving every tour for the best months of the summer. Yet this, in my experience, would be unduly defeatist, nor could it guarantee cloudless skies even then. Long shadows and an early dusk, the smell of wood-smoke and a bite in the air – these are the compensations of winter touring and, believe me, such pleasures are very real. Take yourself to East Anglia in the winter months, or west into Herefordshire and the Marches, and you will miss very little. Kent and Somerset are naturals for the summer.

There are just a few tips I should pass on to you. Throughout my travels, the county gazetteers of Nikolaus Pevsner's great series, *The Buildings of England*, have been my constant and irreplaceable companions. Do buy or borrow the relevant volumes if you can. Church guides too, although of uneven quality, are often very useful as reminders of what you have seen, and you should equip yourself in advance with a pocketful of change if you intend to collect them on your tours. Dress up warmly or those churches will be the death of you; and never be without your flask of tea. I have rarely been as cold as in the churches of Suffolk: they lock the chill within them like a sepulchre.

These tours are a beginning; they are not comprehensive; I have not found a place for everything of interest in my notes. What I have aimed to do here has been to pick out the essentials, to sketch in the background, and to leave the savouring of the atmosphere to you. My hope is that I shall have inspired you to travel further.

Glossary

Advowson   The patronage of a church

Aisle   An extension of the church to north or south of nave or chancel, usually separated off behind columns

Alien priory   A religious establishment, not always conventual, owing allegiance to a mother-house outside England

Ambulatory   The walking-place, or aisle, round the east end of a church, behind the high altar

Appropriation   The formal acquisition of the full rights to a church, including control of its revenues

Apse   The semicircular termination of the chancel or sanctuary at its eastern end

Arcade   A run of columns supporting arches

Augustinian   Communities of clerks (also known as Austin or Regular Canons) who, from the late eleventh century, adopted the Rule of St Augustine

Aumbry   A locker or cupboard for the safe-keeping of books and sacramental vessels, usually in the chancel

Austin Friars   Congregations of hermits brought together as an order in 1256 under the Rule of St Augustine

Bailey   The defended outer ward of a castle

Ballflower   A stylised globular ornament of flower petals round a ball, characteristic of the early fourteenth century

Barbican   The outer work before a castle gate

Barrel-roof   A roof or vault of plain semicircular section, also known as a wagon-roof

Bay   A unit or division of a building

Benedictine   The oldest of the orders, being monks who observed the original Rule of St Benedict

Black-letter text   A post-Reformation wall-painted text, favourite subjects being the Lord's Prayer and the Ten Commandments

Blind arcade   The decorative treatment of a wall surface, characteristically Norman, by setting blank arches (hence also 'blank arcade') against it

Boss   A carved projection at the intersection of vaulting ribs

Bridgettine   A double order of nuns with monks as their spiritual advisers, founded by Bridget of Sweden in the mid-fourteenth century and introduced into England by Henry V

Capital   The head of a column, usually decoratively carved

Carmelite   Founded in the mid-twelfth century as the Order of Our Lady of Mount Carmel, and reorganized as friars ('white friars') in the next century

Carthusian   A contemplative order of monks, bound to silence, founded by St Bruno in 1084 but especially popular in the later Middle Ages

Chancel   The eastern part of the church, usually reserved to the clergy

Chantry   The endowment of a priest (also applied to the altar or chapel) to sing masses for the soul of the founder

Chapter-house   The chamber, usually in the east claustral range, set aside for daily meetings of the monastic community to transact business or receive instruction

Chevron   The zig-zag moulding particularly favoured by the Normans

Choir (quire)   The part of the church, fitted with choir-stalls, where the monks met to sing and to pray

Chrysom child   A child shown in effigy wearing the chrism, or baptismal, robe to indicate death in infancy

Cistercian   Reformed Benedictines, established at Cîteaux in 1098 and later greatly expanded by St Bernard

Clerestory   A line of windows above the nave or chancel arcades, helping to light the church interior

Cluniac   Reformed Benedictines of the 'family' of Cluny (founded in 909)

Commandery   An estate-centre of one of the Military Orders, the Templars or Hospitallers (Knights of St John)

Corbel   A projection or bracket, usually provided to carry a beam and frequently heavily carved

Cornice   The decorative moulding used to finish off the top of a wall

Corona   A crown of radiating chapels, projecting from an ambulatory at the east end of a large church

Corrodian   A pensioner maintained by a religious community as a favour to a patron or in return for a gift of land

Coving   The concave moulding supporting a projection such as a rood loft

Crenellate   To supply with an embattled parapet

Crossing   The intersection in a church of nave, transepts, and chancel, quite frequently capped with a tower

Crown-post   The central post linking tie-beam with collar-beam in a crown-post roof

Crypt   A chamber, usually vaulted and built under the east end of a church, intended for burials and for the display of relics

Cure of souls   The spiritual charge of parishioners

Curtain (wall)   An encircling wall pierced by gates and supplied with interval towers

Decorated   The phase of English Gothic between Early English and Perpendicular, confined largely to the first half of the fourteenth century and characterized by the use of ingenious and extravagant ornament

Dog-tooth   A favourite Early English ornament of raised four-cornered stars

Dominican   Friars Preacher, or 'black friars', founded by St Dominic (d. 1221)

Doom   A Last Judgement painting usually sited over the chancel arch

Drum tower   A circular mural tower

Early English   The phase of English Gothic between Transitional and Decorated, covering the thirteenth century and characterized by lancet windows

Easter Sepulchre   A recess, often in the form of a canopied tomb, in the north wall of the chancel, intended to carry a Christ effigy during the celebration of Easter

Encaustic tile   A tile decorated with an inlay pattern of clay of a different colour

Entablature   The upper part of a classical order, over column and capital, including architrave, frieze, and cornice

Fan-vault   A vault built up of inverted semi-cones, joining at the apex and fan-like in effect

Flushwork   Knapped flint and dressed stone used together to create patterns

Foliated   Covered with ornament in the form of leaves

Franciscan   Friars Minor, or 'grey friars', founded by St Francis in 1209 and vowed to corporate poverty

Friars of the Sack   Otherwise known as the Friars of the Penance of Jesus Christ, a short-lived order which had ceased to exist in England by 1320

Frieze   A decorated band at the top of a wall under the cornice

Galilee   An open porch or vestibule, sometimes used as a chapel, sheltering the west door of a church

Garderobe   A privy or lavatory

Gesso   Plaster sometimes used over wood on an effigy

Gilbertine   A double order of nuns and canons, founded in c. 1131 by St Gilbert of Sempringham and the only home-grown English order

Gothic The style of architecture which, from the later twelfth century, succeeded Romanesque in Western Europe, being characterized especially by the pointed arch

Hammer beam A beam projecting from the wall to form a bracket, sometimes repeated in a double hammer beam, supporting arched braces

Hearse A frame holding candles over an effigy

Hood-mould The projecting moulding over a door or window opening, designed to throw off the rain-water

Hospitallers A military order, also known as the Knights of the Hospital of St John of Jerusalem, founded for the protection of pilgrims to the Holy Land

Iconoclast A breaker of images or idols

Interval tower One of a number of towers set along the length of a curtain wall

Jettying The projection of floor joists in a timber building to create an overhang at first-floor level and above

King-post The central post on a tie-beam, supporting the ridge of the roof

Lancet A narrow pointed window without tracery, often used in multiples of two or three (sometime more), and characteristic of the Early English style

Lantern A polygonal turret over a crossing (also seen on towers) used to finish off a vault and to let in light

Laver The monks' wash-place in the cloister, usually next to the refectory door

Lierne vault A ribbed vault further decorated with liernes, or tertiary ribs, linking the bosses and intersections of the main vaulting ribs to create a complex non-structural pattern

Lintel The beam over a door or other opening

Loop An arrow-slit or loophole

Lucarne A dormer window, frequently used as a form of decoration on fourteenth-century spires

Machicolation An opening in the floor of a projecting fighting gallery, for dropping missiles on an enemy below

Minster A large church, frequently originating as the missionary centre and head-church of a region during the Anglo-Saxon Conversion

Misericord The carved projection on the underside of the hinged seat of a choir-stall, designed as an additional seat or support for monks required to stand for long periods at their devotions; also the chamber in a monastery set aside for the eating of meat

Motte A castle mound

Mullion The vertical bar of wood or stone which divides a window into lights

Murder hole   A hole in the vault of an entrance passage through which defenders could fire on those below

Nave   The body of a church, usually separated from the chancel by an arch

Newel stair   A circular stair winding round a central pillar

Norman   The architectural style described on the Continent as Romanesque and characterized by round-headed arches

Oculus   A round window

Oriel   A projecting upper-storey window supported on brackets

Parclose screen   The screen that shuts off a chapel at the end of an aisle and that may continue the line of the rood screen across the body of the church between nave and chancel

Peculiar   An ecclesiastical division enjoying exemption from the ordinary jurisdiction of the bishop

Perpendicular   The English name for the final phase of Gothic, beginning generally in the mid-fourteenth century

Piscina   A basin, often set in the south wall of the chancel under an ornamental canopy, for the priest's ablutions and for the washing of the chalice and paten

Pluralist   The holder simultaneously of two or more benefices

Poppyhead   A carved finial on a bench-end, approximating in shape to a fleur-de-lis

Prebend   The portion of a cathedral endowment set aside for the support of a member of the chapter (a prebendary)

Preceptory   An estate-centre (also known as a 'commandery') of knights of one of the military orders

Premonstratensian   An order of canons (the 'white canons') founded by St Norbert in 1120 and observing the Rule of St Augustine

Presbytery   The eastern end of the chancel in larger churches, beyond the choir

Quatrefoil   Four lobes separated by cusps in a flower-like ornament or opening, usually enclosed in a circle

Rebus   A word-picture made up out of the elements of a name

Refectory (frater)   The common eating-place of the monks

Reliquary   A container for relics

Rere-dorter   The latrine block of a monastic community, built to adjoin the dormitory

Reredos   A carved screen against the wall behind an altar

Respond   The half-pier against a wall which may support an arch at the end of an arcade

Reticulated tracery   A net-like combination of ogee shapes much favoured in the early fourteenth century

Roll moulding   A plain semicircular moulding

Romanesque   The architectural style, particularly developed in the twelfth century and characterized by round-headed arches, which in England is usually known as Norman

Rood beam   The beam (over the rood screen) which carries the rood loft, on which is placed the rood (cross) itself, usually with supporting figures

Sacristy   The chamber in a church set aside for the safe-keeping of plate and other valuables

Sanctuary   The part of the church next to the high altar

Savigniac   An order of monks founded as a colony of hermits in 1105 and merged with the Cistercians in 1147

Screens passage   A passage between the screen at the lower end of the hall and the entrances to kitchen, buttery, and pantry beyond

Sedile, sedilia (pl.)   A seat or seats built into the south wall of the chancel for the use of clergy

Sexpartite vault   A vault of which the ribs divide each bay into six parts

Shell-keep   The tower on a castle mound made by circling the platform with a stone wall

Soffit   The underside of an arch or other architectural element like a lintel

Solar   A private chamber, usually adjoining the lord's end of the hall

Spandrel   The flat surface squaring off an arch in a feature like a door or separating the upper parts of arches in an arcade

Spiritualities   Revenues arising from the spiritual services of a parish priest, including oblations

Squint   An opening cut obliquely through a wall or pier to give a view of the high altar from an aisle or transept

Star vault   A vault in which the ribs are so arranged as to create an effect like a star; also called a stellar vault

Stiff-leaf   The stylized foliage used on capitals of the late twelfth and early thirteenth centuries

String course   A horizontal moulding across a façade

Templars   A military order, also known as the Poor Knights of Christ and the Temple of Solomon, founded in 1118 for the protection of pilgrims and of the Holy Places, and suppressed in 1312

Tester   A canopy and sounding-board over a pulpit

Tie beam   A horizontal beam laid across the full width of a building at the base of the roof frame

Tomb-chest   The stone coffin on which effigies were laid

Transept(s)   The short arm(s) of a cruciform church, adjoining the crossing

Transom   The horizontal bar of a window

Transitional   The phase of English architecture at the end of the twelfth century when the Gothic style had not yet taken full hold and when Norman and Early English motifs might be used together

Trefoil   Three lobes separated by cusps in a flower-like ornament or opening

Tympanum   The space, frequently carrying sculpture, between the lintel of a door and its arch

Undercroft   A ground-floor chamber or basement, often vaulted

Vesica   A pointed oval quite common as a feature of Late Norman and Transitional façades; also used on tympana to enclose Christ or Virgin figures, where it is known as an 'aureole'

Wagon roof   A closely raftered roof of semicircular section, like the canvas and frame of a covered wagon

Wall plate   The horizontal timber laid on a stone wall to carry the frame of a building or its roof

Ward   The court or bailey of a castle

Weeper   A sculptured mourning figure, usually shown hooded

Westwork   The porch, upper chamber, and tower combined at the west end of an Early Romanesque church

Chapter 1

Introduction

Those broken vistas and shattered fragments which are all we can expect to find of medieval England on our tours, need context and direction to make sense. Take Wilfrid's crypt in the minster church at **Ripon**. Chronologically our starting-point, the crypt might seem of little interest – scarcely worth the extra entrance fee to inspect the undistinguished treasury it now houses – were we not to recall the part it played in the earliest missionary movement of the Anglo-Saxon Church. Ripon under Wilfrid was a fortress of Christianity in a godless and hostile land. Wilfrid fought demons with relics, malignant spirits with the holy bones of Christian martyrs. And he built himself a crypt, as his successors would do in other parts of the land and at a later date, to keep this precious armoury secure. One of the more prominent seventh-century saints, certainly well known to Wilfrid, was the evangelist St Cedd, founder in 659 of another Yorkshire monastery at **Lastingham**. Just a few years after settling there, Cedd and many of his monks were carried off by plague; in the ninth century, his monastery succumbed to the Vikings. Yet in 1078, when the Benedictines returned briefly to Lastingham before moving on to found a great monastery at York, the first thing they did was to construct a grand crypt to hold the relics of their earliest saintly abbot. The crypt remains there intact to this day, unspoilt and highly evocative.

Both Wilfrid, archbishop of York, and Cedd, bishop of the East Saxons, were noted pioneers of that most successful of missionizing techniques, the foundation of self-sustaining monastic communities. Over the dark centuries, as a parish system slowly began to shape itself, this was to be how the Conversion proceeded, locally centred on the minster. Ripon, of course, was one of these centres, **Nassington** and **Bibury** were others. Some of the characteristics of this early organization have left a recognizable imprint on our landscape. The unexpected scale of the still imposing church at Bibury must reflect its ascendancy over satellite chapelries (Winson, Barnsley, and Aldsworth), dating back to the period of missionary expansion and long maintained through later centuries in the 'peculiar' of the

1

abbots of Oseney. Immediately to the east, the two little churches of **Eastleach** Turville and Eastleach Martin confront each other charmingly over a brook. How the Eastleaches came to be built so close together may never be fully resolved. However, the most likely explanation is that they preserve the sites of pre-Conquest estate centres, where the boundary (as now) was the intervening stream and where each lord had built a chapel of his own. The many parish churches of an important Anglo-Saxon borough like **Stamford**, much reduced in number since the Reformation and still on the decline, are again witness to such private initiatives. Compare Stamford even now with the ungenerous church provision of a twelfth-century urban foundation like **King's Lynn**. Stamford's churches are those of its Anglo-Saxon landowners: a chapel for each lord and his men. In contrast, Lynn in the twelfth century was the bishop's town, while private churches were going out of favour. The port's highly successful expansion into the Newland north of the Purfleet was recognized only grudgingly by its priests. St Nicholas stands alone as the church of this quarter; despite its great size, it still ranks ecclesiastically as a 'chapel'.

*   *   *

Certainly the most memorable of the Anglo-Saxon churches you will see is **Deerhurst**, in the broad Vale of Gloucester. Deerhurst is not an easy building to unravel, for it underwent many important structural changes, radically altering the internal plan of the church, during the first centuries of its prominence as a monastery. But concentrate on just two of its more striking features – the great ninth-century font with Pagan Celtic ornament of trumpet spirals, and the strange triangular-headed window-openings in the tower – and you may again experience that same alienation the Normans felt in the presence of an earlier culture. '*Rudes et idiotas*' is how one Norman abbot was accustomed to describe the pre-Conquest holders of his office at St Albans. And even the more temperate Archbishop Lanfranc, real architect of the Anglo-Norman church settlement in these first years, was heard to muse one day: 'These Englishmen among whom we are living have set up for themselves certain saints whom they revere. But sometimes when I turn over in my mind their own accounts of whom they were, I cannot help having doubts about the quality of their sanctity.'

Lanfranc, to his credit, kept his misgivings well concealed. And it may be that the Normans, left on their own, would have changed rather little, apart from gratifying their instinct to build large. Eleventh-century England was more sophisticated artistically than Normandy, and there were anyway many good causes, left behind by the invaders in 1066, which required reward and development back at home. Yet Western Europe generally, at just this time, was experiencing significant change. When

1 The crypt at Lastingham, built in the early 1080s to hold the relics of the seventh-century St Cedd

2 The characteristically lofty Anglo-Saxon nave at Deerhurst, with its distinctive triangular-headed openings into the body of the tower, themselves dating to the early ninth century

3 The remains of the west porch, or Galilee, at Fountains Abbey, such porches (often used for burials) being a characteristic feature of early Cistercian architecture

Richard de Clare, in 1090, chose to bring Norman Benedictines from Le Bec-Hellouin to assist himself and his household in their devotions at the new castle at **Clare**, he was already behaving somewhat conservatively. His associates, the Warenne earls of Surrey, had chosen Cluniacs for Lewes and for **Castle Acre** because they thought them more in touch with the contemporary church reform. And even the Cluniacs would soon look old-fashioned.

Once change begins, its pace may become confusing, to contemporaries at least as much as to ourselves. In the monastic church especially, stability was lost in a bewildering galaxy of new orders, some of them taking shape to cope with special problems, others merely competing in austerity. The Benedictines who left Lastingham in 1088 to settle finally at St Mary's Abbey (York), were to be at war with each other scarcely more than a generation later, when their best spirits split off in 1132 to establish **Fountains** and to join the Cistercians, whose passage through York on the way to **Rievaulx** had been the major inspiration of the rift. Rievaulx itself had been set up under the patronage of a great nobleman, Walter l'Espec, whose castle at **Helmsley** lay just a few miles to the south. Yet Walter, in the previous decade and like many of his class, had favoured the Augustinians, maids-of-all-work in the Church, who had settled under his protection at **Kirkham**. There was talk at Kirkham, though it came to nothing, of a change of allegiance to Cîteaux, and both mergers and take-overs of various kinds were certainly not exceptional at this period. The much-travelled monks of **Byland**, settling there only in the 1170s, had been Savigniacs (an off-shoot from King Stephen's important Savigniac foundation at Furness) before the merger of their order with the Cistercians in 1147. On the county border between Sussex and Kent, **Bayham**'s unusual situation reflects the artificial bringing together of two failing Premonstratensian communities, one in each county, neither of which could have survived on its own. **Creake**, in Norfolk, was an Augustinian house, but it had begun life originally as a hospital. Small wonder, then, that poor Margaret de Lacy, 'in her simplicity', should have become so muddled that she assigned her nuns of Aconbury, by mistake it seems, to the Knights of St John of Jerusalem. She had intended them rather to be Augustinian canonesses, which is what they became in the 1230s.

*   *   *

Monastic reform was one major change in the twelfth-century Church; another was the separation of the parish church from its lay owners. The new look in the Church had begun with papal reforms in the 1070s. At issue then had been the independence of the prelacy at a high level, liberating the metropolitans and their bishops from the king. But once that had been achieved in the concordats of the early twelfth century, the same principles could be seen to apply lower down. Throughout Western Europe, and of course in England too, it became increasingly difficult from the mid-twelfth century for a layman to retain an interest in the church his father or his grandfather might have founded. Tithes, as most came to recognize, belonged not to the original builder of a church, but to God and to his agents on this earth.

The great handing-over of the parish churches coincided in most areas with population expansion and with economic growth; its product can be seen everywhere in the West. Notice how many of the parish churches you will visit are twelfth-century buildings. They probably take the place of earlier churches in the same parish, but it was in the twelfth century that the money was found for a rebuilding in stone, nor was it unusual even within the same century for extra aisles to be added to the main structure. One of the most explicit documents relating to such a transfer and rebuilding concerns the church of **Long Sutton**, in the Lincolnshire fens.

4 The classically inspired arcades in the castle hall at Oakham,
dating to the 1180s

By the late twelfth century, these rich reclaimed silt-lands were coming
to support an unusually dense population, affluent and comparatively free.
Long Sutton's new church, to which a fresh site was assigned by the local
landowner in about 1180, was to take the place (it is clearly stated) of
'the earlier wooden church of the same vill'. The need for a new building
very likely arose from overcrowding at an increasingly inadequate predecessor. But the occasion of the reconstruction (very grand as we now see
it) was the transfer of the church and its rights to the Cluniacs of **Castle
Acre**, into whose charge the cure of souls in the parish was now entrusted.
This marriage of interests, religious and economic, was to be repeated all
over the land.

Long Sutton is not a building at the peak of contemporary taste; it could
even have been a little old-fashioned. However, among the characteristics
it shared with other more up-to-date churches of its time were restraint
and deliberate symmetry. This 'classical' control is something you will meet
again most impressively in the contemporary nave and chancel of the parish

church at **Castle Hedingham**, while there is clear Roman inspiration in the capitals at **Oakham**, although under arches enriched with the familiar dog-tooth ornament more at home in the buildings of the North. Much of the work at Oakham Castle's great hall is related in style to the east end of Canterbury Cathedral, as rebuilt by William of Sens; in the tiny rural church at **Kempley**, the fine Byzantine-inspired murals share a common origin with contemporary paintings at Winchester Cathedral. And all seem to point to that comparatively brief period of heightened contact between England and the South which was the consequence of an Angevin imperial dream and of the dynastic alliances of Henry II.

It was during these years arguably, and scarcely at the Conquest at all, that English architecture experienced its revolution. Contrast the cool discipline of the arcades at late-twelfth-century **Seaton** with the exuberant barbarism, only a few decades earlier, of the stone-carvers of **Kilpeck** or of **Tickencote**. Kilpeck was a focus of Norman settlement; it had a castle, a new stone church, and a Benedictine priory cell all sited within calling distance of each other. Yet still in the mid-twelfth century, as much as three generations from the Conquest, the sources of Kilpeck's art, although perhaps touched by pilgrimage, are essentially Scandinavian. Overseas contacts, ecclesiastical reform, the contemporary expansion of population

5 Mid-twelfth-century stone-carving, still showing Scandinavian influence, on the south door at Kilpeck

and of profits on the land and in the towns – these were to be the circumstances for a new sophistication in art which a military adventure alone could not generate. Take the fine decorative precision of the rebuilt choir and presbytery of the abbey church at **Rievaulx**, or the contemporary bell-tower and arcades of the parish church at **West Walton**: both being buildings we would describe as Early English. They have nothing in common with the rude strength of the Norman naves of **Tewkesbury** or **Great Malvern**, although scarcely a century intervenes. And then notice how ineptly the fourteenth-century vault at Tewkesbury marries up with the Norman work below. At Tewkesbury as elsewhere, Romanesque and Gothic are indeed a world apart. Culturally, there had been a coming of age in the West.

* * *

This coming of age was by no means confined to the Church. And its background, of course, was economic. Even before the Conquest, the boroughs had become an important element in Anglo-Saxon society. **Stamford** certainly had come to great prominence, while the little town of **Milborne Port**, as its great church survives to remind us, was never to be as prosperous (relatively) again. But the reduction of Milborne Port, as **Sherborne** grew alongside it, is itself one of the indicators of that great shaking-out of the towns, characteristic of the twelfth century, for which the Normans alone were no more than partly responsible. **Battle** with its market at the abbey gate, and **Clare** and **Richmond** where the same growth occurred next to a castle, are indeed Norman creations directly attributable to the Conquest. However, it would be much harder to say the same for the entrepreneurial foundations of subsequent decades – the abbot of Evesham's new market centre at **Stow-on-the-Wold**, or the bishop of Norwich's Tuesday Market extension of **King's Lynn** – each of which was an independent response to economic opportunity in an era of better profits and higher prices. There is nothing petty or hesitant about the laying-out of a great market square like Stow's or **Swaffham**'s; wide commercial streets such as those of **Burford** or **Chipping Campden** speak volumes about contemporary business optimism. Before the end of the twelfth century, English burgesses everywhere were claiming rights for themselves, in government and the law, which would give them (if secured) effective independence and the recognition they thought appropriate to their wealth. They did not always succeed, and the deterioration of the partnership between the abbot of **Cirencester** and his townspeople is one of the better known stories of that landowner bullying to which the greater monasteries especially were prone. Yet for the majority of the towns, there was to be a period in the twelfth and thirteenth centuries of maximum

6 Elaborate and high-quality Early English work in the choir and presbytery arcades at Rievaulx Abbey, reversing the austerities of earlier Cistercian practice

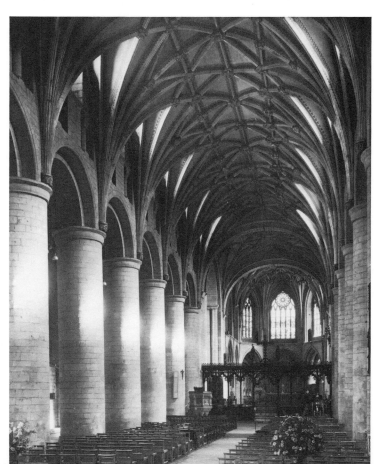

7 Twelfth-century drum columns in the nave at Tewkesbury, supporting a fourteenth-century lierne vault of entirely different character

8 A fifteenth-century timber-framed building on the corner of Lady Street and Water Street, Lavenham, retaining its original shop-front

activity and growth. It was then that almost every town centre you will visit was first shaped.

Like churchmen or like the builders of castles, one of the ways in which England's burgesses could exhibit their wealth might be in the choice of stone instead of timber for their houses. It has been primarily at the greater towns – at Lincoln, at Norwich, and at Southampton especially – that the best examples of such housing have survived, some of them as early as the 1190s. Nevertheless, both **Stamford** and **Rye** preserve thirteenth-century vaulted undercrofts below those choice Georgian town-houses which are now the major ornament of their streets, while Flore's House at **Oakham**, although much tampered with in later years, retains the hall with adjoining chamber blocks typical of the domestic planning of its period. Much the finest of these merchants' houses, and almost intact, is William Grevel's house on the High Street at **Chipping Campden**, grandly placed to take advantage of its long street frontage and handsomely equipped with a two-storeyed bay window to light the principal chambers within. Compare this stone house, dating to the late fourteenth century, with its many fifteenth-century timber-framed equivalents at other prospering cloth towns like **Burford**, **Thaxted**, **Kersey**, and **Lavenham**, and what you will notice is a constantly rising standard of domestic comfort as the austerities of the past were left behind. When Levinus Lemnius, a Zeeland physician, visited England in the sixteenth century, his comments both as tourist and professional man were almost invariably favourable. The English kept their health, he observed, by wholesome living and excellent meat: English roasts, all agreed, were unbeatable. In the English home, what Lemnius remarked was the 'neate cleanlines, the exquisite finenesse, the pleasaunte and delightfull furniture' of his hosts – 'Their chambers and parlours, strawed over with sweete herbes, refreshed me; their nosegayes finely entermingled wyth sundry sortes of fragraunte floures in their bed-chambers and privy roomes, with comfortable smell cheered mee up and entirelye delyghted all my sences.'

*　　*　　*

What had happened in the towns was a development, of course, of what had long been standard practice among the aristocracy. A mid-twelfth-century palace-keep like **Castle Rising**, purpose-built to accommodate a great lord, brings together all the essentials of domestic life, conveniently grouped on one level. It has a hall and great chamber, a chapel and a kitchen, with garderobes in the thickness of the walls. But its arrangements are communal, and its comforts are those of a warehouse unit on an unlettable factory estate. Something like a century and a half would elapse before **Goodrich** was built in the Welsh borderlands. However, in the meantime remarkable changes had taken place. Goodrich's builders, the Valence earls

9 William d'Aubigny's residential keep at Castle Rising, dating probably to the late 1130s and incorporating a spacious residential suite at first-floor level

of Pembroke, were experienced travellers, knowledgeable about the ways of the South. They had spent much time at Court both in England and in France, and the tastes they brought to their new Marcher castle were among the most sophisticated of their time. What you will notice about Goodrich, in particular, is its many separate suites of comfortable private lodgings, each with its garderobe and individual fireplace. Goodrich, which dates to about 1300, already has more in common with castles of chivalry like **Bolton** or **Bodiam** than with an Anglo-Norman fortress like Castle Rising. Its purpose is to accommodate the lord and his retinue in the luxury appropriate to their rank. Privacy had become one of the privileges that money could buy, among its costs being the companionship of the hall.

Nowhere had this hall-centred emphasis on the common life been more emphatic than in the religious houses of the twelfth century and before. Yet here too standards were changing. At many communities, inflated revenues in the thirteenth and early fourteenth centuries had led to massive rebuildings. We can see this plainly enough in the ambitious church of **Abbey Dore**, in **Rievaulx**'s great choir and reconstructed cloister, in the rebuilding of the east ends at **Fountains** and **Bayham**, or of the refectory in early-fourteenth-century **Easby**. Sometimes ambition might soar too high, as in the incomplete remodelling of **Kirkham**. But the inevitable product of all this work, throughout England, was a capital stock of buildings so magnificent as to diminish and overawe those who dwelt there. While recruitment continued brisk, no particular problems arose. When it faltered, as was all too often the case from the time of the Black Death onwards, many communities were to find themselves severely under strain.

There might be nothing especially daunting about an empty church; indeed its resonance, if anything, would improve. But the cold and cavernous halls of half-populated refectories, dormitories, and infirmaries were to be another matter entirely, and it is here that we begin to see changes. **Jervaulx**'s meat kitchen and adjoining misericord are unusually complete survivals of a very typical addition of the fifteenth century, when the stricter dietary regulations of earlier times had been forgotten or were substantially ignored. They lie to the east of the great refectory, used only on feast days and other special occasions, and separate it still from the infirmary complex, where the practice of meat-eating had always been tolerated, although confined to the sick and the old. Another misericord survives at **Fountains**, again next to the infirmary of which it was formerly the reredorter (common lavatory), and a conversion of the fifteenth century. Well before this, and perhaps as far back as the fourteenth century, the partitioning of the infirmary hall itself (unusually large at Fountains) had begun. And this also would have been happening contemporaneously

10 Fine-quality vaulting in the ambulatory at the east end of the church at Abbey Dore, added during the lavish rebuilding programme of the early thirteenth century which completely transformed this originally austere Cistercian house

in the great dormitory in the east range, where wainscotting divided the monks' cubicles.

Related to these alterations were the rebuildings everywhere of cloisters and abbots' lodgings, as glazing was inserted to keep out the cold and as monastic superiors, maintaining great state, took over vacant buildings as their own. The abbot of **Hailes**, for example, was one of those whose conversion of an empty lay brothers' range, west of the cloister, was accompanied by a rebuilding of the cloister arcades. At **Battle**, the abbot's lodgings in the west range were several times extended, to occupy the whole of this quarter of the site. The abbot's great kitchen is the only substantial survival at **Glastonbury** of a fourteenth-century remodelling of his mansion. But at **Muchelney** the abbot's lodgings in the south-west angle of the cloister, and at **Castle Acre** the prior's suite in the west range, are still very much as the last superiors would have left them, with the exception of course of their furnishings. Observe the great comfort of apartments like these. They have fine oriels and handsome fireplaces, window-seats, good detailing on the door-frames, and expensive timber roofs. With wall-paintings and woven hangings, cushions and carved wainscotting, they provided quarters as comfortable as anybody could have expected in the Late Middle Ages, and that most of us would welcome even now.

*   *   *

The prior of Castle Acre was a substantial landowner, drawing the greater part of his revenues from rents. However, his house was known too as a pilgrimage centre, its most precious relic being the arm of St Philip. And its associations with this pious industry had been even greater in the past when it controlled the little priory at Broomholm, near Bacton on the coast, fortunate possessor of a splinter of the True Cross. Fashions change in relics as in everything else, and Broomholm's receipts, having peaked in the thirteenth century, were well down two centuries later. But Broomholm's loss was **Walsingham**'s gain, and the ever strengthening draw of the 'Holy House' there, influential still on the hard-headed Tudors, was one of the more remarkable religious phenomena of the day. Another lastingly popular relic was that 'unctuous gum', the Holy Blood of **Hailes**, experiencing such a boom from the mid-fifteenth century as to encourage the rebuilding of the great cloister. At both houses, as at the 'stations' of each pilgrimage on the way, the marks of public favour remain obvious.

Other contemporary fashions in belief were to have a more general impact on England's late-medieval landscape. The heavy mortalities suffered in the Black Death of 1348–9 were only the first of many such visitations in late-medieval England. Accustomed to sudden death cutting short their span, patrons turned increasingly to thoughts of what might happen in the After-Life, itself more controllable (or so the thinking went) since the Church had refined its doctrine of Purgatory. From the Council of Lyons (1274) as never before, the prayers of the faithful had come to be recognized as particularly efficacious in smoothing the soul's passage through Purgatory. For the first time, both investment and reward were widely understood. The result, at many different levels, was the chantry.

Among those well placed to profit from such beliefs were the religious houses, the abbey church at **Creake** being substantially enlarged before

11 The handsome chimney-piece in the abbot's new lodgings at Muchelney, rebuilt in the early sixteenth century to an altogether higher standard of comfort

the end of the thirteenth century by the addition of the Calthorpes' memorial chapel, adjoining the north aisle of the presbytery. Nor was this the end of the canons' exploitation of the doctrine, for one of the most generous individual gifts Creake ever received was the transfer of lands in 1349, just when the Black Death was afflicting the locality, to maintain 'a canon of the convent to celebrate divine service in the Abbey aforesaid, who shall celebrate each day for the souls of Richard de Redham and Katherine his wife and of all the deceased faithful'. On a much grander scale, the Clare and Despenser rebuilding of the east end of the abbey

12 The presbytery at Tewkesbury, rebuilt on a grand scale in the second quarter of the fourteenth century as a Clare and Despenser tomb-church

church at **Tewkesbury**, another mid-fourteenth-century work, transformed the monks' choir of this important Benedictine house into the most magnificent of family mausolea. But the popularity of the monastic orders was on the slide. A very great man like Thomas de Holand (d. 1400), earl of Kent and duke of Surrey, might still select monks to be the guardians of his soul, much as had once been so generally the practice in the twelfth century. However, Holand's choice in his day was to fall not on any of the greater orders of the twelfth-century reform, but on the austere and isolationist Carthusians. Holand's memorial was the quiet and seclusion of the hermit-monks of **Mount Grace**, monastic less in practice than in name.

Fellow patrons, both then and later, were to turn away from the monks altogether. When **Stoke-by-Clare**, once of Bec, went the way of the other former 'alien' priories in the general suppressions of 1414, what took the place of the Benedictine community was a college of secular priests. Like other contemporary foundations of this kind, the purpose of the new college was to pray for the soul of its founder, Edmund de Mortimer (d. 1425), earl of March and Ulster, and for those of his ancestors and his heirs. Stoke's formal establishment from this time on was to include a dean and six prebendaries, eight vicars, four clerks, and five choristers. On the college's suppression in 1548, as we know from contemporary inventories, the community was richly equipped.

Little survives of Stoke today, and what there is has been muddlingly incorporated in later buildings. However, if you want to obtain some impression of the scale of these establishments, all you need do is contemplate the great chancels – large enough to hold the prebendaries' stalls – at **Sudbury** (St Gregory) or at Lady Botreaux's **North Cadbury**, before going on to inspect what is surely the most magnificent and evocative of all these monuments, the former Yorkist collegiate chantry at **Fotheringhay**. A mere fragment now, for it has lost the spacious choir built there by Edward of York, second duke, before his death in 1415, Fotheringhay's church is nevertheless an impressive building, beautifully sited above the river, where it can be seen for miles around. South of the church are the humps and hollows, yet to be excavated, of the college quadrangle and its associated buildings; away to the east, but on the river still, are the earthworks of a great motte and bailey. This was to be how an ancient and noble family, in the fifteenth century, sought to protect its future, installing a direct line, regardless of cost, to God the Father Almighty.

*   *   *

Lesser men had to settle for less, and the story of lay piety in the Later Middle Ages is of repeated calculations, whether by individuals or by

13 The nave and west tower of the great church of the former Yorkist collegiate chantry at Fotheringhay; the chancel of the church (right) and the collegiate buildings (between the church and the river on the south) were demolished in the sixteenth century

groups, of the price of appropriate intercession. An obvious target for expenditure was the parish church. **Lavenham** and **Long Melford**, **Fairford**, **Chipping Campden**, and **Thirsk** – each of these owes its present form to an exceptionally generous bequest which, if it did not meet the cost of a complete reconstruction, at least primed the pump for such a programme. The inscriptions at Long Melford are unusually full. They allow us to date the separate episodes in the rebuilding, and they urge us repeatedly to pray for the souls of the principal donors and their associates: of the Cloptons and the Dents, the Coupers and the Smiths, the Martyns and the Pies, and all the 'weel disposyd men of this town'.

In many cases, although not in all, these parish church rebuildings were confined to the areas of the parishioners' responsibility – the nave and its aisles, the north and south porches, and the west tower. In **Cirencester**, with its long history of disputes between the abbot (as rector) and his parishioners, the chancel is notably meagre, as it is again at **Northleach** (an appropriated rectory of the abbot of Gloucester) and **Martock** (of the

14 The parish church at Lavenham, rebuilt in all but the chancel during the late fifteenth and early sixteenth centuries on the profits of the East Anglian cloth trade

Treasurer of Wells). An exception was **Swaffham**, where it was the rector himself who led the reconstruction, keeping a record in what has come to be known as the 'Black Book'. John Botright, rector of Swaffham from 1435 to 1474, was a pluralist in the accepted tradition of the late-medieval Church. With other important interests away from the parish, he would have recognized no obligation to be resident there. Yet his notes of Swaffham's donors are impressively full, and they were continued following his death. Botright's associates in the rebuilding included John Chapman, the so-called 'Pedlar of Swaffham', with Catherine his wife, contributors of the north aisle and of a substantial donation towards the west tower; also the Coos, William and Anne, who 'did make the Roffe of the porche', the Payns, John and Catherine, who 'made the little chapel of Corpus Christi and the feretory [shrine] in the same chapel', the Blakes, generous donors to a number of causes including the 'fyndyng of a free mason to the makyng of the Chirche by the space of a yere', and the Langmans, contributors of nave benches. These and many more were to receive their reward in a special recitation of 'the Office of the Dead for the Benefactors of the Church of Swaffham' every Whitsunday in perpetuity. 'It should be noted,' says the Black Book in a later hand, 'that when these prayers are said for the soul of "thy priest", it means for the soul of Mr John Botright, doctor of divinity and rector of this church, who lies buried before the image of St Peter.' He lies there still in the robes of his doctorate, with a demon crushed at his feet. Against the tomb-chest, two of the four shields make characteristically learned play with a rebus of the two elements of his name: three boats for the first, three augers for the second, the latter being the tools of a shipwright.

Included in Botright's Black Book was an inventory of church goods – of books, plate and vestments – taken in 1454. In previous years and under other direction, Swaffham's furnishings had been allowed to deteriorate. Yet they were abundant again by the mid-fifteenth century, and would continue to accumulate until the Reformation brought its own form of spring-cleaning to the parish churches. Some of these goods were deliberate acquisitions, purchased by the churchwardens as replacements. However, most had come to Swaffham as memorial bequests and many bore inscriptions to record their source, urging prayers on the pious *in memoriam*. The Swaffham Pedlar bench-ends, now re-used in clergy stalls, remind us still of John Chapman (humping his pack) and his dog. At **Great Walsingham**, donor initials are carved on the shields borne by angels on the bench-ends of the south aisle; the font at **Walpole St Peter** has a memorial inscription, and so do the brass eagle lecterns at **Oxborough** and at **Wiggenhall St Mary**.

The richer the gift and the more impressive the sacrifice, the higher inevitably would be the reward. Look now at the fine timber roofs – each one a costly masterpiece – at **Woolpit** and **Needham Market**, at **Martock**, **Somerton**, and **Weston Zoyland**; at the beautiful screens, both parclose and rood (with a full set at **Long Sutton**), at **Lavenham** and **Fairford**, at **Thirsk** and **Curry Rivel**, at **South Creake**, **Castle Acre**, and **Walsoken**. All these are late-medieval additions to their churches, and they belong to a period of parishioner investment for which there had been few earlier precedents. One intimation of a Protestant future was the increasing emphasis now coming to be placed on the sermon. Where wall-benches had sufficed (we can see them still at the first Norman church at **Castle Rising**) or seats round the piers as at **Snettisham**, full complements of pews were beginning to be fitted, to survive in such lovely sets as those of **Hessett** and **Isle Abbots**, **Trent** and **North Cadbury**, **Great Walsingham** and **Wiggenhall St Mary**. Pulpits too, although rare as permanent fixtures before the fifteenth century, grew increasingly common and more grand. Compare the delicious little late-fourteenth-century pulpit, north of the chancel arch at **Stanton**, with the great stone pulpit in the

15 The early-sixteenth-century nave roof at Martock: one of the grandest in Somerset

parish church at **Cirencester** or its even grander timber equivalent at **Fotheringhay**. Both are of the fifteenth century, as is the more modest but still expensive pulpit at **Castle Acre**, its panels painted appropriately with the Four Latin Doctors: Ambrose and Augustine, Jerome and Gregory, the most respected theologians of the early Church. Castle Acre's other contemporary church furnishings included fine screens and a telescoping font cover which is one of the best of its kind – all these within a building almost entirely re-shaped in the fifteenth century. While the castle here slept and the priory dozed, the parish church awoke to a flowering it shared with its companions in many parts of England.

*   *   *

Most particularly, this flowering took effect in the regions associated with the cloth trade – in the West Country, the Cotswolds, and East Anglia, and in smaller pockets like **Cranbrook** and its locality in West Kent. English cloth, both at home and abroad, enjoyed a high vogue in the Late Middle Ages. For a century and more, English cloth- and wool-merchants could sell as much as they might reasonably produce. Consider the confident swagger of those memorial brasses at **Stamford** or at **Northleach**, where wealthy civilians (accompanied by their fashionable wives) have their feet firmly planted on the wool-packs that had given them their riches. The Brownes of Stamford, the Forteys of Northleach, the Springs of **Lavenham**: these were the men of late-medieval England who could best afford to invest their surplus wealth in parish church rebuildings, and whose prosperity rubbed off on others in their vicinity like the fortunate cutlers of **Thaxted**. However, to attribute such rebuildings to excessive riches alone would be to miss a good deal of their point. Of course it is true that the woolmen, buttressed by their wealth, built with more ambition and panache than many others. Great churches like **Clare** and **Woolpit**, **Fairford** and **Chipping Campden**, **Martock** and **Weston Zoyland** are their memorial. Nevertheless, they were far from alone in late-medieval England in the overwhelming concern they continued to exhibit for the health of their souls after death. Indeed, it is contemporary practice in the purchase of atonement, much more than wealth, that explains the reconstruction of the English parish churches, never limited to areas of prosperity.

The fashions in religious belief so influential at our churches had an equivalent in chivalry and the castle. If heraldry mattered in Anglo-Norman England, it found little architectural expression. Yet from the mid-thirteenth century we begin to discover it everywhere – in the wall paintings and the floor-tiles at **Hailes** before 1300, in the frescoes of the lord's chamber at **Longthorpe Tower** early in the fourteenth century, at **Kirkham** on the priory gatehouse at much the same period, at **Tewkesbury** in the fine glass and monuments of a slightly later Despenser rebuilding. Then **Bodiam**, in the 1380s, would be fashionably got up with Knollys and Dalyngrigge escutcheons over each of the main entrances of the fortress. In the next generation, **Herstmonceux**'s prominent heraldic panel, the Fiennes arms proudly displayed, was one of many contemporary adaptations of a practice of high chivalry most developed at the castle-palaces of Louis d'Orléans at Pierrefonds and La Ferté-Milon.

Bodiam and Herstmonceux are picture-book castles, and what we must appreciate is that it was exactly this effect which was sought by the builders of the day. The same taste for display may be recognized again in the aggressive French-style machicolations of the fortalices at **Nunney** and at **Scotney**. Yet formidable though every one of these castles may

16 The great entrance tower, with heraldic panel over the gate, of Sir Roger Fiennes's castle at Herstmonceux, built in the 1440s

appear on first sight, only Bodiam had the makings of an effective fortress, and even that was an old soldier's toy. Most important to their builders – to Sir Edward Dalyngrigge at Bodiam, Sir Roger Fiennes at Herstmonceux, Roger Ashburnham at Scotney, and Sir John de la Mare at Nunney – was the opportunity the new castle immediately afforded them for an exhibition of great wealth and for the practice of conspicuous waste. Keeping the required chivalric life-style in late-medieval Europe would be governed by considerations like these, and a man might beggar himself to achieve it. In the North, Baron Scrope's **Bolton** may be superficially grimmer and more obviously purposeful than the others. However, Bolton too, like Bodiam, its precise contemporary, was the pride and joy of an old campaigner's heart, not unmindful of the comforts age had earned. Bolton's

17 French-style machicolations and water defences at Roger Ashburnham's late-fourteenth-century castle at Scotney

furnishings, some of the more valuable of which are listed in Scrope's will, were lavish even by the already generous standards of his class. Moreover, they equipped a building designed not merely to house the former Treasurer and his immediate family but to accommodate his considerable entourage. It was Richard, first Baron Scrope of Bolton (d. 1403), whose extreme sensitivity about the arms he bore engaged him in a dispute with Sir Robert Grosvenor which was to become one of the major *causes célèbres* of late-fourteenth-century heraldry. Getting and keeping the state he deserved was to trouble Scrope the rest of his life.

*　　*　　*

Personal wealth, we can now be sure, was not the only determinant of building preferences in late-medieval England, nor was it invariably the most important. Influential everywhere was the very understandable desire, increasing over the years, for individual privacy – for the facilities to pursue devotions and to consort with the family away from the turbulent crowd. We can see this obviously in a castle like Bolton, yet the same impulses are there in the desire of the monks to rid themselves of the disturbance of a lay congregation, even at the heavy cost of building another (and separate) church, as at **Winchcombe**, at **Sherborne**, or at **Muchelney**.

Still more crucial to the Church was the refined doctrine of Purgatory and its promise of redemption through good works. No greater encouragement to practical piety has existed in England either before or after the Late Middle Ages. With few exceptions, our parish churches throughout the country were transformed by it.

Then, as always in England, there was class. The Nevilles of the Northern Marches had climbed high already and were still on the ascent when Ralph Neville (d. 1425), first earl of Westmorland, built the family another castle at **Sheriff Hutton**. He made it lofty and imposing, with four great angle-towers, an appropriate vehicle for the dignity of his line. As at Bolton and Bodiam, Nunney, Scotney and Herstmonceux, quite as important as the defensive capability of Sheriff Hutton was the first impression it created on the beholder. Castle-builders of the late fourteenth and the fifteenth centuries commonly made use of the very latest defensive gimmickry from France; they built high to be noticed, filling their moats with the clear water which, then as now, reflected and exaggerated their investment. By utilitarian standards, these were not sensible buildings. In England, away from the coast, there was not much to be feared from an aggressive intruder. Machicolated towers and gatehouses were just another expression of that extravagant lifestyle that was costing the aristocracy so dear. But who at any period has ever determined his expenditure according only to what he could afford? Ralph Boteler, a former Treasurer of England and war captain, poured money into **Sudeley** in turbulent times, and then lost it all before his death in circumstances still imperfectly understood. As an investment, Sudeley was misconceived; as a memorial, it still works its charm.

Investment and memorial were to be united more successfully at **Oxborough**, in remote rural Norfolk. There have been Bedingfelds at Oxborough since the not untypical (for its period) merging of two landed interests when Margaret Tuddenham, widow of Edmund Bedingfeld, inherited the estate from her brother, Thomas, on his execution in 1461 for treason. Margaret's grandson, another Edmund, made a fortune in war-service for the Yorkist Edward IV, and then kept it (unlike Boteler) when the parties changed, after the triumph of Henry Tudor at Bosworth (1485). In the meantime, from 1482, he had begun the building of a fashionable new mansion at Oxburgh Hall, adjoining the parish church of which his second son, Robert, was to be rector for three decades and which was to be made into the tomb-church of their line. No family in residence for as long as the Bedingfelds can be blamed for tampering with and modernizing its home, and there is little of Oxburgh, as we see it now, that goes back to its original builder. Nevertheless, the conception is Sir Edmund's – the moat is his, and so is the great entrance tower – and Oxburgh still ranks today as one of the finer examples of what a wealthy country gentleman, of more than local interests, might consider appropriate to his standing at the end of the Middle Ages, just before the social revolution of the Tudors.

Oxburgh Hall, of which it is not too difficult to reconstruct the medieval domestic arrangements, was a comfortable house: well lit, well heated, and ambitiously built of a material (brick) which, although used before at great houses like Herstmonceux, was still on its way into fashion. It was also one of the final monuments of chivalry. In the middle of its show-front, facing the road, an impressive entrance tower, turreted and boldly crenellated, with the now obligatory gun-ports towards ground level, is decorated overall with vestigial machicolations, a triumph of the brickworker's craft. Behind this pseudo-military display, the courtyard mansion of traditional plan preserved the great hall (since demolished) of Oxburgh's feudal past, even then an anachronistic survival which country-houses generally would take another full century to shed. Luxurious and lordly, Oxburgh Hall was associated with that third driving force in contemporary patronage, the parish church seen as memorial. Immediately south of the chancel at Oxborough Church, the Bedingfelds built themselves a chapel which, from the early sixteenth century, would serve and commemorate their clan. Never reluctant to experiment with the latest materials, they chose terracotta for two of their most impressive family monuments, in keeping with one of the shorter-lived fashions of the English Renaissance when (briefly) all influences from the Continent were acceptable. On each of these monuments, a capricious pot-pourri of Renaissance motifs exhibits the continuing determination of this Norfolk gentry family not to be left behind by the times.

*   *   *

Architecturally *à la mode*, the Bedingfelds became partners in religion with the dinosaurs. When every man of ambition in Tudor and Stuart England was scrambling for a place among the Protestants, the Bedingfelds adhered to the Old Faith. They paid for it in the comparative poverty which then kept Sir Edmund's mansion substantially unharmed until the antiquarians could take a hand in its preservation. Others, of course, paid more dearly, and the landscape of England remains a graveyard today of the greatest period of English monasticism.

The collapse of the monasteries had begun much earlier. It had been foreshadowed in Henry V's suppression of such alien houses as **Stoke-by-Clare** (a dependency of Le Bec-Hellouin) and **Newent** (of the Benedictines of Cormeilles). Stoke had been re-founded immediately as a nobleman's collegiate chantry; Newent went a similar way in the endowment of the new Yorkist college at **Fotheringhay**. Steadily, during the fifteenth century and through the first three decades of the next, this re-direction of Church resources gathered pace. At first the wealthier houses were safe enough, and it was the smaller communities, in particular the already weak and under-populated Augustinian foundations, that went down: **Kersey** in favour of King's College, Cambridge (1443), **Creake** towards the endowment of Christ's College in the same university (1506/7), being one of the works of piety of Margaret Beaufort. But as whispers of the Reformation began to penetrate England, the monks found themselves with few sympathizers. Those who had objected to Cardinal Wolsey's suppression of the comparatively prosperous Premonstratensian community at **Bayham** in 1525 were easily put down. In all, Wolsey suppressed no fewer than thirty houses for the support of his collegiate foundations. He blazed the trail which the king and Thomas Cromwell were glad to follow.

Michelham Priory was just one of those houses which Cromwell marked out as his own; it fell among the first in 1536. Contemporaneously, many were to use position at court or local knowledge to lay a finger on the best of the spoils. In August 1539, Henry VIII granted **Battle Abbey**, its site and buildings, to Sir Anthony Browne, master of the king's horse. Just a few months later, Jack Horner, lately steward of **Glastonbury Abbey**, pulled out the plum of **Doulting**. At Battle, Sir Anthony was to keep the abbot's lodgings for his own, afterwards rebuilding the guest-house for his ward, the young Princess Elizabeth. Jack Horner had the great abbey barn at Doulting on his property: it stands there majestically to this day.

Generally, what was potentially valuable to the post-Dissolution owner and his tenants was kept. The rest, usually the church first and then the east claustral range, was deliberately demolished rather than let fall to ruin, thus destroying the nest, as one owner put it, 'for fear the Birds should build therein again'. Of course, the superior's lodgings, so frequently rebuilt in the Later Middle Ages, survived better than most: at **Clare** and at **Tewkesbury**, at **Sherborne** and **Battle**, **Michelham** and **Castle Acre** among others. **Muchelney**'s former abbot's lodgings, after long duty as a farmhouse, have only recently been restored to something approaching the condition in which their builder, Abbot Broke (d. 1522) would have left them. However, there were occasions too when a monastic church, despite its great scale, could still serve the needs of a lay community. A number of our finest cathedrals have survived in this way, as the king and his advisers, after the Dissolution, reorganized the Anglican episco-

18 Glastonbury Abbey's barn at Doulting: one of Jack Horner's plums at the Dissolution

pacy. More haphazard was the preservation of such fine monuments as **Tewkesbury**, **Sherborne**, and **Great Malvern**, each of them now an exceptionally grand church, out of scale with the congregations of today. The nave of Tewkesbury had served as the parish church; after the Dissolution, the townsmen bought the choir as well, moving up to where, amongst the tombs of the Despensers, they could carry on their Protestant devotions. At Sherborne and Great Malvern, the purchase of the monastic churches, from which the townspeople had been excluded, was clearly seen as an investment, remedying an old grievance at Sherborne (where the exclusion had been especially resented) and side-stepping a pressing need for repairs to Great Malvern's parish church (so derelict as to be ripe for demolition). The bargain in each case was a happy one. Both at Sherborne and Great Malvern, great rebuilding programmes on the churches had only just been completed when Henry VIII's commissioners dismissed the communities. If the parishioners had purchased a church that was too big for them, they had nevertheless got one that was new.

*   *   *

Prominent in the former choir of Great Malvern, south of the high altar and just to the east of the monks' stalls, is the tomb of John Knotsford (d. 1589), himself one of the principal despoilers of the priory. It is a magnificent monument, Renaissance in some respects but traditional also, revealing that hesitation between the old and the new so characteristic of the England of Elizabeth. Look at other tombs of the period and you will recognize the same thing – in the Bellasis monument (1603) to the demolisher of Newburgh Priory, now in the parish church at **Coxwold**, in the old-fashioned Colt (1570) and Kervil (1625) monuments at **Cavendish** and **Wiggenhall St Mary**, and even in the more firmly classical tombs at **Whaplode** and **Chipping Campden** of Sir Anthony Irby (d. 1610) and Sir Baptist Hicks (d. 1629) respectively. Certainly the grandest of these memorials is the great Burghley monument at St Martin's, **Stamford** Baron, to Sir William Cecil (d. 1598), Treasurer of England. Cecil's long service at Court had brought him into contact, since as far back as the mid-century, with every man of consequence in the arts. His monument, like Burghley House itself, is a fine confection of Renaissance motifs, put together (as one might expect) with more sympathy and good taste than was usual in such exercises at that period. Nevertheless, the Treasurer's effigy, in the plate armour of high chivalry, remains entirely medieval. North of the tomb, the Burghley Chapel carries on the old tradition of the family chantry, while down the road next to the bridge are the Burghley Alms-houses, re-founded by Cecil just before his death in a final gesture of self-commemorative piety.

Cecil's conservatism was widely shared. Take the entrance tower of Sir Richard Baker's courtyard mansion at **Sissinghurst**, dating to the 1560s or later: it has all the panoply of a late-medieval gatehouse without the defensive capability that had justified it. Or consider the anachronistic survival of the great hall at **Kirby**, traditionally placed at the south-west angle of a court which, with its Mediterranean open loggia and giant pilaster ornament, is aggressively Renaissance in its taste. Burghley House had its great hall also, and even **Montacute**, built in the very last years of the century, kept a vestigial hall (complete with screens passage) compressed behind the symmetry of its show-front. Of course, all these buildings looked forward too, and the future belonged clearly to the innovators. Way back in pre-Reformation times, the visual word-play of the rebus – John Cammell's at **Glastonbury** (St John Baptist), Abbot Ramsam's at

19 The very un-military entrance tower of Sir Richard Baker's late-sixteenth-century courtyard mansion (now almost totally demolished) at Sissinghurst

Sherborne, Abbot Thornton's on his grave slab at **Middleham** – had suggested something of that delight in verbal and decorative ingenuity that would flower fully in late Tudor England. By the time we get to Montacute almost everything is a conceit, sometimes handled a little heavily (as in the statues of the Nine Worthies in their Roman attire) but nevertheless ingenious and allusive, like the dinner-table conversation of over-educated literary men. Montacute's gardens and its gallery are the perfect setting for a parade of fashion; they provoke the wit and inspire the raconteur. This indeed is a new world of leisure and security, even if its roots were planted firmly in the old.

20 The show-front of Montacute: an architectural exercise of very special charm in the English Renaissance manner, complete with statues of the Nine Worthies as Ancient Romans

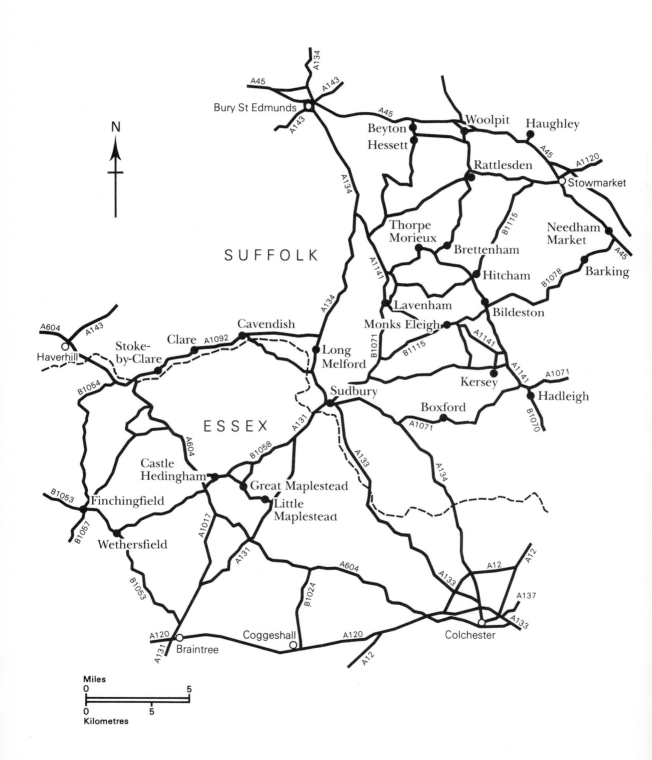

Chapter 2

South-West Suffolk and North Essex

This pleasant late-medieval landscape of handsome churches, of picture-postcard villages, and of pretty but stunted little towns, is the East Anglia we have come to expect. Certainly, these are the characteristics we are sure to remember, and rightly so. But every landscape has its earlier layers that contribute to an explanation of the later. We may usefully unpeel some of them on the way.

Nobody, for example, would visit this region for its castles. It is not by a sea-coast; it is nowhere near a border; these are not Marcher lands. Yet it is at **Castle Hedingham** that we recognize what is probably the finest of all twelfth-century stone keeps, while at **Clare** the earthworks of a great motte and bailey, not very much earlier in date, are both acces-

21 The fine Anglo-Norman keep at Castle Hedingham, dating to the second quarter of the twelfth century and one of the best of its kind

sible and splendidly preserved. Stand on the summit of Clare motte, too, and you will see laid out below you, barely altered by time, a model medieval town plan. To the north of the castle and in its shadow, is the great market square. It has been 'colonized' since the sixteenth century by permanent shops, but its outline is still recognizable. To the north again, in its traditional location, is the parish church, with a short extension of the main street beyond. To the south, tucked under the castle's protection but on the side away from the town, is the thirteenth-century Austin priory, to which the friars have lately returned. Contrast this cluster, evidence of insecurity when the king's law ran but lightly in the land, with the confident commercial straggle of a **Hadleigh** or a **Long Melford**, where it was the shop-keeper's interest in a viable road frontage that principally determined the plan. Ribbon developments are not now considered attractive; we avoid them where we can. In the Middle Ages, though, they spoke of law and order, only recently and most arduously achieved.

Much of the essential crystallization of the English law occurred in Henry II's reign (1154–89) and in those of his sons Richard (d. 1199) and John (d. 1216). Property rights, formally acknowledged, were to be protected henceforth by the king. Meanwhile other interests, including political and trading links overseas, were promoted by Angevin ambitions. Externally, the fine parish church at **Castle Hedingham** is typically late-medieval, one of many such buildings throughout the region. Yet only look inside and a different world unfolds, where the king of England, Henry II, was also (and more vitally) duke of Normandy and count of Anjou, where one of his daughters (Matilda) married the duke of Saxony, another (Eleanor) became queen of Castile, and a third (Joan) was the wife successively of William II, king of Sicily, and of Raymond, count of Toulouse. Aubrey de Vere (d. 1194), first earl of Oxford and lord of Hedingham, was a man very much of this circle. He had fought on Matilda's side in the recent civil wars against Stephen, and he had been richly rewarded for his loyalty to the Angevin interest. Perhaps inevitably, his own parish church, when rebuilt on a lavish scale in the late twelfth century, came to display all the sophistication familiar to the international aristocracy of Henry's court, especially visible in the typically 'classical' flavour of its beautifully proportioned arcades. This style, not repeated again by English architects and masons before its very different re-emergence at the Renaissance, owed much to the king's interests in the South. The interests failed and the style was short-lived. But we can see another reason for its disappearance in the profile of the chancel arch at Hedingham, decorated with the zigzag work of Norman England, yet pointed where all the other arches are round. Only recently imported from its breeding-ground in France, Gothic had come to stay.

Just a few miles to the south-east, and well worth the diversion from

22 The former Hospitaller church at Little Maplestead, retaining its original (much restored) fourteenth-century circular nave

the main road, is a further reminder of the larger world system into which the English aristocracy had been drawn. **Little Maplestead**, despite a heavy-handed restoration in the last century, is still identifiably the former estate chapel of a commandery of the knights of St John. These knights, also known as the Hospitallers, had been organized as a military order for the protection of pilgrims to the Holy Land. After the First Crusade, as the Latin kingdom of Jerusalem had continued to hold its own against Islam, the Hospitallers had prospered, building up an endowment of lands all over Europe which included their Little Maplestead estates. It was common Hospitaller practice, as it was with the Templars, to model their chapels on the circular church of the Holy Sepulchre at Jerusalem, and it is this that explains the unusual plan (a hexagon within a circle) of the main body of Little Maplestead's parish church.

You will not find, in the churches of this region, much of the date of Castle Hedingham. So extensive were the late-medieval rebuildings that even work of the early fourteenth century (as at Little Maplestead) is comparatively rare. But the cloth trade, usually the explanation of these rebuildings, was already prospering in Suffolk before the Black Death

23 A view of the southern end of the village street at Kersey, one of the centres of the late-medieval cloth-making industry, especially prosperous in the fifteenth century

24 The late-medieval panelled roof of the south porch at Kersey: a wood-carver's *tour de force* only possible in a region of high prosperity

(1349). And at **Kersey**, one of its centres, the handsome north aisle of the weavers' great church must actually have been in the very course of construction when the plague carried off the skilled masons. The aisle arcade is unfinished, and so in some details is the fine set of piscina and sedilia which is the ornament still of the north chapel. In due course, work would be resumed at Kersey. However, the objectives of the later builders were to prove very different, and the church remains curiously lopsided.

With Kersey's second-stage rebuilding – and indeed somewhat before it – we enter the period for which the region is chiefly remembered. The Black Death itself, with its many successor epidemics, had focused men's minds on mortality. Surplus wealth found a natural outlet in the protection of souls. To this end, a wealthy individual might endow a chantry, or even (if he were rich enough) a commemorative college; collectively, well-off craftsmen banded together to organize parochial gilds, again chiefly with a memorial purpose. Both institutions, familiar throughout England, are well represented in our area. Chancels (the responsibility of the rector) were not usually rebuilt on any great scale during the later Middle Ages – rectors had other financial worries to preoccupy them. Yet **Cavendish** and **Sudbury** (St Gregory) were each to be supplied with a fine new east end before 1400, the former as the chantry chapel and last place of rest of Sir John Cavendish, chief justice of the king's bench, the latter as the choir and presbytery of Archbishop Sudbury's memorial college, established where his family home had once been. In much the same way and with the same object, **Lavenham Church** was to owe its rebuilding to the generosity of Thomas Spring III, one of the wealthiest clothiers of his day; **Long Melford**, in its present form, is the church very largely of the Cloptons. At **Thaxted**, it was the Gild of Cutlers (responsible also for the fine fifteenth-century gildhall in the town) who assisted in the rebuilding of the parish church; at **Finchingfield**, the Holy Trinity Gild; at **Boxford**, the Gild of St John Baptist; at **Woolpit**, the Trinity Gild and the Gild of the Nativity of the Blessed Virgin Mary.

Large churches grew quickly in these circumstances, for a spirit of competition was abroad. **Hadleigh** had not long been established as a market town when the cloth trade gave it an opening. Soon it had become an important regional centre of the industry, with only Ipswich and Bury St Edmunds as its rivals. Its great church, surrounded by a churchyard so generous as to be almost a close, is among the more spacious in East Anglia. Immediately to the south, Hadleigh's five parochial gilds built their gildhall. It is still in place, forming one of a remarkable group which, with the church itself, includes as its third element the proud gate-tower of Archdeacon William Pykenham's once palatial rectory, boldly embattled in the manner of the day.

Scarcely less grand among the greater urban churches was **Clare**, where the burgesses' rebuilding of an already handsome nave could perhaps be seen as a gesture of independence from the yoke of the castellans, long the dominant element in their parish. Certainly, when the men of **Woolpit** joined together in a lavish contemporary reconstruction of their church, they cannot have been unaware that their magnificent nave would entirely out-class the adjoining chancel, for which the abbot of Bury was responsible. At Woolpit, a fine double hammer-beam roof is the most remarkable feature of the new building; expensively enriched with elaborate carving, it appears to have been commissioned with little regard to the cost. But consider also, at a church of this standing, the resort of what was never more than a village, the decorative elaboration of the great south porch, the grand clerestory, the carved bench-ends, and the intricate work on the screen. Some part of this extravagance may well have been owed to the gifts of pilgrims, rewarding the church for a favour granted by its miracle-working image of Our Lady. Yet the rebuilding of Woolpit, as we know very well from frequent clauses in its parishioners' wills, was a cause both heavy on the consciences and dear to the hearts of the community. No pilgrim, we may guess, would have gone readily to **Needham Market**; it is difficult to make time for this featureless little town even today. Nevertheless, it is at Needham Market that one of Suffolk's least distinguished churches conceals within it the most splendid of all East Anglian timber roofs. Here again the community, not the rector, would have paid.

It is the skill and ambition of the East Anglian joiner that combine to make this corner of England most memorable. At Needham Market, a true master of his craft built himself a church all over again in the air. Elsewhere, contemporary joiners almost equal in skill were creating a tradition of vernacular architecture that would persist little changed well into the seventeenth century. Even now, as much as five hundred years later, many of the houses they built are still in occupation — indeed, remain greatly in demand. Moreover, these buildings' long life has at least as much to do with their comfort and convenience as with the picturesque qualities we applaud. Go to the market-place at **Lavenham** today and the first building you will notice is the proud gildhall of the Corpus Christi Gild, a pious association and mutual benefit society to which the town's wealthier clothiers all belonged. Yet almost next to it also is a comparatively modest town house of fifteenth-century date, as representative as one could wish of the better-quality housing which the Lavenham burgess of some substance and standing could reasonably afford by this period. It makes a comfortable home, with a hall in the middle (open to the rafters) and with chamber blocks — one of later build — at each end. Lavenham's 'Little House', as it is now rather misleadingly called, is set sideways to the street, making extravagant use of what must always have been a valuable market frontage. And if we want to appreciate the more usual practice of the late-

25 The astounding fifteenth-century roof – a church again in the air – at the otherwise unremarkable parish church of Needham Market

medieval craftsman-shopkeeper in the region, we would do better perhaps to go to **Thaxted**, where three terraced houses, planned vertically rather than horizontally, front on the lane to the church, behind the gildhall. Characteristically, the top two storeys of these houses are jettied forward over the lane, making spacious upper chambers in finely crafted timber structures which actually gain in rigidity by this device. They exemplify that combination of prosperity and skill which is the hallmark of late-medieval East Anglia.

*Barking   This interesting church is set at the east end of the village, north of (and above) the main road. Next to it, the handsome early-nineteenth-century rectory, with its grand Tuscan columns, will evoke a response among readers of Jane Austen, and both church and churchyard are exceptionally prettily sited. But the isolation of the church has caused it to be kept locked, and this may deter the hurried visitor. For those who persevere and who obtain the key, the rewards include a good-quality late-fifteenth-century font cover, original timber roofs of some distinction, and a particularly fine set of screens (both parclose and rood). An unusual feature of the church is the use of terracotta detail in one of the north windows, being a short-lived fashion of the 1530s and 1540s as England dragged itself, with the help of Italian craftsmen, into its long-delayed Renaissance.

Beyton   The church at Beyton lies next to the road which runs north from Hesset to link with the A45 (Bury–Stowmarket). Much of the present building is Victorian. However, the circular west tower is of some interest, being unusual in this part of the county. Towers of this plan are very much more common in the north-eastern estuarine quarter of Suffolk. Some of them, certainly, are Anglo-Saxon in origin, and they have been thought to have been associated with the defence of East Anglia against Viking raids on the coast. Beyton's tower is probably Norman rather than Anglo-Saxon, both the buttresses and the large west window being late-medieval additions. Pause but do not stop for long; there is little to be gained by going inside.

**Bildeston   The pleasant village, with its many fine timber-framed houses, is separated from its church by a stretch of open country to the west. On the hill and in isolation, the church achieves a particular calm, now its principal virtue. It is a large building, made more impressive internally by the lack of division between chancel and nave. Notice especially the good south doorway, with its heraldic decoration (a characteristic fifteenth-century touch) and fine surviving woodwork. The roofs are original throughout, but look bare without the angels. Handsome but rather featureless, it is the setting of this church and its relationship to the village that claim our attention. Prominent hilltop sites were frequently favoured by Suffolk church-builders, even at the expense (as here) of a quite considerable separation from the community. At Bildeston, both church and village are worth a visit; they seem to gain by the division.

**Boxford   This delightful village, in its peaceful situation just off the main Hadleigh–Sudbury road (A1071), is well worth the diversion. It was a former centre of the woollen-cloth industry of the region, remaining prosperous well into the eighteenth century, although in Victorian times much reduced. There are many good houses of the sixteenth to eighteenth centuries lining its streets, with an attractive stream (the Box) channelled through the heart of the village, and fine views to tempt the photographer. The handsome church gains much internally by the continuation of the fifteenth-century nave arcades through at the same scale into the chancel, thus giving the whole building an impressive unity. In addition, the church has a quite extraordinary feature in the fourteenth-century timber porch, vaulted internally, now sheltering the north door. It is possible that the porch has been moved from elsewhere, but a timber survival of this kind and date is in any event very rare, being preserved at Boxford by a happy but unusual chance. The fifteenth-century south porch, although less exceptional, is very fine; the pairs of four-light windows on either side are a rare feature, as is the lavishness of the overall decoration, financed by John Cowper and his family, wealthy clothiers of Boxford in the mid-century. Worth noting also is the south chapel, with tiered niches on either side of the east window, formerly holding images of Our Lady and three saints. Next to the window is a contemporary fifteenth-century painting of a royal saint, the locally renowned Edmund, king of East Anglia (841-69), captured and killed by Ingwar's Viking army. A matching painting on the other side of the window might either have been Edward the Confessor (d. 1066) or the more recent Henry VI (d. 1471), around whose memory a cult grew swiftly in the late fifteenth and early sixteenth centuries, zealously fostered by the Lancastrians as a weapon against the Yorkists who had deposed him. North of the chancel, where the organ and vestry are now sited, was the gild chapel of St John the Baptist, Boxford having had at least four trade or parish gilds before their suppression in the mid-sixteenth century, each of which would have taken an interest in the fabric and furnishings of the church.

Brettenham   The church stands boldly at a junction on the road between Thorpe Morieux and Rattlesden, having the somewhat unusual (and spectacular) feature of a south porch tower which gives the building its solid, well-founded look. Within the porch, the late-medieval church door is still intact; otherwise, points of interest include the grandly placed fourteenth-century (Decorated) font and a contemporary angle-piscina (with heraldry) in the chancel. This is a pleasant building, inside and out, but undistinguished – its font compares unfavourably with the font at Rattlesden, its piscina with that at Thorpe Morieux. Stop only if you have plenty of time.

***Castle Hedingham   The great castle that still dominates this pretty town, being privately owned, is one of the least well known of the twelfth-century Anglo-Norman square keeps; it is also arguably the finest. Currently, it is open only in the summer, but a good view of it can be obtained from the churchyard below, and this is certainly better than nothing. If you are lucky enough to gain admittance, notice especially the very high quality of the masonry: in the many decorated window openings, in the fireplaces and doors, and in the great arches that supported the floors. The finest apartment at Hedingham (as at Rochester, which it resembles in so many ways) was the great second-floor hall, rising through two storeys with another floor above it, under the roof. Entrance was gained at first-floor level, through a single door formerly protected by a forebuilding; below this again, there was a store. Hedingham was the principal seat of the de Vere family, whose fortunes expanded particularly under the second Aubrey de Vere, sheriff of eleven counties under Henry I in 1130 and subsequently Great Chamberlain of England. As a trusted servant of the king, Aubrey II was able to build on a scale rarely permitted by the crown. Hedingham is a remarkable testimony to the wealth of the Great Chamberlain and of Aubrey III, his son, the first of a long line of de Vere earls of Oxford, extinguished only in the early eighteenth century. Of the other castle buildings, little or nothing remains; but the scale of the surviving earthworks is impressive.

Scarcely less important than the castle at Hedingham is the very remarkable parish church. Obviously, it owes much of its splendour to de Vere patronage, continuing still in the sixteenth century with John de Vere, thirteenth earl and hereditary Great Chamberlain (d. 1513), to whom was due, in all probability, the rebuilding of the west tower and other works, including the clerestory and south porch. A fine black marble monument to the fifteenth earl (d. 1540) is preserved in the chancel at Hedingham, though his ancestors had preferred burial at the Benedictine priory of Earl's Colne, a few miles to the south-east, suppressed with the other 'lesser' monasteries in 1536. Hedingham has a fine double-hammerbeam roof attributable to the early-sixteenth-century rebuilding, with some chancel stalls and a good rood screen of about this period. However, the glory of the church is the Late Norman work in the nave arcades, in the chancel arch, and in the blank arches which frame the windows of the chancel. As rebuilt in the last two decades of the twelfth century, this is work of the very highest quality, with that classical flavour visible also at contemporary Canterbury. On no account should you miss it.

**Cavendish A fine large church is loftily placed behind the village green and some pretty thatched cottages to the north of the Clare–Long Melford road (A1092). Among the many notable features of this well-maintained church are a very grand fifteenth-century clerestory (the gift of the Smyth family) and good contemporary timber roofs to the nave and north aisle. However, most remarkable at Cavendish is the great late-fourteenth-century chancel, with its huge east window, rebuilt by the executors of Sir John Cavendish, chief justice of the king's bench, murdered by peasant rebels at Bury St Edmunds in June 1381. Sir John, who had made his will shortly before his death, clearly intended the chancel to serve as a mortuary chapel for himself and for his wife, through whom he had acquired the manor. His tomb has not survived, the only major monument in the chancel at Cavendish being the tomb-chest of Sir George Colt (d. 1570), itself handsome enough in an old-fashioned heraldic idiom. The great brass lectern, dating to the early sixteenth century, is one of the grandest in the county.

***Clare The little town of Clare has the misfortune to be placed on the busy A1092. Yet it is full of features of interest, not least a fine collection of timber-framed buildings of the fifteenth and sixteenth centuries. The massive motte-and-bailey castle at the southern end of the town is probably the work of Richard de Clare, companion of the Conqueror and founder of the great house of Clare. Now made accessible as a 'country park', it preserves the original motte to its full height, with a fragment of the later shell-keep still in place on the top. From this vantage point, the very substantial remaining castle earthworks can be viewed, as can the town itself, with the parish church prominent to the north, and

with what is left of the medieval Austin friary to the south, just beyond the boundaries of the castle. Another religious community, recruited from the Norman Benedictine abbey of Le Bec-Hellouin, at first sheltered (from 1090) in the north bailey. In the more secure times of Henry I, it was re-sited at Stoke-by-Clare, along the main road to the west, leaving Clare itself open to the friars a century later. At the friary, recovered by the Austin friars in 1953 and now freely open to visitors, several buildings and other fragments survive. The brothers have restored the former infirmary range as their church; only the south wall of the original church remains, but what is still recognizably the cloister is now a rose garden, with a building on the west which (especially on its own buttressed west front) preserves many of the features of the late-medieval prior's lodging. Like many such lodgings, it was saved from destruction in 1538 to become the private house of the site's new owners, returning recently to the friars as their residence.

The fine parish church at Clare is best viewed from the north, where its full length can be seen uninterrupted by other buildings. As remodelled in the late fifteenth and early sixteenth centuries, it is a spacious and light building of very grand proportions, skilfully incorporating fourteenth-century work, including the piers of the nave arcades. Notice especially the richly carved string-course over the arches of these arcades (a very individual feature of Clare); also the interesting fourteenth-century south porch, with its adjoining chapel, and bone-hole under them both. The chancel, largely rebuilt in the early seventeenth century in a close copy of the late-medieval style, holds a fine collection of Jacobean church furniture, including a complete set of choir stalls and the communion rail before the high altar. The early-sixteenth-century eagle lectern is one of the better examples of its class.

**Finchingfield The village at Finchingfield is a total (and most satisfying) composition – a green with duckpond, a bridge, timber-framed and other attractive period houses, and a church rising above the whole, with the gildhall of the late-medieval Holy Trinity Gild sheltering the approaches to the churchyard. There are good pubs and every incentive to linger. In the church, look especially at the excellent (if restored) rood screen, with an interesting earlier screen in the south aisle still in place and mainly fourteenth-century work. Behind this screen, there is a handsome monument to Sir John Berners and Elizabeth, his wife (d. 1523), with fine brasses paired on a Purbeck marble slab and with heraldry and weepers on the tomb-chest. The clerestory in the chancel is an unusual feature, bringing the chancel roof up to the same height as that of the nave, and increasing the sense of light and space in what is already an attractive and an interesting building.

*Great Maplestead   Like its sister church at Little Maplestead, this building suffered gravely at the hands of Victorian restorers, though it still possesses several features of interest. The earliest parts of the church are the west tower and the little apse at the east end of the chancel, both of early-twelfth-century date. Later improvements and additions included the rebuilding of the chancel in the early thirteenth century (leaving the apse intact) and the extension of the church southwards in the fourteenth century by the addition (probably at different times) of a south aisle and transeptal chapel. The vestry, the south porch, and the north transept and aisle are Victorian. In the early seventeenth century, the south transept was extended to make a mortuary chapel for the Deane family of Dynes Hall, a handsome house of that period a mile or so south of the parish church. It is the magnificent memorials they put up in the chapel – to Sir John Deane (1625) and to Lady Anne Deane (1633) – that now give Great Maplestead its special interest. Notice particularly the macabre figure of Lady Anne, rising in her shroud behind her reclining son. It recalls the widespread taste

26 The late-fifteenth-century gatehouse tower of William Pykenham's rectory at Hadleigh

for such memorials in the later Middle Ages, as witnessed particularly in shroud brasses and in skeletal effigies of a grisliness much greater than this.

**Hadleigh   Cloth-making brought prosperity to Hadleigh in the later Middle Ages, with the result that the town, strung out along its everlasting High Street, is rich in timber-framed buildings both of this and of the early-modern period. In the centre, an exceptionally grand urban church (remodelled, of course, in the fifteenth century, but with a spectacular earlier western tower and spire) stands in what is almost a close of its own. To the south of the churchyard, a fifteenth-century building, three-storeyed at the centre, incorporates a first-floor gildhall at its eastern end; to the west, the church approaches are dominated by the great brick gatehouse (typically arrogant pseudo-military work) of the deanery, built in 1495 for William Pykenham, rector of Hadleigh and archdeacon of Suffolk (1472-97). Of the church itself, the most important characteristic is its great size, spelling out, as little else can do, the wealth of the clothiers who built it. Town, church, gildhall, and gatehouse must be seen as a group. Together, they make Hadleigh worth the longer visit that the inside of the church, sadly over-restored by the Victorians, might in other circumstances have discouraged. Once within, individual features worth noting include a very handsome late-fourteenth-century octagonal font (the cover is modern), some good parclose screens, a bench-end in the south chapel with a carving of St Edmund's head found by a wolf (in monk's clothing!), and a recess north of the high altar which appears to have done double duty as a monument and an Easter Sepulchre.

*Haughley A pleasant village with a wide street and a number of timber-framed houses, nicely placed to the north of the thunderous A45. Behind the church and reasonably visible from the churchyard are the earthworks of the bailey of a large twelfth-century motte-and-bailey castle; the motte itself is inaccessibly placed to the north-west but, should you get a glimpse of it, is tall and grand, if overgrown. At the church, notice the comparatively rare fourteenth-century porch tower, the unusually broad south aisle, and the good late-medieval timber roofs to both this aisle and the nave. The font, with Evangelist symbols on the bowl and lions and Wild Men against the stem, is of the characteristically elaborate East Anglian form.

**Hessett Few churches, even in Suffolk, concentrate so many points of interest as Hessett. The chancel is comparatively modest work of the fourteenth century, with a handsome Decorated east window;

everything else was rebuilt in the fifteenth century at the expense of the parishioners, some of whose names are recorded. We know, for example, that it was John Bacon (d. 1513) who finished off the tower with its pinnacled and crenellated parapet, and it was probably the same benefactor, then lord of the manor, who funded the building of the south porch. John Hoo (d. 1492) and Katherine, his wife, paid for the addition of a new north-east chapel (or vestry), with a room over it, and for the embattling and embellishment of the whole. Shortly afterwards, Robert and Agnes Hoo contributed a new font. The font is still in place; so is the fifteenth-century rood screen (now missing its loft, though the rood stair and rood loft door are preserved), and so also is much of the contemporary stained glass. But look here especially at the late-medieval benches – a complete set in both chancel and nave, with cross-benches against the aisle walls. And give some time also to the important wall-paintings: a large St Christopher over the north door and another (less well preserved) above the south door, a Seven Deadly Sins in the north aisle, with a later Christ of the Trades painted below it. St Christopher, usually shown with his staff and with the Christ Child on his shoulder, was the patron saint of travellers: they would have seen him as they entered or left the church. Both the Seven Deadly Sins and the Christ of the Trades would have been useful aids to the eloquence of the preacher, warnings to his flock against temptations, including the practice of working on the sabbath by which Our Saviour was continually re-injured. On no account should you miss this church; opposite, there is a well-kept pub (The Five Bells) further to reward the diversion.

*Hitcham Just north of Bildeston, and worth the short diversion through pretty country, is the parish church of Hitcham, with what may have been the late-medieval gildhall next to the church gate (much altered since and restored). The church is on a prominent elevated site at the south end of the village. It is spacious, light, and well maintained, being notable especially for the fine roofs to nave and aisles, perhaps as late as the early seventeenth century though very much in the vernacular tradition. Notice also the comparatively rare survival of the lower painted panels of an early-sixteenth-century rood screen, with angels carrying emblems of the Passion (among them the pillar, the spear, and the crown of thorns). The south porch is particularly handsome.

***Kersey** Do not miss this village. The heavy woollen cloths known as 'kerseys' were famous throughout medieval England, bringing a prosperity that still shows to this day. Late-medieval timber-framed houses line a long street which dips attractively to a ford at the bottom before rising again to the loftily placed and very grand parish church to the south. Just to the north, an Augustinian priory once confronted the church across the valley. Some part of its buildings remain, but are now private property; it was one of the smaller and later Augustinian foundations, being suppressed as early as 1443/4 in favour of Henry VI's King's College, Cambridge. The college also became patron of the parish church at Kersey, but is unlikely to have contributed to its late-medieval rebuilding, which would have been owed rather to wealthy parishioners. Two clear stages in this rebuilding are recognizable, the first pre-dating the Black Death and being left incomplete in a number of details when the plague visited the parish. It is to the 1330s and 1340s that the unusually broad north aisle belongs. Next to the altar, a fine set of piscina and sedilia belongs to this period, as does the extraordinary carved stone cornice just below roof-level, much mutilated but still recognizably designed to tell a long story, the subject of which is not known. There is no corresponding aisle to the south of the nave, giving the church a somewhat lop-sided feel, particularly marked as one enters the building from the north. In the second phase of the rebuilding, dating to the fifteenth century, the nave was

reconstructed, porches were added to the north and south, and the great tower (a prominent local landmark) was completed. The nave roof is contemporary and must have been, as originally conceived, very fine. Look especially, however, at the very remarkable panelled roofs of the south and north porches, being work (in the south porch particularly) of the highest quality. Other features of the late-medieval church are the well preserved rood-loft stair and door, the unusually intact figure paintings (three prophets and three kings) on six surviving panels of the former rood screen, and the original fifteenth-century shaft, architecturally conceived, of the wooden lectern. A fragmentary St George and the Dragon painting has been preserved on the south wall of the church, with many broken mouldings and other bits and pieces collected together (in a rather haphazard and antiquarian way) in the north aisle.

***Lavenham** This unique little town deserves its reputation as the show-piece of late-medieval Suffolk. Right at its centre, the splendid Swan Hotel is one of many timber-framed buildings of the fifteenth and sixteenth centuries, testifying to the wealth of Lavenham as a cloth-making centre throughout this period, the home of great clothier families like the Springs. Indeed, it is for its domestic architecture that Lavenham is particularly memorable. Incorporated in the Swan Hotel, for example, is the Old Wool Hall, a perfect hall-house of the fifteenth century, with a contemporary shop-front just across the road on the corner of Lady Street and Water Street. Further down Water Street is the De Vere House, again of the fifteenth century and richly carved; in Market Place, the fine Gildhall is a good assemblage (now in National Trust ownership) of the early sixteenth century, put up for the Corpus Christi Gild which would shortly be suppressed at the Reformation; facing the same open market, the Little House (now carefully restored) is a splendidly preserved burgess house of Lavenham's wealthiest

27 The Spring Chantry in the north aisle at Lavenham: a fine example of pre-Reformation church furnishings

period, with its two-storeyed hall and adjoining solar block, exactly as most men of comfortable means would have chosen to live in the fifteenth century.

Other good timber-framed houses, some of them terraced and very small, climb the hill westwards towards the great church, which, as so often is the case in Suffolk communities, is sited on the extreme perimeter of the town. Lavenham's church, of which only the chancel is as early as the fourteenth century, is as much a product of clothier prosperity as are the houses in the town itself. As at Long Melford, its precise contemporary, the rebuilding was a cooperative venture. However, two donors stand out as especially generous, being

John de Vere (d. 1513), lord of the manor and thirteenth earl of Oxford (also a patron of the parish church at Castle Hedingham), and Thomas Spring III (d. 1523), one of the wealthiest clothiers of his day. De Vere and Spring heraldry decorates the church: together on the great west tower, de Vere alone on the fine south porch. The grand Spring chapel, at the east end of the south aisle, was built in Thomas Spring's memory by Alice, his widow, and completed in 1525. Spring and Oxford chantries, with fine timber screens, survive in the north and south aisles respectively. Notice also the excellent fourteenth-century rood screen in the most splendidly ornate Decorated style, the good set of misericords preserved in the chancel stalls, and the handsome clerestory which lights the contemporary nave roof. Like the town itself, Lavenham Church is not to be missed.

*Little Maplestead A disastrous mid-nineteenth-century restoration, leaving little of the original stonework untouched, has made this interesting and perfectly genuine church one of the least authentically 'medieval' in north Essex. However, its plan remains as before, and it is this that will reward a diversion. Little Maplestead is one of only four medieval round churches still in use in England (the others are in London, Cambridge, and Northampton, with the now roofless round chapel at Ludlow Castle making a fifth standing building of this kind). Moreover, as built or reconstructed in about 1335, it is by far the latest of the group. Its peculiar plan, with long rectangular chancel terminating in an apse, and with a hexagonal 'nave' surrounded by a circular 'aisle', is owed to the fact that from the late twelfth century until the suppression of the English Grand Priory in 1540, Little Maplestead was a possession of the Knights of St John (the Hospitallers). Like their rival order, the Templars, the Hospitallers quite frequently built round chapels, modelled on the church of the Holy Sepulchre at Jerusalem, at their major estate centres, or commanderies. At Little Maplestead, the chancel would have served as the knights' choir, a screen separating it from the body of the nave, which, even in the Middle Ages, would probably have done duty as a more open place of worship for the parish. Parochial use, certainly, is the most likely explanation for the survival of the building when everything else round about it was destroyed after the crown's sale of the manor in the early 1540s. Notice the grace of the fourteenth-century nave arcade (over-restored but still authentic in flavour) and its contrast with the primitive simplicity of the rudely carved font, perhaps as early as the late eleventh century.

***Long Melford The busy road (A134) from Sudbury to Bury St Edmunds runs the full length of Long Melford, but even this cannot spoil the attractions of a village (really a small town) which is one of the most interesting in England. Approach it, if you can, from the Sudbury end. Many timber-framed and later period houses will prepare you for a view (at last) of the splendid parish church at the north end of the street, behind and above the wide green. Long Melford is justly famous for its restaurants, antique shops, and pubs. Among its buildings, the timber-framed Bull Hotel is certainly one of the best. Melford Hall (at the north end of the village, opposite the green) and Kentwell Hall (just beyond it, to the north again) are both fine buildings of the mid-sixteenth century, the latter retaining its earlier moat. Neither should be missed, if the time can be spared to visit them. However, the glory of Long Melford is its church. The tower is modern, but it harmonizes well with a building which, externally at least, is entirely of the late fifteenth and early sixteenth centuries. Notice the way that the handsome flushwork decoration is on the village side of the church, not on the north. Yet economy, if this is what prompted the difference, is certainly not apparent inside. It was the Cloptons of Kentwell who, before they rebuilt their own country mansion, contributed most to the construction of the church. They have their private chantry chapel, north of the high altar; they are represented in the stained-glass donor figures preserved in the windows of the north aisle; and it was John Clopton, the most generous of them all, whose 'goods' financed (among many other works) the unique Lady Chapel, attached to the church at its east end. Most striking in the church is the spacious nave, with its broad flanking aisles, running without the interruption of a chancel arch straight through to the original east end. A splendid clerestory lights the fine original roof, and there are good roofs too in the aisles and (on an especially attractive domestic scale) in the encircling aisle, or ambulatory, of the Lady Chapel. Notice particularly the good collection of

28 The Lady Chapel at Long Melford, a work of piety financed out of John Clopton's estate and remarkable especially for its unique encircling ambulatory

late-fifteenth-century stained glass; the fine fourteenth-century alabaster relief of the Adoration of the Magi, perhaps originally part of an altar or reredos, now built into the wall of the north aisle; the painted cornice in the Clopton Chantry, with verses attributed to John Lydgate, a fifteenth-century monk of Bury; and the tombs of John Clopton (d. 1497), to the north of the high altar, and of Sir William Cordell (d. 1580), builder of Melford Hall, to the south. Donor inscriptions, portraits, and monuments are everywhere a feature of the church, recording a genuine cooperative effort in which the whole community, at one time or another, became engaged.

*Monks Eleigh The well-placed church lies above and to the north of the main street of the village, itself a pretty straggle along the line of the Lavenham–Hadleigh road (A1141). The most obvious feature of the church is its handsome west tower, but

notice also the little late-medieval pulpit, being a characteristic addition to church furnishings in the fifteenth century, as preaching in the vernacular became more popular and as fixed seating in the form of pews was supplied. The chancel is a mid-nineteenth-century rebuild.

*Needham Market This is not a remarkable town in any way, and neither it nor its church would be worth a visit had it not been for the work of a carpenter of genius, employed on the church roof during a rebuilding of the later fifteenth century. The church, which is centrally placed on the main street of the town, could easily be mistaken for a Victorian chapel, nor is its interior (below roof level) any more interesting. Above, the carpenter takes over with an individual creation hardly less, as Pevsner says, than 'a whole church with nave and aisles and clerestory seemingly in the air'. Most remarkable in what is already a fine hammer-beam roof is the clerestory, built into the top of the roof itself and not, as was customary, lighting the roof from below. It is this especially that gives the impression of a separate building, floating high over the floor of the nave, and it is for this effect that (on a bright sunny day) a stop at Needham Market is to be recommended. Certainly, the roof has been claimed by those who should know as the best of its kind in England.

**Rattlesden   Although somewhat marred by its mean west tower, this is a fine church, well set above the road at the east end of an attractive village and photogenically placed behind a timber-framed cottage at the churchyard gate. Externally, the church is already very handsome; internally, the double hammer-beam nave roof (although extensively restored in the nineteenth century) is breathtaking, and there is another good roof of sixteenth-century date in the chancel. Undoubtedly the single most interesting feature of the church interior is the fourteenth-century (Decorated) aumbry in the north wall of the chancel; such cupboards for holding sacred vessels, especially as elaborate as the one at Rattlesden, are not all that common, and it has been suggested that the aumbry may also have served as an Easter Sepulchre. Worth noticing also are the good thirteenth-century south door, with an unusual circular window above it, the fine fourteenth-century octagonal font (as well placed as, and very similar to, the font at Brettenham), and the fragmentary, although still interesting, surviving timber furnishings, including six of the lower panels of the late-medieval rood screen (now at the west end of the church behind the font) and some contemporary bench-ends (in the chancel). In this church, the fourteenth-century nave arcades and chancel arch marry particularly well with the fifteenth-century (Perpendicular) clerestory, contriving between them a spacious and entirely harmonious interior. The rood screen, although modern, is both impressive and reasonably authentic in form.

*Stoke-by-Clare   One of the nicest features of this church is the approach from the road, with timber-framed cottages on the left, a shaded green, and an interesting early-sixteenth-century brick-built dovecot at the college entrance to the right. Notice the off-centre siting of the fourteenth-century western tower, the product of an almost total rebuilding of the church in the following century on a new line slightly to the north. However, most important here are the surviving fifteenth-century church furnishings – a fine little pulpit (in excellent condition) of the very end of the century, and a number of good (although damaged) benches, now grouped together in the chancel.

Behind the church, and clearly visible from the churchyard, are eighteenth-century buildings incorporating some fragments of the priory which moved to this site from Clare in 1124. Stoke-by-Clare Priory, as an 'alien' priory dependent on the Norman abbey of Bec, was dissolved with the other such houses in 1414-15 in the first major suppression of religious communities, brought on by Anglo-French rivalry. It became at that date a college of secular (i.e. not monastic) priests.

*Sudbury   Much time could be spent to advantage in Sudbury. There are three important medieval churches (St Gregory, St Peter, and All Saints), and a number of interesting late-medieval buildings (especially in Stour Street). But Sudbury is also a busy market town. You may not feel disposed to give it as much time as an adequate inspection would require. Happily, one of the most interesting buildings (the parish church of St Gregory), being sited on the western perimeter of the old town and on the road out to Long Melford, is also one of the easier to get at. This fine well-cared-for church owes much to a famous native of the town, Simon Sudbury (bishop of London, 1361-75, then archbishop of Canterbury, 1375 until his murder by rebels on 14 June 1381). It was Simon who, with his brother John, founded a college on a site next to St Gregory's, the establishment initially (from 1374) including a warden,

29 The lofty nave at Thaxted, largely rebuilt out of the pious donations of local gildsmen and equipped with a fine early-sixteenth-century clerestory, flooding the church with light

five secular canons, and three chaplains. The first major rebuilding of St Gregory's – a second occurred at the end of the fifteenth century – was undertaken in connection with the new foundation, one consequence being that the chancel had to be extended to its present unusual length to accommodate the fellows of the college. Their stalls, complete with some interesting carved misericords, are still in place. Outside the church and opposite its west end, the gate of Sudbury's college (suppressed in 1544) survives in the precinct wall of the present-day Walnut Tree Hospital. Notable features of St Gregory's include a handsome chapel, attached (as at Clare) to the south porch, and original roofs to nave and aisles. But most remarkable, and certainly worth the stop to see it, is the late-medieval archi-

tectural font cover, somewhat gaudily painted, as is the nave roof, but authentic and justifiably well known.

Of the other Sudbury churches, St Peter's (on its island site in the very centre of the town) is no longer in use as a church but is opened regularly for concerts, lectures, and exhibitions. Its best features are the fine parclose screens on either side of the chancel and some good surviving roofs. On the way out towards Chelmsford, All Saints again has exactly these qualities, with a fifteenth-century pulpit in addition. It is probably worth pausing if you are leaving the town in this direction, there being a number of timber-framed houses in Friars Street also, including part of the gatehouse of the former Dominican priory (the Blackfriars), dissolved in 1538.

***Thaxted A little town of great individuality and charm, Thaxted is worth a prolonged pause; you will find it rich in licensed restaurants, but short on attractive pubs. There are two major monuments (the church and the gildhall), with a scatter of timber-framed buildings, including three good fifteenth-century town-houses terraced immediately behind the gildhall itself. Thaxted was a clothiers' town, like many in the area, but much of its late-medieval prosperity derived also from the cutlery trade. The three-storeyed gildhall, grandly placed at the top of Town Street with the parish church rising splendidly beyond it, was the hall of the Cutlers' Gild. It has lost something of its medieval flavour in successive restorations, but is nevertheless authentically fifteenth-century, being one of the finest such buildings to survive in England. The church is no less important. It is dedicated, among others, to St Lawrence (patron saint of cutlers), and was extensively rebuilt and enlarged in the late fourteenth and fifteenth centuries, the last additions being the chancel and its chapels, the clerestory and nave roof – all of the first decade of the sixteenth century. Apart from the interesting font case and cover (restored late-medieval work), the church is largely bare of furnishings. A consequence of this, and of the clear glass used in the great windows of the aisles and clerestory, is that the whole church appears extraordinarily spacious and light. This was not as its medieval congregations saw it, yet it enables us now to appreciate the quality of the heavy timber roofs, original throughout, lit with unexpected and exceptional brilliance. This is a church to linger in and to savour: not, perhaps, for any individual feature but for the completely satisfying harmony of the whole. Its light and bareness are those of the Protestant Reformation. They have a Lutheran quality, and Thaxted indeed, in its present condition, is just what the most ardent of the reformers would have wanted.

*Thorpe Morieux Among Suffolk churches, Thorpe Morieux is the exception in being hardly touched by late-medieval rebuilding. In consequence, Thorpe Morieux is less spectacular than many, though its wholly rural setting is particularly charming and it possesses several features of interest. Among these, the fourteenth-century timber south porch is a pleasant surprise, and there is a handsome angle-piscina in the south wall of the chancel, of exceptional quality for a church of this size, with a foliated capital in the characteristic stiff-leaf Early English style.

Wethersfield A nicely placed although not especially interesting church, Wethersfield owes much of its charm to a pleasant village setting. The chancel is ill lit but contains in its south wall a good fourteenth-century piscina and blank arcading; also a fifteenth-century tomb-chest with paired alabaster effigies. The rood screen is graceful and original, if much restored. Stop only if you have time to spare.

**Woolpit The parish church at Woolpit, with its handsome nineteenth-century spire, makes a prominent local landmark. But avoid approaching it from the north if you can, for the A45 has so scarred the landscape as to make that quarter the worst possible introduction to a medieval monument of very considerable distinction. Woolpit itself is a delightful village, complete with timber-framed houses, a nice pub (The Swan), and a parish pump on the green. The church, however, is outstanding. One of its chief glories is the mid-fifteenth-century south porch, embellished with decorative panelling and niches. Like the rest of the church (with the exception, as at Hessett, of the chancel), it was financed by the legacies and other contributions of Woolpit parishioners. Prospering in the fifteenth century, they rebuilt the nave, equipping it further with the great clerestory which now lights a contemporary double hammer-beam roof, rightly described by Pevsner as 'one of the proudest in Suffolk'. To their generosity also can be attributed the elaborate rood screen (unfortunately repainted) and the fine set of late-medieval benches (restored extensively but still essentially fifteenth-century in form). The brass lectern, of similar date and design to the lectern at Cavendish, is worth noting; so also is the chapel at the east end of the south aisle, being the most likely site of the former miracle-working image of Our Lady of Woolpit, a widely known local focus of pilgrimage before the iconoclasts of the Reformation did away with it.

HOTELS AND ITINERARIES

To my mind, there could be no better centre for this tour than Lavenham, nor any finer hotel than the **Swan**. Certainly, you will find the Swan expensive; in the summer tourist season, it will be noisy and packed. However, as a winter base for a tour which, with the exception of the keep at Castle Hedingham, might as well be made at this season as any other, the Swan is beyond compare. In the reception areas, great wood fires are kept burning continuously; there is much genuine late-medieval timbering, with modern additions sympathetically contrived; if the food is over-ambitious, it is a small enough price to pay for dining in such delightful surroundings.

A distinct second-best, although again this is a building of considerable period charm, is the **Bull** at Long Melford. Like Lavenham, Long Melford is a famous tourist centre; and with good reason. Although there are many other hotels along the line of its lengthy street, the Bull is the obvious place to stay. Its splendid timberwork of the sixteenth and seventeenth centuries is incentive enough from the start; there are some particularly fine oak-beamed interiors. But Long Melford is on a busy road, and the Bull itself is on a junction which exposes it to traffic on two sides. This is a good hotel, reliable and handsome; it is simply not as good as the Swan.

Much lower down the scale is the **Bell** at Clare. It is a sixteenth-century timber-framed building, slightly ramshackle but full of charm; it is friendly and on a more intimate scale than the Swan or the Bull, both of which are part of the Trusthouse chain; Clare itself, with its many interesting medieval features, would be an excellent place to stay. But the Bell is a turning-post for the A1092, with all that that means in noise and confusion. Ask for a room away from the road.

Do not be seduced by what others write about the **Mill Hotel** at Sudbury. If rooms are short in the area, this is a large hotel and might do. The site by the river is quiet and appealing; the conversion has been done with imagination and at great cost; it looks especially good after dark. But the decor is steak-house. What a pity!

*　　*　　*

There are two obvious parts to this tour, south-west and north-east of **Lavenham**. The division works as conveniently if you stay at Long Melford, although it is clearly less meaningful if the base you decide upon is Clare.

From Lavenham, **Thorpe Morieux** and **Brettenham** (neither of major interest) can be taken in conveniently on the way to **Rattlesden**, which must be seen. The short diversion to **Hessett** is well worth the extra mileage to the north-west, but return the same way (even at the cost of missing the round tower at **Beyton**) so as to be able to approach **Woolpit** from the south. **Haughley** is not top priority, but is now too close to miss. However, you will have a much more difficult decision when it comes to striking south again, for **Needham Market** ought to be seen, yet its situation on a busy road and amidst commercial squalor would be quite enough to break your lyrical mood. Unless you have plenty of time, leave Needham Market to the photographers and perhaps jettison Haughley too, joining the B1115 (Stowmarket to Hadleigh) to stop at **Hitcham** and **Bildeston**, both of them quite quickly, before making your major pauses at **Hadleigh** and then

30 The fifteenth-century gildhall at Thaxted, with contemporary terraced town-houses adjoining it on the right

(returning north towards Lavenham again) at the very delightful **Kersey**. Out of the way, but well worth a visit even at the cost of missing out some of the lesser churches like Hitcham and Bildeston, is **Boxford**. And stop, if you still have the time, at **Monks Eleigh**, the church of which is a prominent landmark on the Hadleigh to Lavenham road (A1141).

If you approach the region from the west, or if you leave that way, it would seem sensible to take in the churches, gildhalls, and charming village settings of **Thaxted** and **Finchingfield** on your journey. For the rest of the tour, **Long Melford** makes a good beginning for a circuit which includes **Cavendish, Clare**, and **Stoke-by-Clare**, then pushing south to **Castle Hedingham**. There is much to see at both Clare and Castle Hedingham; after the latter, you may wish to head west, whereupon **Wethersfield**, although of not enough importance to deserve a diversion, is conveniently on the way out to Finchingfield. Should you be returning to Long Melford with time to spare, do not miss the strange round church of the Hospitallers at **Little Maplestead**, pausing too (although for no more than a moment) at **Great Maplestead** on the same diversion. The A131 will bring you in to **Sudbury** close to All Saints Church (turn right just after the bridge), but you may wish to save your remaining energies for the more elegant St Gregory's, conveniently placed with easy parking just to the left of the A134 as it leaves the town centre for Long Melford.

Nobody's priorities are ever the same, but mine undoubtedly are Castle Hedingham, Clare, Kersey, Lavenham, Long Melford, and Thaxted in the front rank, with Bildeston, Boxford, Cavendish, Finchingfield, Hadleigh, Hessett, Rattlesden, and Woolpit in the second. On my visits, I conceived a perhaps irrational affection for Boxford and Hessett especially.

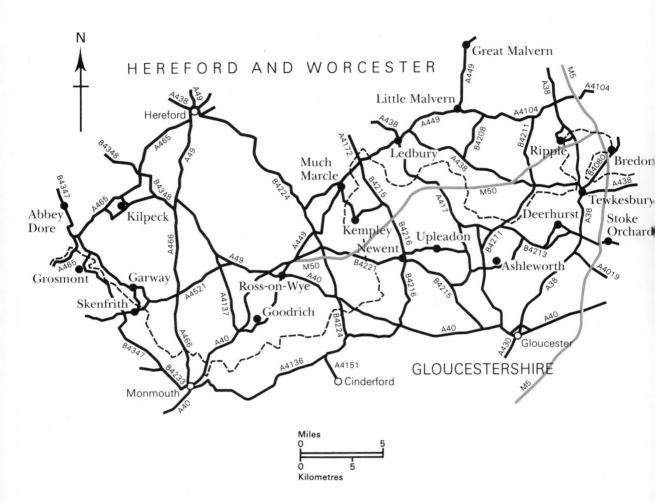

Chapter 3

The Vale of Gloucester, Herefordshire, and the March

Some landscapes have a very special antiquity; one can sense that they have been prayed and fought over for centuries. Here, on the flat plain of Gloucester and on the increasingly hilly margins of Wales, we are in one of them. At Anglo-Saxon **Deerhurst**, the former monastic church is a building substantially of the eighth century. Its great stone baptismal font – most potent symbol, after the cross, of the new faith that had lately swept the region – carries trumpet-spiral ornament reaching back yet further to a Celtic twilight and beyond into the pre-Christian Iron Age.

By the early ninth century, Deerhurst was already at its most prosperous. From that time, its problems multiplied as ascendancy slipped from the Mercian kings and as Viking warriors ravished its estates. It was Edward the Confessor, last-but-one king of Wessex, who divided this Mercian monastery's lands between Westminster Abbey, his own favoured tomb-church, and the Benedictine community of St Denis, near Paris, of which Deerhurst was subsequently a cell. They were not happy times for Deerhurst or for England, launching this island on an association with France that would trouble its politics for generations.

In our region there are many memorials to the events of these years, starting with the Norman Conquest and with its aftermath. Take, for example, the monumental drum columns, characteristically arrogant, of the Early Norman naves at **Tewkesbury** and **Great Malvern**. Better still, go to **Kilpeck**, where all the main elements of the post-Conquest settlement – castle, monastery, and rebuilt parish church – cluster together in self-protection. The church at Kilpeck is deservedly well known for its stone-carvings, Viking-influenced in their use of animal interlaces and themselves powerfully evocative of the past. But consider what it must have meant to a small rural community – the earthworks of the deserted village are still visible to the north-east of Kilpeck Church – when William fitz Norman's French-speaking soldiery first arrived in the locality, shortly to be followed there by the monks of Gloucester, with the rebuilding of the parish church not long after. Contemporaneously, other parish churches

31 Kilpeck's chancel arch, with chancel and sanctuary beyond, showing the important mid-twelfth-century figure-carving on the north and south responds of the arch

throughout the region were similarly (if not always as extravagantly) transformed. It was in the twelfth century that the church at **Ledbury**, the bishop of Hereford's newly prospering market town, was laid out at its present great length. **Ripple**, the mother-church of a sprawling parish, had grown very grand already before 1200. **Bredon** at this time acquired its splendid north porch; **Kempley**, its high-quality paintings.

The Kempley frescoes show Byzantine influence, and they seem to stem from a very different culture from that of the stone-carvers of Kilpeck. Yet at **Stoke Orchard**, intriguingly, the two traditions are seen to coincide. Here the St James narrative, although probably the work of local painters, clearly derives from an imported model. Not so, however, the decorative bands above and below the cycle, nor the ironwork still remaining on the church door; for on both of these the animal ornament is of Viking or even Celtic inspiration. Little or nothing of this regional tradition survives at **Abbey Dore**, and here we may contemplate, on the very border of Wales, a building that is thoroughly French. Abbey Dore belongs, as a Cistercian church, to that second invasion – this time monastic – of an England still bearing the scars of the first. Of course, the Cistercians recruited locally. Their first great abbot, Stephen Harding of Cîteaux, had indeed himself been an Englishman. But the culture they imported was Burgundian, from their homeland, and Abbey Dore's Frenchness very precisely reflects the strongly centralizing tendencies of their order.

By the late twelfth century, when the rebuilding of Abbey Dore began, Cistercian practice had lost its rigour, in architecture as in much else. St Bernard, certainly, would not have approved of the beautiful ambulatory at Dore (far removed from the austerity he had urged on his monks), nor could he have endorsed the growing custom, again evident at Dore, of the burial of important local laymen in the presbytery. Yet for us, the two knight effigies of Dore, fully armed with their hands on their swords as if ready to spring from the tomb, are a useful reminder of the troubles of the March and of the perils of the abbey's situation. Abbey Dore lies next to the last main road running approximately parallel to the Welsh border. Immediately to the west rise the Black Mountains; to the south, the castles of Hubert de Burgh, **Grosmont** and **Skenfrith**, guard the same river valley, with **Garway**, an important preceptory of the Knights Templar (the 'Poor Knights of Christ and of the Temple of Solomon'), just over the Monnow to the east. Compared with Goodrich, built to the advanced standards of almost a century later, neither Grosmont nor Skenfrith could be said to be especially sophisticated. Yet both are the product of a keen military intelligence, being prized possessions of one of the more experienced soldiers of the day. And both make it plain, as does the Templar establishment at Garway, that the English had come to the region to remain there. Inspect the churches associated with each fortress. At Garway and at Skenfrith there are strong west towers, massively constructed in their lower stages and readily defendable in an emergency. Grosmont, in contrast, is a great garrison church, far too grand – as is now evident – for the needs of the parish, but well suited to the castle it adjoined.

Garrison duties imply permanent residence, and it is already clear at Grosmont by the early thirteenth century that the comforts of the lord required attention. Hubert de Burgh's domestic range, well placed to take advantage of the fine prospect over the valley, is still the most important single element in the castle. But look too at the very sophisticated stone chimney, with fireplaces one above the other, of the Lancastrian lodgings at Grosmont, beyond the north curtain. And compare this facility with the brave display of fireplaces, window-seats, hand-basins, and garderobes at a new castle of the period like **Goodrich**. The defences of Goodrich are, of course, well developed. Its formidable angle-towers and complex approaches are characteristic of our best period of castle-building, towards the end of Edward I's reign. They rank with similar work at the late-thirteenth-century castles of the king, over the border in North Wales. However, Grosmont was expected to do duty too as the country house of the Valence earls of Pembroke and of their considerable entourage. Notice especially the way that the accommodation at Goodrich has been designed as a series of comfortable self-contained suites – we would now call them flats, and this indeed is how they functioned. William de Valence, half-brother of Henry III and one of that weak-willed king's notorious foreign favourites, had married into the Pembroke inheritance in 1247 when still a very young man. Always a close associate of the king, he and his son, Aymer de Valence (d. 1324), were great noblemen; they held widely scattered lands and were regularly summoned to the wars. In the circumstances and in accordance with the growing custom of the day, they needed to surround themselves with men of skill and position, both soldiers and administrators, only a rank or so lower than themselves. All of these required accommodation at Goodrich, and none could be evilly housed.

The Valence line ended with Aymer. Ten years before, at Bannockburn, another great dynasty had been cut off abruptly on the death in battle of Gilbert de Clare, earl of Gloucester and third of his name. Such dynastic failures, and the implacable laws of forfeiture, inheritance, and dower, were among the chief encouragements of a preoccupation with nobility to which heraldry had added new glamour. At **Much Marcle**, it is the realism of Blanche Mortimer's effigy, her robe trailing over the tomb-chest, that initially attracts our attention. But prominent also is the heraldry of Mortimer and Grandison, the two families with which Blanche was associated. Compare this with the heraldic elaboration of Eleanor de Clare's rebuilding, also datable to the mid-fourteenth century, of the east end of the abbey church at **Tewkesbury**. Eleanor de Clare had lost a brother at Bannockburn and a husband, Hugh le Despenser the Younger (executed in 1326), in the coup d'état that brought Edward II's reign to an end. As coheiress of the Clare estates, Eleanor was independently wealthy. Together with her son, the third Hugh le Despenser (d. 1349), she deployed her great fortune in commemorative work of a seldom paralleled magnificence, building a resting-place for generations of her family in the care of the Tewkesbury Benedictines. At Tewkesbury to this day, Despenser tombs occupy places of honour to the right and left of the high altar. Above them, splendidly portrayed in the magnificent glass of Eleanor's presbytery windows, Despensers and Clares (in heraldic surcoats and with their hands

32 The former priory church at Deerhurst, with what remains of the east claustral range on the right; note the characteristically tall Anglo-Saxon tower and nave

on their swords) share the company of Christ with the Virgin, St John Baptist, and the Apostles.

Tewkesbury's latter-day prosperity had much to do with the continuing patronage of its magnate lords of the manor. With an annual income at the time of its suppression of almost £1,600, it was one of the wealthiest Benedictine communities, well able to survive the economic blight of the Late Middle Ages and to emerge with its fortune intact. Not so the lesser houses – the former alien priories like **Deerhurst** (granted to Tewkesbury in 1467) and **Newent** (assigned in 1411 to Fotheringhay College), or the cradle-sick children of the great communities, among them **Kilpeck** (resumed by Gloucester Abbey in 1428 after an independent life of almost exactly three centuries). Yet by the late fifteenth century, the return of prosperity to landowners everywhere was having its effect on the monks. There are many indications in late-medieval England of the resilience of monasticism throughout its final decades. From the mid-fifteenth century, the canons of Bristol Abbey were to enlarge their church at **Ashleworth**, to rebuild their manor-house on an adjoining site, and to put up a grand new tithe barn. At **Great Malvern**, the near total reconstruction of the priory church was contemporaneously under way in a building programme that lasted the better part of the century. It was not that the monks of Great Malvern were especially rich: they had time and good friends on their side. Malvern parish church, as it has since become, is a building of considerable splendour, exceptionally well maintained. It brings together in happy association a near-unique assemblage of fifteenth-century church fittings, especially notable for its encaustic tiles and for the fine surviving glass of its magnificent windows, one of them the gift of Henry VII in memory of Prince Arthur, his son. By a curious irony, Great Malvern remains to this day the tomb-church and shrine of the priory's most active despoiler. John Knotsford, purchaser of the site soon after the dismissal of the monks, lived to enjoy the profits of his initiative for almost another half-century. It was his daughter and heiress Anne who, on her father's death in 1589, commissioned the fine monument just south of the altar in which she is to be seen, in life-size effigy, kneeling at the feet of her parents. All three Knotsfords — John, Jane, and Anne — are frozen in attitudes of prayer. Come the Last Judgement, they will need whatever intercession they can get.

***Abbey Dore   With its slightly absurd seventeenth-century tower, more like a chimney at the angle of industrial buildings, Abbey Dore is a disappointment from the outside. But look above the porch as you approach it from the road, and the two great lancets with vesica between them will take you back immediately to the late twelfth century and to France, the home of the new Gothic style. Dore was founded from Morimond, one of the three great founding abbeys (with Cîteaux and Clairvaux) of the Cistercian order. However, nothing remains of the original buildings on the site, begun in 1147. And what we see now is a fragment only—transepts, crossing, chancel, and ambulatory—of the great church put up in the second and third building campaigns of the late twelfth and early thirteenth centuries. It was the pressures of this exceptionally costly building programme that were probably responsible for the reputation for greed that came to attach to the monks of Dore at this period. Nor, as you will notice especially in the east bay of the chancel and in its surrounding ambulatory (both of the early thirteenth century), was any expense spared to contrive an effect scarcely less impressive than

that achieved a few years before in the rebuilding of the church at Cîteaux itself, identically remodelled at the east end. Mercifully little has happened at Dore since the early seventeenth century, when John Lord Scudamore, a descendant of the John Scudamore who had bought the abbey site and buildings shortly after Dore's suppression in 1536, re-roofed and completely re-fitted the church in the form in which it remains equipped to this day. The ambulatory preserves its fine thirteenth-century vault, but notice the way that Lord Scudamore's carpenter, John Abel, has laid his own timber roof on the broken vaults of the crossing, transepts, and presbytery (chancel); other works of this period include the pompous but charming screen, the stalls, pulpit, communion rail, and west gallery (against the former arch from the crossing into the nave), all the work of John Abel (1632–4); the glass in the east window is also Lord Scudamore's, though the painted texts, which are such a feature of the transepts now, belong to the reign of Queen Anne. Of the furnishings of the Cistercian church, the heraldic tiles of the floor on either side of the altar commemorate donors of the late thirteenth century, and it is to this date also that the two good knight effigies belong; the altar, restored to its former position by Lord Scudamore, is medieval. But feast your eyes chiefly on the mighty clustered columns of the presbytery arcade and on the vaulting (of the highest quality) in the ambulatory. To see a Cistercian building of this splendour still in use, with all the added visual delight of the seventeenth-century refurbishing, is a quite exceptional treat.

Ashleworth The church and its associated buildings at Ashleworth, detached from and well away to the east of the village, have benefited greatly by their isolation. As it is, they constitute a rare rectorial group (church, manor-house, and tithe-barn) little changed since the late fifteenth century. Ashleworth was an important rectory and manor of the Augustinian canons of Bristol, being one of their most valuable possessions. With other former properties of the canons, it became part of the original endowment of Henry VIII's new bishopric of Bristol, which may certainly have assisted its survival. At Ashleworth, the church is not without features of interest. There is good fifteenth-century woodwork, including both the screen and the roof (with panelled canopy over the screen) of the unusually spacious south aisle; the other roofs also are of this period. And take a good look especially at the rare early example of the royal arms of Elizabeth, now placed inappropriately at the west end of the south aisle but probably intended for a grander location at the east end, over the rood-beam. Royal arms of this sort, intended to emphasize the recent change in authority in the church, were not infrequently painted over an earlier doom or sometimes (as at Ludham, in Suffolk, on a movable panel similar to Ashleworth's) on the back of one. It is quite possible that Ashleworth's royal arms hide a fifteenth-century doom, contemporary with the screen and other woodwork.

Next to the church, and easily studied from the churchyard on its east front as well as its west, the rectorial manor-house is a

33 The crossing at Abbey Dore, re-roofed in the early seventeenth century, to which period the west gallery (left) and screen (right) also belong

well-preserved late-medieval building of conventional plan, with central hall open to the roof, a solar block (upper and lower chamber) on the north, and a kitchen and service rooms (with chamber over) on the south, beyond the screens passage. Dated to the mid-fifteenth century, it is about half a century earlier than the tithe-barn at Ashleworth, thought to have been built in Abbot Newland's time, in c. 1500. The barn has the usual pair of transeptal porches on its west side, towards the road, and is the same length as the bishop of Worcester's much earlier and loftier tithe-barn at Bredon. Like Bredon, it is now the property of the National Trust.

**Bredon The parish church at Bredon is pleasantly situated, away from the main road (which runs to the south) and with interesting buildings on all sides. Almost next door is the handsome rectory, a sixteenth-century stone building to the north of the church, with the eighteenth-century manor-house off to the west, and the great medieval tithe-barn just a little beyond it. Throughout the Middle Ages, from the tenth century until the sixteenth, both the manor of Bredon and the advowson of the church belonged to the bishops of Worcester, and it is the personal interest of individual bishops in their turn that must explain some of the more lavish characteristics of Bredon's buildings. At the church, this interest is immediately obvious in the handsome twelfth-century north porch, expensively decorated and vaulted in a fashion most unusual in a building of this status. But observe also the very high quality of the paired lancet windows in the beautiful protruding south chapel, datable to the mid-thirteenth century, and notice the fine display of heraldry on the tiles of the sanctuary steps, celebrating the great families of the early fourteenth century – the Mortimers and de Veres, the Beauchamps and Warennes, the Clares, fitz Alans, and Berkeleys, with the royal arms of England and of France, and of the kingdoms of Castile and Leon. In the chancel, the Easter Sepulchre is a handsome tomb-like recess in the north wall, datable to about 1300, while against the south wall there is a very fine grave-slab (up-ended and carved with a cross and portrait busts) of the early fourteenth century, and a good contemporary piscina and sedilia. Of the early glass, two saints' figures in the north-west chancel window are attributable to the early fourteenth century; opposite, the curious scaled-down monument to a couple and their child is of *c.* 1500. Finally, do not leave the church without pausing to admire the splendidly pompous monument, dominating the south chapel, to Giles and Catherine Reed (both of whom died in 1611), with the eight children of their union.

To the west of the church, approached from the Tewkesbury road, is the bishops' tithe-barn, dated to the fourteenth century and one of the finest in the country. Its tall gables and steep roof are typical of the earlier tithe-barns (cf. the mid-thirteenth-century Cistercian barns at Great Coxwell and Beaulieu-St Leonards), and distinguish Bredon from the less imposing style adopted towards the end of the Middle Ages at Ashleworth. At Bredon, in the fifteenth century, the south porch was heightened to accommodate an upper chamber, with outer stair and fireplace, for the barn-ward. The barn, recently gutted by fire and rebuilt, is now in the care of the National Trust.

***Deerhurst The former priory church of St Mary, Deerhurst, is one of the most important Early Christian monuments in England. A complex and still tentative building sequence has been suggested for the church. However, it is certain that a good part of the present nave, choir (now chancel), and former apse (its foundations exposed at the east end of the church) is as early as the eighth century in date. Very probably, a Christian place of worship has existed at Deerhurst since the seventh-century conversion of the Anglo-Saxons. Characteristic of pre-Conquest monastic building is the great height of the nave, for such churches were frequently of several storeys. As you enter the church, look back at the lofty west wall. You will see a blocked door, half-way up and originally opening into a chamber or gallery at this end of the nave. Above it, the twin triangular-headed windows near the top of the wall are of early-ninth-century date; with the unique ninth-century font, ornamented with trumpet spirals of clearly Celtic inspiration, they are the most memorable Anglo-Saxon features of the building. Much of the early character of the pre-Conquest church was lost when the fine nave arcades (Early English and *c.* 1200) were inserted and the aisles finished off symmetrically on north and south. The east end, squared off, has long been deprived of its apse. But spare at least some of your attention for Deerhurst's later periods: the

34 The fourteenth-century tithe-barn of the bishops of Worcester at Bredon, showing the open stair to the barn-ward's chamber over the south porch

fine brass, surrounded by other family memorials at the east end of the north aisle, to Sir John Cassey and Alice, his wife, datable to c. 1400; the lovely early-fourteenth-century figure of St Catherine (holding her wheel) in the west window of the aisle to the south; the marvellously evocative Puritan disposition of the pews on three sides of the altar-table in the present chancel, pre-Laudian and dating to the early seventeenth century – how came they to survive the indignation of later Anglican restorers and divines?

Immediately south of the church, a late-medieval domestic building (hall with solar to the north) is the only survival of the Benedictine priory – in its last years, a priory cell of Tewkesbury – of which it was once the east claustral range. A cloister, for which there is evidence to the west of this building, would have completed the monastic plan at an earlier period, although Deerhurst Priory at the end of the Middle Ages was more manorial than conventual in organization. Further to the west again,

on the other side of the road, Odda's Chapel is the third element at Deerhurst, identified by inscription as the chapel erected by Earl Odda in memory of his brother, Aelfric, who died at Deerhurst in 1053. Dedicated on 12 April 1056, it is a simple little building only recently sorted out and restored.

*Garway This remote and diminutive church is nevertheless well worth a visit. An ancient holy place with a pre-Conquest religious community, Garway became Templar property in the 1180s, being the site of an important preceptory in the area, later (in the 1310s) taken over by the Hospitallers. Like many Templar churches, Garway was built initially with a circular nave, modelled on the church of the Holy Sepulchre at Jerusalem (cf. the Hospitaller church at Little Maplestead). It had lost this plan by the late thirteenth century, when the present rectangular nave was built. However, the fine Late Norman chancel arch survives from the first period, while a portion of the original nave may still be

35 Late-thirteenth-century angle-towers at Goodrich Castle, with the twelfth-century tower keep rising beyond

seen at foundation level north of the church, as excavated in 1927. The squat west tower is of early-thirteenth-century date, belonging to the first phase of Templar building at Garway; it is sited away from the nave in a detached position which relates it to the circular church, and may also have been intended to play a role in the defence of the Templar preceptory, for its lower walls are exceptionally thick. Notice the good medieval chancel roof, the surviving open stairs (east of the chancel arch) to the rood loft door, and the rugged carpentry of the benches in the nave (a complete set, probably of the seventeenth century). A massive round dovecot to the south of the church is dated by inscription to 1326, soon after the Hospitallers came into the estate, which they then held for another two centuries.

***Goodrich   There is nothing exciting about the approaches to Goodrich, but this makes the castle all the more impressive when it stands at last fully revealed. You will want to linger at Goodrich and to work round it systematically with a guide-book. But notice particularly the following points, roughly in the order in which you will reach them. First, the exceptionally

elaborate gatehouse defences (barbican, stepped approach, and long gate-passage) which are characteristic refinements of England's greatest period of castle-building. Then, as you enter the courtyard, look left and you will see an intriguing and somewhat bizarre survival − a Norman square keep of the mid-twelfth century, built of a grey masonry quite unlike the red sandstone of the rest of the castle: it could have had little role in the later defensive system at Goodrich and was probably preserved only for its value as a watch-tower and because of the problems it would have posed in demolition. One good use for it now is to make the contrast between the quality of accommodation at the twelfth-century castle and that of a century later. As you go through the great hall on the west side of the court and make the circuit round each of the towers, notice the lavish provision of fireplaces and window-seats, the great windows at all but the lower levels, and the frequent occurrence of garderobes − these last being given additionally their own garderobe tower on the east side of the court, with three separate chambers draining out into the moat below. After the hall, the finest accommodation is in the north-west corner of the castle, where the lord's

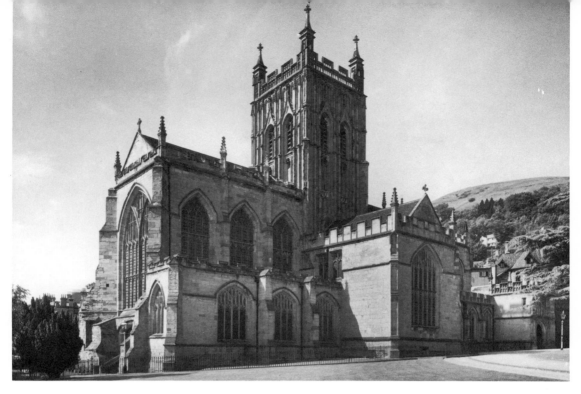

36 The former priory church at Great Malvern, bought by the parishioners shortly after the Dissolution to replace a derelict church of their own

solar commanded the best view of the valley. But the lodgings in the two southern towers are almost equally grand, standing at the beginning of a very general tradition in late-medieval castle architecture, according to which great emphasis was placed on the provision of good quarters for the more prominent members of the lord's household and for his guests. Goodrich was the castle of an important baron, William de Valence (d.1296), half-brother of Henry III. William was an experienced soldier, who had fought in France and in the Holy Land as well as in Wales, and it was probably he who laid out the new castle in the 1280s. His son Aymer (d. 1324) made the second and final major contribution to the fortress by completing the barbican and by adding an outer ward to the west and north, being the quarters least well protected by the moat. Both the barbican and these elements of concentric defence are again typical of the military architecture of the period – just what any professional soldier of the early fourteenth century would have thought to be necessary at his castle.

***Great Malvern Only the church and the gatehouse of what was once an important and wealthy Benedictine priory survive at Malvern, now surrounded by the evidence of the town's spectacular nineteenth-century development as a spa. The gatehouse, as became customary in the period, is a pompous late-medieval building, especially ornate on its outer front. However, it is the church that we have come to Malvern to see, and this is truly sensational. On the exterior, restoration work has been so thorough that Great Malvern Priory, in its Victorian setting with the mighty Abbey Hotel next door, cannot help looking a little bogus. But notice especially the handsome central tower, with its expensive panelling and delicately pierced battlements. And if the two-storeyed north porch is a nineteenth-century addition, the great set of windows on all sides of the church is genuine Perpendicular at its most ambitious, a fitting setting for the magnificent fifteenth-century stained glass which is the principal glory of the interior. As you enter the nave, what will strike you immediately

37 Painted glass, including a Virgin and Child, from one of the pre-Dissolution windows at Great Malvern

is the contrast between the comparatively modest Early Norman arcading and the soaring mid-fifteenth-century clerestory above it. The nave itself is not long: in a monastic church, it did not need to be so. But an impression of size is created most vividly by the identical proportions of the lofty chancel, entered through crossing arches so generous as to do nothing to spoil the unity of the interior. Great Malvern became a parish church only at the Dissolution, when the comparatively newly completed priory church was sold to Malvern's small lay community to replace a derelict church of its own. The purchase has since proved our great good fortune, for it has preserved precious features of the earlier building which would otherwise certainly have been destroyed. These include a fine set of choir stalls, many of them preserving their original misericords and usually remembered for an almost complete *Tasks of the Months*. But it is the fifteenth-century tiles at Malvern, and especially the glass, that deserve attention. These tiles, which include the unique wall-tiles best seen on the back of the choir screen, were manufactured on the site and are sophisticated products, characterized by elaborate inscriptions and ambitious architectural

motifs, of the final generations of the English floor-tiling industry. The contemporary glass is as fine a set as you will see anywhere in England, among its triumphs being the *Joys of Mary* window in the north wall of the transept, paid for by Henry VII as one of several memorials to his son Prince Arthur (d. 1502), elder brother of the priory's despoiler, Henry VIII. John Knotsford, another plunderer of the site, is commemorated in a handsome alabaster tomb of the late sixteenth century, immediately south of the high altar. One feels like spitting on it.

**Grosmont For all its impressive dry moat and the bold drum towers of its western front, facing the main road and the village, Grosmont Castle was always very much a domestic building, with little of the soldierly regularity of plan that characterized neighbouring Skenfrith. Both castles were rebuilt almost completely by Hubert de Burgh (d.1234), earl of Kent. However at Grosmont, Earl Hubert's work started not with the defences (already deeply ditched) but with the reconstruction from the ground of the eastern hall and solar range, overlooking the valley below. Much of this range is still intact, providing an excellent example of the comfortable suite of first-floor apartments – great hall and adjoining private chamber – now becoming standard for a magnate: note especially the fine side-wall fireplace of the hall and the handsome windows provided on all sides. Earl Hubert's hall can be dated to around 1210. About a decade later, he began the remodelling of the castle's defences, building strong drum towers to protect the angles to the north and west, and fortifying the entrance with a three-storeyed gatehouse (two chambers over a long vaulted passage). Both these elements – the angle towers and the increasingly sophisticated gatehouse – were to be developed further in castles of later-thirteenth-century England, to become the chief features of the defensive systems of the more costly fortresses like Goodrich. Subsequently, Grosmont's popularity with its Lancastrian owners (Henry 'of Grosmont', the fourth earl, was born there in c. 1300) was probably owed at least as much to the excellence of Hubert de Burgh's domestic arrangements as to the outstanding natural beauty of the site. Certainly, neither the earls nor their ladies did much to change Grosmont, their only major contribution being a much smaller range to the north of the curtain, of which the high-quality early-fourteenth-century chimney (serving two floors) is now the most important survival.

Across the road, in an attractive village setting, Grosmont Church is of great size and importance, clearly owing these to the patronage of the castellans. It is of cruciform plan, with a fine tower over the crossing, and its outstanding feature is the large Early English chancel (built in the period of Earl Hubert's lordship), with its excellent thirteenth-century arcading. Two good piscinas have survived the sometimes brutal Victorian restorations: one on the south wall of the chancel, the other in the north transept, to which it is said to have been moved from Queen Eleanor's Chapel (now the vestry). The disused nave and splendid octagonal tower are attributable to the Lancastrian ownership of Grosmont.

***Kempley** Between Much Marcle and Kempley village, the old church of St Mary is set in near-isolation, which of course increases its charm. But there is little reason to linger outside, for the great glory of this most remarkable twelfth-century monument is the set of contemporary frescoes in its chancel. These have been variously dated earlier or later in the century. However, their pronounced Byzantine quality suggests that they belong most probably to the second half of the century and to that period of contact with the Mediterranean world introduced by our first Angevin kings. Notice especially the seated figure of Christ, at the centre of the tunnel vault, surrounded by symbols of the evangelists; he is accompanied on the vault by figures of St Peter and of the Virgin; below these are the twelve apostles, with other figures, including a pilgrim and a bishop, and with architectural paintings set off by a complex and intriguing chequer pattern. In such a remote setting and in so diminutive a rural church, the quality of these paintings is especially remarkable. But take time off also to inspect the twelfth-century Tree of Life tympanum over the south door, the enclosing fourteenth-century timber south porch, and the paintings in the nave (a century or more later than those in the chancel) which feature, among other things, a good and clearly visible Wheel of Life.

***Kilpeck** The church at Kilpeck must not be missed. It is a complete and scarcely altered rural church – diminutive nave, smaller chancel, and apse of jewel-like perfection – of the mid-twelfth century. However, its chief claim to fame is the prolific and very high quality stone-carving with which it is decorated inside and out: a masterpiece of the so-called Herefordshire School. Buy the guide and take yourself round, ornament by ornament. But notice especially the complex beauty of the fine south door, the occurrence of Scandinavian-style animal interlaces even at this late date, and the unique arrangement of figures, one above the other and perhaps a recollection (it has been suggested) of the

38 Church Lane, Ledbury, notable for its timber-framed houses

Santiago pilgrimage, on the responds of the great chancel arch. The east end of Kilpeck must be among the most photographed in England, and deservedly so. Its symmetry, its simplicity, and its appealing touch of barbarity, only slightly marred by Pugin's gaudy glass (1849), are uniquely evocative of the period.

To the north-east of the church are the earthworks of the village that once supported it. However, the quality of the workmanship at Kilpeck is such that it could only have resulted from the patronage of the lord of the castle, immediately to the west, and of the monks of Gloucester Abbey, owners of an adjoining priory cell to the south-east. Kilpeck Castle is a well-preserved motte and bailey, with two fragments of the stone walling of a polygonal shell-keep (probably late-twelfth-century) surviving on the summit of the motte. It is thought that Hugh de Kilpeck, grandson of the original post-

Conquest landowner, William fitz Norman, built the church, and that he did so with the cooperation of the monks at Kilpeck Priory, founded just a few years earlier in 1134. Walk over the motte if you can spare the time, or at least study it carefully from the churchyard. In addition to the prominent mound, well-protected by a deep ditch, Kilpeck has two baileys – one kidney-shaped between the motte and the church, the other a larger almost square enclosure to the south. Nothing remains of the Benedictine priory, placed away to the south-east of the village. It is likely in any event that the conventual life had ceased at Kilpeck some years before 1428, at which time (fully a century before the general Dissolution of 1536–40) the cell was merged with its mother-community at Gloucester.

***Ledbury** The parish church of this very attractive market town lies a little up the hill, east of the High Street, and is best approached up the narrow cobbled Church Lane, entirely late-medieval in character. The church is exceptionally large. With the support of the bishops of Hereford, whose manor this was, Ledbury Church was greatly extended in the thirteenth and early fourteenth centuries. But its huge length, in nave and chancel, dates back to the original campaign of the first half of the twelfth century (see the twelfth-century west façade and the still largely contemporary chancel and sanctuary) and to the development of Ledbury as an important market centre for the region. Of this earliest period, the chancel arcades, with the rare circular openings (formerly a clerestory) surviving above them, are the most notable reminder. For the later work, ignore (if you can) the over-zealous nineteenth-century restorations and concentrate on the very remarkable outer north chapel, now called the baptistery and thought to have been built as the chapter-house of a college, projected at Ledbury in the early fourteenth century but never fully established. Here the work, with its finely carved ballflower ornament so characteristic of the period, is of exceptional quality and richness. And here too,

built upright in the wall just east of the arch into the north chancel chapel, is Ledbury's most interesting monument, the late-thirteenth-century slab (formerly laid flat) and effigy of a praying priest – an early example of the new realism beginning to characterize monumental sculpture in the later Middle Ages. This realism is again apparent in the Pauncefoot monument in the curtained-off section of the north chapel now used as a vestry. Datable to about 1360, it shares many characteristics with the contemporary Grandison tomb at Much Marcle, including the illusionistic drapery hanging over the tomb-chest; unfortunately, it is not in good condition.

Among Ledbury's good secular buildings are the Old Council Offices and Old Grammar School, both in Church Lane and datable to c. 1500. In that lane too, one of the late-medieval shops from Butcher Row (a former colonization of the open market on the High Street), has been preserved and reconstructed on a new site. The prominent timber-framed Market House is no earlier than the seventeenth century. But the southern half of the appealing Feathers Hotel is of the late sixteenth century, and there is an especially fine fifteenth-century house and shop, with prominent overhang, on the busy High Street/New Street corner. St Katherine's Hospital, founded by Bishop Hugh Foliot in 1232, is a rare survival (also on the High Street) of an early-fourteenth-century retreat for the aged and infirm: at its east end, a chapel, with a hall at the west, both under the same great roof.

*Little Malvern This pleasing fragment, prominently placed next to the A4104 as it rises towards the turning north to Great Malvern, is the greater part of what is left of one of the lesser Benedictine houses, a dependency of the cathedral priory at Worcester. It consists of the former choir and presbytery, shorn of transepts and chapels, of the priory church, with a grand central tower rising over the crossing. The nave has gone, as has all but the west range of the cloister (now the earliest part of the neighbouring Little Malvern Court), and

most of what remains shows the hand of Bishop Alcock of Worcester, an energetic reformer of Little Malvern in the early 1480s. It was Bishop Alcock who, after conducting a visitation of the community in 1480, dismissed the monks to Gloucester Abbey for a period of disciplining, not allowing their return until two years later, by which time he had begun a process of restoration of their buildings. The fine external panelling on the upper stage of the tower could date a little earlier than Alcock's time. However, it was the bishop certainly who reconstructed the east end of the priory church, rebuilding the chapels (now ruined) north and south of the chancel, and supplying the great east window. The church these days is more impressive outside than in. Its features, which include royal donor glass in the east window and late-medieval floor-tiles of the Malvern school, are better seen in Malvern itself, where they escaped more successfully the attentions of iconoclastic reformers. It was such reformers again who hacked off the misericords on the surviving choir stalls, five on either side of the chancel, though these retain interesting figure-carving on the arms. The rood screen, re-sited in its present position to mark the division not otherwise apparent between nave and chancel, is crude fifteenth-century work; its head, much better carved, is probably part of the contemporary rood-beam.

Behind the church and a little to the west, the fourteenth-century prior's hall (with roof intact) has survived – and may be visited from time to time – in the present Little Malvern Court. It provides one of many examples of such re-use at the Dissolution of the more comfortable elements of a suppressed monastic house to provide the core of a much modified and extended Tudor mansion.

**Much Marcle The parish church at Much Marcle has been sadly brutalized by Victorian restorers, and for this reason is bound to be something of a disappointment. Notice, however, the good thirteenth-century nave arcades, with a contemporary clerestory; also the handsome Perpendicular central tower and the unusually long chancel, extended in the late thirteenth century, at which time the north chapel was also added, presumably for a chantry of some kind. But the reason for taking time over Much Marcle is its monuments. Most remarkable of these is the stately tomb of Blanche Mortimer, daughter of Roger Mortimer (first earl of March) and wife of Sir Peter Grandison, himself buried at Hereford Cathedral. Ignore the wavy cresting, which is later, but study especially the outstanding realism of the effigy (the drapery flows over the tomb chest at Lady Grandison's feet) and the insistent Mortimer and Grandison heraldry. The Grandison monument is set against the north wall of the chancel, towards the tower arch. In the north-west corner of the north chapel, there is another fine aristocratic monument, dating to about 1400 (a generation or so after the Grandison tomb), and again of memorable realism, particularly in the effigy of the fashionably dressed lady accompanied by her dogs. This important monument is dwarfed by the grand tomb of Sir John Kyrle (d. 1650), at one time high sheriff of Herefordshire and a prominent local sympathizer with the parliamentary cause. Even the names of the earlier knight and his lady are not now known. However, it is thought that we do know the name of the man who commissioned the third important effigy at Much Marcle, a rare oak figure (now in the nave) of Walter de Helyon (d. about 1360), recently re-painted as near as may be to the original colours. Walter de Helyon, usually described as a franklin of Much Marcle, was a member of the lesser country gentry, scarcely more (despite his knightly pose) than a jumped-up yeoman. The simplicity of his effigy makes a most striking contrast with the heraldic elaboration and expensive realism of the other two monuments of the period. North of the churchyard are the plainly visible remains of a small motte-and-bailey castle. It can never have been of great significance as a fortress, though

it is still known rather grandly as 'Mortimer's Castle'.

*Newent This is a pretty little town, mainly eighteenth-century along a main street of which the focal point (seen from the east) is a handsome timber-framed market hall (c. 1600). Towards the eastern end of that street also is the well-kept George Hotel, a good example of an early-nineteenth-century post-house, conveniently placed almost opposite the entrance to the churchyard. Only the east end and porch tower of Newent Church are medieval, and the whole has been dreadfully scraped within as one element in a drastic late-nineteenth-century restoration. Nevertheless, the church is worth a visit if only to experience the cultural shock of walking under a fourteenth-century tower straight into the age of Wren. What happened at Newent was that the medieval nave, of which nothing remains, collapsed on 18 January 1674, to be almost immediately rebuilt. A local master-carpenter, Edward Taylor, had worked for Wren. It is to him that the character of the present nave is chiefly owed, for it was he who designed and constructed the broad-span timber roof, unsupported by central pillars, which gives the body of the church its auditorium-like quality. Other striking elements in the design are the equal-sized openings to the chancel and Lady Chapel, to its south, while the eye is drawn especially to the great pilasters, with Ionic capitals, which frame these openings and appear to support the main roof.

Next to the church, the Old Court marks the site of a priory cell of Cormeilles Abbey (Normandy), to which the church and manor of Newent belonged from soon after the Conquest. This was later to become, shortly before the suppression of the alien priories early in the fifteenth century, part of the founding endowment of Fotheringhay College (Northamptonshire), the great collegiate chantry of the Yorkists.

*Ripple In this attractive village, the church and very splendid early-Georgian rectory make an excellent group of their own. Formerly the mother-church of a much larger parish, Ripple Church is an impressive building, already very grand in the late twelfth century, to which period the nave, the transepts, and the base of the tower all belong. The contemporary lancet windows of the nave clerestory let in little light, with the result that the body of the church appears gloomy. However, this effect is a consequence also of the exceptionally well-lit and spacious chancel, rebuilt a century later. Notice the great Perpendicular windows in the east and west walls of the church; and take time especially to study the fine set of misericords of the sixteen surviving stalls in the chancel, twelve of the carvings being a complete rendering of the *Tasks of the Months*, from cutting wood in January to fireside spinning in December. They are more accessible than most misericord series of this kind and, because of the excellent light in the chancel, are a particular temptation to the photographer. Why the chancel at Ripple should have been so grand, and why in the fifteenth century it should have been equipped with stalls of this quality and number, remain a mystery. Conceivably, both may result from the foundation here of a chantry in the early fourteenth century, with altars in the transepts dedicated to St Mary and St Peter; alternatively, the stalls could have been brought to Ripple in the sixteenth century, on the suppression of a neighbouring monastic or collegiate community.

Ross-on-Wye   Although pleasantly sited and equipped with some interesting buildings of the sixteenth century and later, including the handsome late-seventeenth-century market hall, Ross is now a rather scruffy town, being certainly a disappointment to the medievalist. Visit the parish church if you happen to be staying at Ross – the splendidly Victorian Royal Hotel, next to the church and with a fine prospect towards the west, is quite an inducement to do so – but avoid the town centre otherwise: you could well use the time saved elsewhere. In the church, which Pevsner finds 'large and interesting' but which has suffered from successive rebuildings and restorations, notice particularly the alabaster monument to William Rudhall (d. 1530), one of Henry VIII's attorney generals. The effigies of Rudhall and his wife are good, but it is the pre-Reformation religious imagery on the tomb-chest (the Trinity, the Annunciation, and massed saints) that is particularly interesting here. Within a very few years, representations of this kind would at best be in poor taste, at worst could be counted as heresy.

**Skenfrith   What remains of Skenfrith has a naked look which does little justice to a castle among the more advanced of its day. Built in a single programme of work between 1228 and 1232, Skenfrith was one of the castles (others in the area included Grosmont and White Castle) of Hubert de Burgh (d. 1234), justiciar of England and earl of Kent, a soldier of wide experience and great skill. Notice especially the geometric plan, with drum towers at the angles (already fashionable in France, where Earl Hubert had fought). But the particular feature of Skenfrith is the cylinder keep, an apparent anachronism in a castle of this date which nevertheless has many parallels in contemporary France. The keep was residential – there was a comfortable chamber on the second floor, with two large windows, a fireplace, and a garderobe – but the principal accommodation of the castle was sited in the ward below, in particular in the well-built western range, next to the keep, the lower floor of which has now been exposed. In effect, Skenfrith stands at a point of transition from the keep-based castles of twelfth-century England to the curtain-wall castle of the later thirteenth century where it was the mural tower and the multiplication of defences that received and deserved most prominence. Strong towers of the Skenfrith style never entirely lost favour so long as castles continued to be built; indeed, they were to experience a widespread revival in the later Middle Ages, as much for their symbolic as for their military qualities. However, Skenfrith's cylinder keep remains recognizably at the end of a fading tradition, not at the beginning of a new one. The chief strength of Earl Hubert's castle lay not in the keep but in the curtain.

Just to the north-west of the castle, the church at Skenfrith is well worth a visit. Its handsome west tower, like that at neighbouring Garway, is unusually strongly built, probably with a defensive purpose in these vulnerable Marcher lands. Inside, the thirteenth-century stone altar has recently been restored, having been demolished presumably at the Reformation, to which period belong also the Ten Commandment texts painted on either side of the east window (and now reproduced on two panels on the north aisle wall). The late-sixteenth-century John Morgan tomb is a curiosity, as is the seventeenth-century box pew of the Morgan family of Skenfrith; both are in the north aisle.

**Stoke Orchard   Motorway noise from the M5 (just to the west) and a scrappy suburban setting have done much to destroy the charm of this little country church. But just open the door, and you will find yourself surrounded by a wall-painting cycle of very great interest and importance. Datable to the early thirteenth century and thus a little later than the Kempley paintings, the Stoke Orchard cycle commemorates (in a continuous band of paintings at head-height round the nave walls) the life and miracles of St James of Spain, whose relics and shrine at Compostela became a major focal-point of pilgrimage in the West from as early as the tenth century, as indeed they remain to this day. The paintings, it must be said, are of poor quality; they have also been much damaged over the years. However, popular though the pilgrimage to Santiago de Compostela became, a St James cycle of this completeness is unparalleled in England and is rare even on the Continent. It links this small rural community in the most evocative way with that great tide of pilgrimage in medieval Europe, triumphing over the difficulties of the way,

which is perhaps better known to us in the pilgrimage to St Thomas of Canterbury. Stoke Orchard, it is thought, may itself have been a stopping-place for pilgrims *en route* for Bristol, where they would have taken ship for Spain. But the cycle could also have been commissioned by a returned lord of the manor, perhaps John the Archer (died *c.* 1234), in pious commemoration of a pilgrimage to Santiago of his own. Whatever the circumstances, take note especially of the comprehensiveness of the cycle, its unusual band-like form, and the frequently changing character of the borders. In these last, the use of animal motifs recalls the Kilpeck Viking-influenced carvings, as do the animal heads on the contemporary ironwork of the surviving medieval north door. This is a lovely little church, notable also for a good quality twelfth-century font and for a complete set of sixteenth-century benches in the nave. You will certainly not regret the short diversion.

***Tewkesbury   As at Great Malvern, the purchase for parochial use of the former monastic church at Tewkesbury has preserved many features, in particular of the late-medieval building, which would otherwise certainly have been lost. Buy a good guide, and take yourself round this splendid building carefully. Your first impression of the great drum columns of the nave, supporting a fourteenth-century lierne vault of equally magnificent but very different character, may well be the memory of Tewkesbury you carry away with you. But persevere. Only dimly seen at the end of the Norman arcade, the presbytery (with surrounding ambulatory) is both one of the greatest architectural marvels of fourteenth-century England and a social document of unique and very special importance. Here a late-medieval aristocratic tomb-church, commemorating the wealth and status of the Clare earls of Gloucester, stands virtually entire. The tombs and chantry chapels of Beauchamp, fitz Hamon, and Despenser (to the north of the altar), of Despenser again (to the south), are grandly placed in a privileged setting

39 The high-quality stellar vault of the four-teenth-century presbytery at Tewkesbury

40 The tomb of Hugh Despenser, next to the high altar at Tewkesbury

to which the pious generosity of Eleanor de Clare, sister of Earl Gilbert (d. 1314) and widow of Hugh le Despenser (d. 1326), had entitled them, and to which the entire rebuilding of the eastern end of the abbey church had been directed. The Clare line, at its greatest with Eleanor's father Gilbert (d. 1295), builder of Caerphilly, had been brought to a sudden end on the death of her brother at Bannockburn. Eleanor made it live on through the Despensers, one of whom, Edward Despenser (d. 1375 and commemorated by the chantry chapel south of the high altar), was among the original knights of the Garter. Study the heraldic and other memorial glass, datable to the early 1340s, in the windows of Eleanor's presbytery, and make a conscientious circuit of the finely vaulted ambulatory, with its unique gallery of chapels – tomb-churches in miniature – and the monuments and effigies they enclose. One out-standing effigy, not of this group, depicts the emaciated corpse of John Wakeman

(d. 1549), last abbot of Tewkesbury and (from 1541) first bishop of the newly created see of Gloucester. In its gruesome representation of extreme decay, it belongs to a tradition of mortality art familiar throughout Western Europe in the Late Middle Ages, but everywhere on the wane by this period.

There are many interesting late-medieval timber-framed buildings in Tewkesbury, with some other fragments of the abbey, including the west gatehouse and the former abbot's lodgings just to the east of it. Look especially at 82-83 Church Street (jettied fifteenth-century houses with filled-in first-floor windows) and at the restored cottage row (numbers 34 to 50) on the abbey side of the street, known to have been a speculative development by the monks.

*Upleadon A very typical twelfth-century rural church, Upleadon is unusual for two things: its remote farmyard setting, away to the east of the present village, and its timber-framed west tower (an addition of about 1500). There is a handsome Norman north door, but the nineteenth-century rebuilding of the chancel has deprived the interior of much of its character, in particular by the widening of the chancel arch. Look west, however, and you will see exposed the internal bracing of the tower, making an interesting composition in black-and-white, complemented by the slightly later timbering of the nave roof. It was at Upleadon that Matthew Price, a local man, indulged in one of the more disreputable pranks of the Reformation period. Holding advanced and irreverent opinions, he had gone to this remote church with his friend William Baker and had there – so the bishop's court was told in 1541 – 'spryncled & cast holy water upon the saide William Bakers ars', calling upon him to 'remember thy baptysm'. Another of Price's beliefs, reported at the time, was that 'hit was as goode to confesse hym to a tree, as to a prest'.

HOTELS AND ITINERARIES

At Ledbury, the **Feathers Hotel** is one of the focal points of life in this small country town. Its bar is lively and local; its rooms, heavily timbered and with authentically creaking floorboards, look out directly on Ledbury's main street, where the butcher may start work at four in the morning and a chiming clock keeps the visitor awake. The food, as one might expect, is variable. However, there are bistro-type restaurants elsewhere in the town, and the wise tourist does not need to book in at the Feathers for its dinners. Go there instead for the period atmosphere – a late-sixteenth-century building in the black-and-white Herefordshire style, with seventeenth-century additions and an eighteenth-century ground-floor interior. This is certainly the place to stay, if you can.

Otherwise, the **Royal Hop Pole** at Tewkesbury, although on the edge of the tour district, is a building with many attractions, eighteenth-century on an earlier frame. Unfortunately, a professional decorator has been set to work, and the interiors are now rather in the road-house tradition. But even he has been unable to destroy the charm of the eighteenth-century staircase and approaches. This is not the only attractive hotel in a town of considerable character. But it is undoubtedly one of the nicest.

The motorways (M5 and M50) pass close to Tewkesbury, and this is not, in consequence, the most restful headquarters for the tour. Very different are the attractions of the **Royal** at Ross-on-Wye, a large and comfortable Victorian hotel, quietly situated on a hill-top next to the church, with views over the Wye valley towards the west. Ross has few of the charms of Ledbury or of Tewkesbury. Yet the Royal is well placed at the centre of our region, in by far the most relaxing location. It is a Trust House hotel, and is as reliably professional as are the other establishments of this chain.

*   *   *

With Ledbury or Ross as your centre, the natural division between the days of your tour is approximately the line of the Wye. However, there is a good deal to be seen to the east of this river, and it makes sense to take in **Much Marcle** and **Kempley** with the western group, along with **Goodrich** as high priority. The other castles, **Skenfrith** and **Grosmont**, are open-access; you can visit them whenever you want. Do not miss **Kilpeck**, and whatever else you may sacrifice, spare the time for a visit to **Abbey Dore**. Neither church will occupy you for long. Yet both, you will find, will remain in the memory as particular peaks of the tour. **Garway**, although not far from either Skenfrith or Grosmont and on a most beautiful road, is perhaps the least rewarding of the buildings on this western itinerary. Go there if you have time to spare, or if you have a special interest in the Templars. Otherwise, put it aside for another day. Overall, this is an ideal tour for a winter break, but daylight hours are in short supply at this season, and there will be Abbey Dore and Kilpeck, at the north-west limits of the itinerary, probably still to be visited.

How you start the tour the next morning will depend naturally on where you have chosen to stay. But remember that **Great Malvern** and **Ledbury**, as major urban churches, will remain open and accessible later than most others, which makes it reasonable to begin in the south. **Newent** and **Upleadon** both have points of interest. However, they are of low priority by comparison with **Ashleworth, Deerhurst,** and the little church at **Stoke Orchard,** all of which should be seen before the long visit (perhaps for lunch as well?) to **Tewkesbury**. If you find yourself having to choose between **Ripple** and **Bredon**, take the latter, for both the tithe-barn and church of this pretty little village are important not just for themselves but for the comparisons they allow us with Ashleworth. You will not fail to see **Little Malvern** from the road if you are heading west again on the A4104 to Ledbury or Great Malvern, to the north. Stop if you can, for although most of its elements are repeated more grandly at Great Malvern, just up the road, there is much that is memorable in this fragmentary priory, not least the rural isolation of its hillside situation, which Great Malvern once had and has now lost.

There is much to be experienced on each day of the tour, and my inclination would be to rank Abbey Dore, Deerhurst, Goodrich, Great Malvern, Kempley, Kilpeck, Ledbury, and Tewkesbury with the best. Second to these, Ashleworth, Bredon, Grosmont, Much Marcle, Skenfrith, and Stoke Orchard each have much to offer; Garway, Little Malvern, Newent, Ripple, and Upleadon somewhat less. To my mind, the late Cistercian and Laudian amalgam at Abbey Dore, the Anglo-Saxon echoes of the priory church at Deerhurst, and the twelfth-century wall-paintings of the chancel at Kempley stand out as the most memorable of them all.

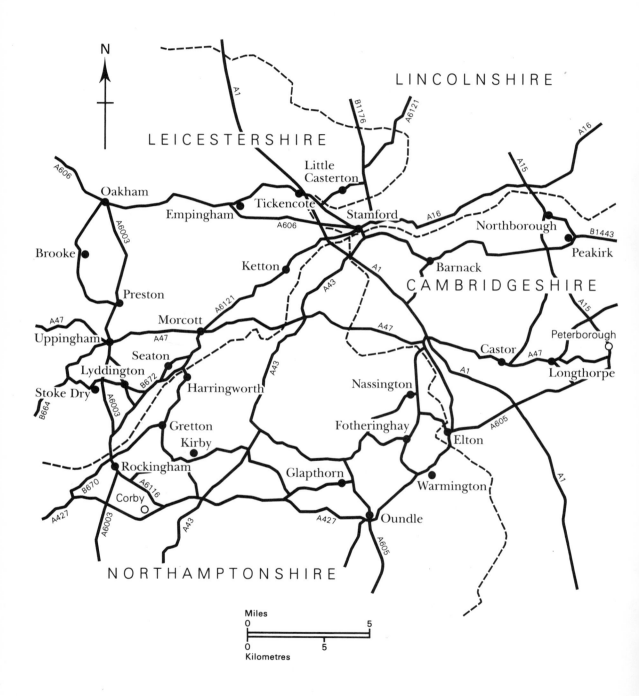

Chapter 4

Rutland, Northamptonshire, and the Soke of Peterborough

Stamford is a border town: one ward in Northamptonshire, five north of the river in Lincolnshire. It never made shire-town status on its own. Yet, for all that, every road in the region has Stamford at its end. Even today, it is harder to be directed to Peterborough, much less Corby, than to this venerable focal point of the ways.

Stamford's centrality goes back well beyond Domesday. With Lincoln and Nottingham, Derby and Leicester, it was one of the Five Boroughs of the Danelaw. In the West Saxon re-conquests and in the building of a single English state, Stamford was to assume a key role. True, even by 1086 some of this early promise had drained away. However, what Domesday records for us is a community at Stamford which, well before the formal incorporation of the borough in the later Middle Ages, already enjoyed exceptional privileges. Stamford's twelve 'lawmen' (Danish in origin) and the more numerous 'sokemen' whom, as early as this, we can reasonably identify as free burgesses, held tenements of their own – they 'have their lands in demesne and seek lords where they will'. Great local landowners retained important interests in Stamford. But their properties were divided and their authority splintered. It was the burgesses, not their overlords, who mattered.

Stamford, until very recently, was on the main road to the North. It was exceptionally well placed to market the goods of the rich fenlands to the east and of the wealthy farming country of Leicestershire and North-amptonshire to the west and south. In these respects, the comparison with **Oakham**, its nearest shire-town, may seem unfair. Yet the essential separation between the two boroughs was a distinction, still more crucial, in lordship. Rutland, and Oakham with it, was the dowry of the late West Saxon queens. Queen Edith, widow of Edward the Confessor, was the sole landowner in Oakham; at Stamford, she was one among many. Accordingly, Oakham was to have just one parish church on a site adjoining the castle; in the entire county of Rutland, there were to be no more than two religious houses, at **Brooke** and at Edith Weston, neither of any great

41 The west front of the nave of St Leonard's Priory, Stamford, formerly a dependency of the great Benedictine house at Durham

substance. The contrast with Stamford is significant. In Stamford's finest hour, divided lordship would result in the building of a church to serve each major estate in the borough – fourteen in all, of which five still survive to this day. Benedictines, both nuns and monks, settled in Stamford and its immediate vicinity. From the thirteenth century, all four orders of friars would find a home there, while late in that same century and early in the next, it would be the free air of the town and its rich religious life that would draw break-away scholars to Stamford in increasing numbers, viewing it as an alternative to Oxford.

English towns, with very few exceptions, were doing well by the late twelfth century; most had at least a century of growth still ahead. At Stamford, one memorial to this prosperity is the extravagant Early English blind arcade round the base of the walls of All Saints; another is the fine early-thirteenth-century vaulted undercroft of a merchant house (Scotneys) on St Mary's Hill; a third, only a little later in date, is the Brazenose Gate in St Paul's Street, which would derive its name from the residence behind it, some decades subsequently, of a migrant Oxford society. Oakham, if we were to accept Flore's House and the rebuilding of the parish church (both of the early fourteenth century) as our evidence, would seem to have enjoyed its boom rather later. Yet at Oakham too, in the hall of **Oakham Castle**, we have what is certainly the prize specimen of late-twelfth-century English domestic architecture, and most immediately striking here is the scale of the building and its cost. Oakham's own emergence as a shire town is datable to precisely this period. In the event, Walkelin de Ferrers' great building was to be saved till our time by its continued suitability for formal proceedings, in particular for the business of the sheriffs (now the magistrates) and their courts. The ring-work at Oakham – perhaps, although not certainly, originally a motte and bailey – was never a castle on the same scale as **Fotheringhay**, away to the south-east. But where it did have a purpose was as a venue for administrators and as the centre of a far-flung estate. Like many such centres in the comparatively peaceful late twelfth century, it was only lightly defended.

The arcades at Oakham, with their handsome capitals, are a fine example of the most sophisticated late-twelfth-century classicizing taste. Furthermore, they illustrate the suddenness (French-inspired *via* Canterbury) of that remarkable transition from the vigorous barbarity of Anglo-Norman stone-carving to the disciplined restraint of Early English. Compare the huge chancel arch, in its five carved orders, of the mid-twelfth-century village church at **Tickencote** with the cool classicism of the capitals at **Peakirk**, ornamenting the chancel arch of a church just as rural and only half-a-century later in date. Separated by more years, but on an especially powerful scale, are the tower and chancel of the great church at **Castor**, the one in the most ornamental Anglo-Norman taste, the other in the purest Early Gothic. And take a church like **Seaton**, entirely rebuilt in this period, with its richly carved Late Norman south door and chancel arch, its classicized nave arcades to north and south, its sophisticated paired Gothic lancets to the east.

Early in the thirteenth century, as rebuildings were completed while prosperity continued to increase, attention began to shift in church architecture to the extras. **Barnack**'s handsome nave arcades, the north of which is classically inspired, had been finished by about 1200. Within a few years, the already impressive Saxon west tower had been strengthened to carry a short stone spire and a new porch had been added to the south, both pioneers of their separate traditions. At Barnack, demand held up for the stone from its quarries, and the greatly enlarged and lavishly furnished fourteenth-century chancel is a token of undiminished prosperity. Through these decades too, a community like **Ketton** might still find the funds to purchase Barnack stone and to build with it a steeple which, in Early English bell-stage and Decorated spire, remains one of the most satisfying in England. Nevertheless, many could feel the chill in the air already before 1300, and within decades a frost would lay its finger on their enterprises. One of these, the incomplete vault of **Warmington Church** which had later to be finished in timber, probably reflects a merely local set-back in the village economy. More certainly, the permanent halt put to the ambitious rebuilding of the parish church at **Northborough**, with only the grand south transept to show for its first phase, was the consequence of a recession in Delamere family fortunes for which the Black Death must surely have been to blame. Northborough's transept, now the Delamere chantry chapel, most appropriately celebrates mortality.

It is not alone in this region in doing so. **Peakirk**, one of the churches in the immediate vicinity, preserves a particularly gruesome representation of that popular legend, the Three Living and Three Dead, where three kings, in all the trappings of their earthly dignity, experience a vision of the fate that would befall them − 'As you are, so once were we. As we are, so shall you be.' The painting dates to the mid-fourteenth century, and may indeed be a record of the Black Death. Of course, analogous morality paintings had been familiar for some time, there being a pre-plague version of the same terrible legend among the many fine paintings at **Longthorpe Tower**, commissioned by Robert Thorpe to decorate his Great Chamber in the early years of the century. However, it was the arbitrary character of the confrontation with death, as brought about by plague and well depicted at Peakirk, which gave mortality its horrid fascination. To the south-west of Peakirk, across the border in Northamptonshire, the son of a king was to establish a college, next to his castle at **Fotheringhay**, the sole purpose of which was to pray for himself and his kin. Edmund of Langley, next after John of Gaunt among the sons of Edward III, died in 1402, having done no more than initiate the project. It was left to Edward, second duke of York (killed at Agincourt in 1415), to begin work on the great choir at Fotheringhay, and then to Richard Plantagenet, third duke and principal generator of the Wars of the Roses, to complete the college buildings and their church. Nevertheless, this very loyalty of the Yorkist princes to their family resting-place at Fotheringhay is a characteristic reflection of the contemporary obsession with Death and with its aftermath which everywhere clouded men's judgement. We can see the same thing, of course, in works of useful piety like the handsome Browne's Hospital at **Stamford**. Many parish churches, among them Stamford's St George (rebuilt out of a legacy from Sir William de Bruges), benefited substantially from these beliefs. However, the great chantries of the period − the Wyatt chantry at **Oundle**, the Walcot chantry at **Barnack** − were to become little more in their day than over-endowed factories of intercession. The product of these building-works is pleasant enough, and we should be grateful to their originators for financing them; their purpose is better forgotten.

42 Early-fourteenth-century wall-paintings in the Great Chamber at Long-thorpe Tower, being part of a complete decorative scheme

Habits, of course, die hard. And the cold Protestant wind, that blew away the medieval doctrine of Purgatory with much else, failed to dislodge the memorial. In the little parish church at **Brooke**, in Rutland, the pompous alabaster tomb-chest and effigy of Charles Noel (d. 1619), of the local landowning family, is a blatant impertinence and corruption. A few years later, towards the middle of the same century, the Tryons of **Har-ringworth** would still feel able to take over the east end of the north aisle of the church, railing it off as a monstrous family vault. Indeed, should you want to get the feel of this little-changed world, there is no better place than St Martin's, **Stamford Baron**, church of the Cecils of Burghley. Here, for all the fine Renaissance detail of his tomb-chest and canopy, the great Lord Burghley lies north of the altar in the traditional place of honour, in full armour and with a lion at his feet. Burghley died old, after a life of achievement during which he had done much to shape the thinking of his countrymen. He had made his fortune, had built his great mansion, and had secured his line; but still the things of this world were not enough. Among many good works of which the future purpose was clear, Burghley re-founded, just the year before his death, the ancient hospital, or alms-house, in St Martin's parish. It was an action precisely paralleling William Browne's foundation, a full century earlier, of the hospital which survives in northern Stamford. Furthermore, Burghley's son and heir, Thomas Cecil, first earl of Exeter, would imitate his father a few years later, establishing an almshouse at **Lyddington**, in Rutland, in what remained of the former bishop's palace. Neither the first Lord Burghley nor the second were unaware of the traditional advantages accruing to a founder in the collective memory and perpetual prayers of his bedesmen.

***Barnack** The monumental Late Saxon west tower of Barnack Church is one of the better-known architectural survivals from this period. Capping it, the octagonal bell-stage and short spire are of early-thirteenth-century date, right at the beginning of the spire-building tradition. Below these, note the characteristically Saxon 'long-and-short work' on the quoins of the tower, the ornamental pilaster strips, triangular-headed windows, and panels of decorative sculpture – on the south face especially, a copy-book example of Saxon building. Internally, the great tower arch, with its odd sandwich-like imposts rounded at the corners, is a highly individual but again clearly Saxon feature, the only other relic of the time being the high-quality stone effigy (a Christ in Majesty) found in 1931 under the church floor and now re-set in a modern niche towards the east end of the north aisle wall. A rebuilding of the Saxon church began towards the end of the twelfth century. Note the north arcade with its classicized capitals and the stiff-leaf ornament of the south arcade, only a few years later in date. Shortly after this, the strange south porch, vaulted into the ridge, is as much a pioneering venture in new styles of church embellishment as is the near-contemporary spire. The thirteenth-century font is an unusual and very handsome specimen, with an especially attractive trefoil-headed arcade round the pedestal. However, the next major stage in the rebuilding of the church

was the reconstruction and extension of the chancel, undertaken in the early fourteenth century. Here the great east window is particularly fine, while the canopied piscina and triple sedilia, richly carved and highly ornamental, are similarly good products of the Decorated tradition. South of the chancel, the early-sixteenth-century Walcot Chapel is a good specimen of the late-medieval chantry nearing the end of its life. It is expensively embattled externally; inside, a Walcot family monument dates to c. 1520, but the most interesting feature of the chapel is the pair of canopied niches, to left and right of the east window, the northern of which retains, most exceptionally, its original early-sixteenth-century Annunciation.

Barnack Church is built of the hard local stone much prized by medieval masons and exported through a wide region, both for normal building work and for monuments. West of the village and just off the Wittering road to the south, a nature reserve known as 'Barnack Hills and Holes' preserves the site of the medieval quarrying: a good picnic spot with a view of Barnack Church in the distance.

***Brooke** Nobody should miss this unique little church, still prettily set in a situation as rustic as are the building and the furnishings it houses. At Brooke, twelfth-century work survives in the south door and in the north arcade; the font also is Norman. In the next century, a west tower was added, retaining still a good arch of the period into the body of the nave. But Brooke's character today is not medieval, and what will confront us now as we enter the church is an interior authentically Elizabethan. The Tudor reconstruction of Brooke, beginning in 1579 after some decades of neglect, included the total rebuilding of the north aisle and chancel, with the addition of a new south porch. Note the unexpectedly classical or 'Tuscan' arches which mark the divisions within the church everywhere except in the nave arcade. Nothing like this had been seen in English church architecture since as far back as the late twelfth century. And study particularly the remarkable set of contemporary church furnishings, bringing to life (as few documents can do) the pressures of the Elizabethan Church Settlement. Since the Reformation, much emphasis had come to be placed by Protestant divines on regular instruction, whether by sermons or by readings from the scriptures. At Brooke, the requisite pulpit, the reading desk, the stalls and family pews are all here, although both pulpit and desk back up against a screen which an Edwardian reformer would have found repugnant but which Elizabeth had restored to her churches. In its simple domestic character and rejection of surplus ornament, Brooke Church is a Protestant building, very obviously a product of the reform. Yet it is also, as was indeed its 'supreme governor' Elizabeth herself, essentially conservative, retaining just that separation between chancel and nave which the zealots had been so eager to remove. Sit for a while in one of Brooke's pews, and soak in the atmosphere of the reform. You will find little else of the period as pure.

On the road out to Oakham, less than a mile from the church, Brooke Priory Farm preserves both the name and the site of one of those lesser institutions of the monastic church which had done most to provoke a reform. Brooke was a priory-cell of the Augustinians of Kenilworth, never having more than three canons in residence and, although not poor by the standards of its day, never rich enough to contemplate

expansion. Brooke was suppressed in 1535, and some of the stonework of the medieval priory remains in the present farm-buildings. Its prominent lodge, however, and the gateway adjoining it, are post-Dissolution embellishments.

Castor   Over the south priest's door on the outside wall of the chancel of this fine large church, an inscription records the consecration of the building in 1124. It was (and remains) of cruciform plan, with much emphasis being placed on an ornate central tower, later equipped with its present fourteenth-century parapet and spire. Inside and out, the tower is still the most impressive individual feature of the church. Its decorative external arcading is of incomparable richness and complexity; internally, although some of the sculptured capitals of the fine Norman crossing have been renewed, many remain to testify to the vigour of Anglo-Norman stone-carving at this period, featuring scenes of great activity including a boar hunt and a contest between a man and a lion. In the early thirteenth century, at the same time that the south aisle was added to the nave, the chancel was rebuilt, again on a grand scale. Now attractively bare and austere, the chancel is brilliantly lit by a great Perpendicular east window, replacing the original triple lancets. In the usual position on the south wall, a handsome double piscina and two-seat sedilia are neatly framed under the continuous string course much favoured by Early English masons. The roofs of the nave and its aisles (recently re-painted with much gilt on the bosses and angels) are fifteenth-century and very spectacular. Worth noting too is the survival of three painted scenes from a fourteenth-century St Catherine Cycle, well lit at the west end of the north aisle. At the other end of the same aisle, a late medieval reredos (itself a rare survival in this position) probably belonged to the shrine here of Saint Cyneswith, one of the daughters of King Penda (d. 654) of Mercia and sister of Saint Cyniburg, also a nun, to whom Castor Church is dedicated.

*Elton   A noble west tower is the first impressive feature of this large country church, but its interior is hardly less grand. Go first to the chancel. Here you will find a good set, datable to *c.* 1300, of aumbry in the north wall, piscina and sedilia in the south, all under identical arches. The same symmetry applies to the nave arcades, contemporary with the chancel, which are best viewed through the broad chancel arch, framing a tall Perpendicular tower arch at the west end. Centrally placed in front of the tower arch and opposite the main entrance through the south door, the font is again of *c.* 1300. Its simplicity accords well with the general composition of the building: very English, very satisfying, very complete.

**Empingham   The church at Empingham is unusually large, reflecting its status (shared with Lyddington and Nassington) as a prebend, or peculiar, of Lincoln. It has an especially handsome and prominent west tower, crowned at the top with battlements and surging pinnacles, and equipped with a pretty little spire in the local Decorated tradition. Entrance to the church is through the west door, and first impressions of a rather plain interior may do Empingham less than full justice. Notice the difference in the nave arcades: round-headed arches of classical simplicity (*c.* 1200) to the right, later pointed arches (still thirteenth century) to the left. Over the easternmost arch of the north arcade, one of the original circular clerestory windows has survived, though the present clerestory, with the good timber roof it supports, is fifteenth-century. Of the same late date is the roof of the north transept, visually the most satisfying part of the interior. The transept has two east windows, next to each of which a piscina establishes the former siting there of an altar. In the later Middle Ages, as the demand rose for altar-space for the celebration of obits and other special masses, such east walls were to become especially precious. At Empingham, we can see how the demand was met. Earlier in date are the mid-thirteenth-

century piscina and sedilia in the south wall of the chancel, a very handsome set which is individually the best feature of the church. Worth noting too is the painting of the Virgin in the eastern splay of one of the south transept windows, overpainted later in the Middle Ages with a non-representational decorative pattern; also the medieval cross-slabs preserved in the north transept, and some fifteenth-century heraldic glass still intact in the heads of the same transept's east windows.

***Fotheringhay   You should approach Fotheringhay, if you possibly can, from the south-east. From there, seen over the flood-meadows of the Nene, the great west tower of Fotheringhay Church, with its noble octagonal lantern-like upper stage, rises to particular advantage. Yet this, even with the nave it adjoins, is a fragment only of the wealthy Yorkist collegiate foundation established by Edmund of Langley (d. 1402), fifth son of Edward III, earl of Cambridge (from 1362) and first duke of York (from 1385). Immediately to its south, the collegiate buildings are mere humps in the grass: they are known to have had a fine cloister with painted glass windows, a library, and other accommodation on a scale appropriate to the importance of the family for which Fotheringhay was to serve as a memorial. Today, the church's incomplete look is owed to the loss of the second duke's choir, demolished shortly after the college's suppression, where Edward and his kin lay buried. The austere, brilliantly lit nave is the work of Richard Plantagenet, third duke of York and father of the Yorkist usurper Edward IV, who died at Wakefield in 1460, defeated by the Lancastrians in one of the more memorable encounters of the disruptive Wars of the Roses. Fotheringhay is now equipped with a nice set of eighteenth-century box pews, but little is left of its original furnishings, the one major exception being a magnificent Perpendicular pulpit, rather gaudily repainted, with its vaulted tester still in place under a larger Jacobean canopy. There is a good Perpendicular font, well placed under the tower

43 The Perpendicular pulpit, before re-painting, at Fotheringhay; note the original vaulted tester still in place under the much larger Jacobean canopy

44 The west tower, with its distinctive octagonal lantern, of the former Yorkist collegiate chantry at Fotheringhay

arch at the west end of the nave. Towards the east, in the substitute Elizabethan chancel, two classical-inspired monuments, paid for by the queen herself in 1573 and in a very low-key idiom, commemorate Edward (the second duke) and Richard (the third), with Cicely Nevill, Richard's widow, herself once resident at Fotheringhay.

Cicely, for the first eight years of her long widowhood, lived at Fotheringhay Castle, next to the river and a short way to the east of the college. On the way there, just before the village street swings south to the bridge, the houses on both sides of the road (Old Inn to south; New Inn to north) still display many fifteenth-century features, most notably a good Perpendicular gate arch at what is now Garden Farm. At the

castle itself, only one fragment of masonry survives. But the site may be walked over and is worth the excursion, for it preserves still intact the major motte-and-bailey earthworks of the twelfth-century earls of Huntingdon and Northampton. On the right day too, from the summit of the motte, you can enjoy what must surely be one of the most beautiful prospects in England. It is a place for reflection, rich in nostalgia for the past.

*Glapthorn A nice little village church with a Perpendicular west tower but otherwise largely of the thirteenth century, making a pleasant contrast with the grandiose urban church at neighbouring Oundle. The varying heights of the nave arcades (the south being earlier than the north) and of the chancel arch, together with the change in style from round to pointed arches, add interest to the interior. There is a good Perpendicular font, and a large St Christopher painting survives on the north wall of the north aisle, somewhat unexpectedly hidden from the south door (from which it would usually have been viewed by departing travellers) by the nave arcades.

Just north of Glapthorn, providing another justification for the diversion, is Southwick, where hall and church make an attractive group, easily seen from the road. Southwick Church has a pretty Decorated west tower and spire, but is otherwise an eighteenth- and nineteenth-century rebuild, not worth a visit. As for Southwick Hall, you can see its fourteenth-century residential tower from a distance and may be able to inspect the interior of this very charming mixed-period house should you happen to coincide with one of its (not too frequent) summer visit days. The same can be said for the much more important but equally inaccessible Deene Park, a major sixteenth-century (and later) country house, between Southwick and Kirby Hall to the west. Like Kirby, this is another great courtyard-plan residence in the late-medieval manner, with a hall on the far side of the court from the gate. It was extensively rebuilt at later periods, with major works in the nineteenth century, and lacks the purity of Kirby. However, you should stop at Deene if both time and its owners permit. The church is of interest for its sixteenth- and seventeenth-century Brudenell monuments, but was largely rebuilt in the late 1860s and is probably best left alone.

*Gretton The parish church at Gretton, on the northern edge of the village, is well placed on the hillside, with a fine prospect north over the Welland. Not a remarkable building in any way, its interior is nevertheless given great character by a splendidly cock-eyed Decorated east window, by thirteenth-century transeptal chapels, to north and south of the eastern-

most bay of the nave, and by sturdy mid-twelfth-century nave arcades, characteristically massive and low. Today, the strongest impression Gretton leaves is of a conspicuously well-furnished church. This it owes to a fine set of eighteenth-century box pews, elegantly curved in the best of taste in front of the chancel arch, and to the contemporary pulpit and chancel panelling. Overall, the effect of the east end – panelled and railed – is a trifle operatic. But this, of course, constitutes a great part of Gretton's charm.

*Harringworth Nicely sited towards the river, Harringworth Church is a memorably pleasant and spacious building, possessing several features of interest. What you will notice first is the pretty west tower, neatly finished off in the early fourteenth century with an appropriately proportioned little stone spire, carrying three tiers of lucarnes, or dormers. When inside, inspect the noble fifteenth-century screen; it preserves (as few now do) the coving that once carried the rood loft, while in the wall to one side, the rood loft door and its stairs are still in place. At the east end of the south aisle, most unusually located, are a diminutive piscina and sedilia, approximately contemporary with the spire. The font, of about 1300, is oddly barbaric in style. But quite another sort of barbarism is displayed, much more prominently, in the monumental collective vault of the Tryon family, which occupies the entire east end of the north aisle. This is work of the mid-seventeenth century, handsomely railed about in the unselfconscious manner of the period. Yet it carries with it the chill of the churchyard. Harringworth would be better without it.

*Ketton Extensive nineteenth-century restorations have stripped this great church of many of its original features. Today, the interior is notable only for its tall late-thirteenth-century nave arcades, for the fine matching tower arches, and for the roof-lines (still showing as cuts against the west face of the tower) of the twelfth- and thirteenth-century gables, before the final fifteenth-century re-roofing. Externally, much more has survived, owing its freshness to the hard Barnack stone of which Ketton Church was constructed. Look at the interesting west front, with its Late Norman door flanked on either side by a range of Early English blind arches. But give most of your time to the very remarkable central tower, once the core and pivot of a cruciform church, which is beyond question one of the finest in England. Norman at the bottom, its handsome bell-stage, with great triple lancets on each face, is a triumph of the later thirteenth-century Early English style. To crown the whole, a glorious early-fourteenth-century spire, with three tiers of lucarnes and with stone figures (the Virgin, Gabriel, St Peter, and St Paul) under canopies at the angles, rises in perfect proportion. It is in the best and the most elaborate Decorated tradition: a very costly work, surely far beyond the ordinary means of such a small community as Ketton, of which the circumstances and occasion are unknown.

***Kirby Although more Renaissance than medieval in character, this most haunting of ruins must be visited. Kirby Hall is a building of three main phases. Started by Sir Humphrey Stafford in 1570, it was completed by Sir Christopher Hatton in the later 1570s and 1580s, and then modified by another Christopher Hatton, the third of his name, in 1638-40. Adjoining it on the west, the late Tudor or Jacobean garden retains its plan, shorn only of those stone ornaments, characteristic of the period, which once gave it an architectural flavour. Kirby Hall, which was allowed to fall into decay in the nineteenth century, is now in the guardianship of the Historic Buildings Commission. There are good explanatory displays in the still roofed south-west wing, formerly the family's residential range, and an excellent guide may be bought at the ticket office. Take your time over the visit, but notice especially the way that the typical late-medieval courtyard plan – great court entered through prominent gatehouse, with hall on the far side and lodgings occupying the remaining ranges – has been retained by the Elizabethan architect (thought to be Thomas Thorpe, father of the noted surveyor John Thorpe, and himself a local mason of distinction). The differences, though, are at least as important as the similarities. Kirby Hall is famous for its display of Renaissance decorative devices, some of them taken from contemporary pattern books, others modelled on buildings Thorpe must have known about in France. Especially individual are the giant pilasters of the inner court, familiar enough in sixteenth-century France but hitherto unparalleled in England. They rest strangely against the medieval fenestration of the great hall at Kirby, itself repeated exactly on the other side of the porch (to the east) where the tall windows back only on domestic offices and are there to furnish symmetry to the façade. Late-medieval domestic building had been characterized by a functional irregularity: a hall might need great windows, whereas a buttery or pantry neither needed them nor got them in the event. By the late sixteenth century, the fashion for symmetry had taken hold while still having to accommodate a great hall in the old manner – a traditional apartment required by the patron, but having little use by this period. Up-to-date was the southern-style open loggia backing the north range at Kirby, the long first-floor gallery in the west range, the Renaissance ornament (sometimes tentatively used), and the over-riding symmetry of house and garden, achieved at whatever the cost. Medieval was the retention of the great hall, with porch and screens passage, and the framing of the court between ranges of lodgings, being a harking back to the day when every great man kept his own large retinue to demonstrate his wealth and importance. Go to Kirby to savour these contradictions.

*Little Casterton On the right summer day, Little Casterton could be an ideal picnic spot, its pretty church tucked away to the north of the village in an especially welcoming riverside setting. A good Perpendicular timber roof, well lit by the clerestory of the same period, adds charm to the interior. Other noteworthy features include a twelfth-century Tree of Life tympanum, re-set in the north aisle, and two very splendid late-thirteenth-century figures (Ecclesia and Synagogue) in the west window jambs, with other paintings (representing part of a Life of Christ cycle) also surviving along the south aisle wall. In the chancel, the handsome piscina came there from Pickworth Church, demolished in the early nineteenth century. A tomb recess in the south aisle, datable to the late thirteenth century, holds two contemporary cross-slabs, the bottom in excellent condition and very ornate. The double brass (to Thomas Burton (d. 1381) and his wife) is also of very good quality.

Longthorpe Dismally set on the suburban margins of Peterborough, Longthorpe Tower is nevertheless well worth a visit. The tower itself, although not the manor-house to which it is attached, is now in the care of the Historic Buildings Commission, and is open throughout the year. At Longthorpe, the tower was added in about 1300 to an existing late-thirteenth-century stone manor-house. It is one of the better examples of the more intensive fortification of such sites characteristic of this period of mounting disorder. In addition, the tower illustrates the growing sophistication of domestic accommodation in the later Middle Ages. It has a fine vaulted Great Chamber on the first floor, formerly entered at this level from the adjoining hall and heated by a fireplace of its own; above this, the lord's private bedchamber is equipped with a garderobe, of which the pierced stone seat, although not now in place, has been preserved. Yet it is neither as a defensive building nor as an illustration of fourteenth-century life and manners that Longthorpe sticks in the memory. The tower's great feature, rather, is the remarkably complete set of wall-paintings, decorating the Great Chamber and, for a

secular building of this kind and date, absolutely unique. The paintings are well described and illustrated in the guide that may now be bought from the custodian of the tower. They seem to have been commissioned by one or other of the Robert Thorpes, father and son, who were stewards in succession of Peterborough Abbey for much of the first half of the fourteenth century. Whoever ordered them was a man of evident piety and of very educated tastes. The themes chosen are both religious and secular. They include biblical scenes (a Nativity on the north wall; a King David on the vault next to it), popular moralities and symbols (a Three Living and Three Dead in one of the window recesses, with a fine Wheel of the Five Senses over the fireplace), heraldry (the Thorpe arms on the south wall, under throned figures of Edward II and his half-brother, Edmund of Woodstock), and such well-known sequences as the familiar Labours of the Months. It is thought that the general theme of the paintings, taken as a whole, was the contrast between the material and the spiritual life. Certainly, they illustrate very fully the traps of the one and the rewards, worth aspiring to, of the other.

Lyddington The size and importance of the church at Lyddington is at least partly explained by its special status as a prebend of Lincoln. However, Lyddington was also the site of one of the principal manor-houses, or country palaces, of the medieval bishops of Lincoln, who might rest there to conduct a visitation in the area or to attend to the business of their great diocese. Today, in consequence, the village's most notable feature is the so-called Bede House, just north of the church. It is a conversion of the former solar range of the bishop's palace into an almshouse, financed by Thomas Lord Burghley (d. 1623). On the north face of the building, protected by a short timber gallery or cloister, are the doors of the bedesmen's individual chambers. They share that side with an earlier stone staircase which still leads to what was formerly the bishop's Great

Chamber on the first floor. Towards the church, facing south, are the fine windows (with central oriel) of Bishop John Russell's late-fifteenth-century rebuilding of the solar range, while under the grass to the north of the building are the foundations of a substantial hall (at right-angles to the chamber and linked to it by the existing stair) built very probably in the early fourteenth century when Bishop Burghersh (1320-40) transformed and fortified his palace. The existing circuit wall, with its nice little late-fifteenth-century angle tower at the south-west corner, follows the line of Bishop Burghersh's enclosure. Beyond it, to the north-east, the earthworks of the bishop's fish-ponds are another prominent survival, with the contemporary enclosures of the episcopal deer park still traceable in the fields to the west.

The massive fourteenth-century west tower of Lyddington's church is not helped by its diminutive spirelet, more like a party-hat than a roof. But the Perpendicular nave arcades are symmetrical and handsome, and the interior is well lit by an effective clerestory of the same period. Individual features include a fifteenth-century rood screen, still fitted with the coving that supported a rood loft; also some wall-paintings, the best of which (behind the pulpit) represents a king, probably Edward the Confessor. In the chancel, notice the rare survival of acoustic jars (for voice amplification) set high in the north and south walls, under the roof. Still more important and individual at Lyddington, and not to be missed on any account, is the arrangement of the altar with rails on all sides, datable to 1635 and the result of a compromise between Laudian and Puritan views at that fraught period, sanctioned by Bishop John Williams (1621-41), an opponent of Archbishop Laud and later himself archbishop of York.

*Morcott   The setting of Morcott Church is not especially attractive, and a visit could be urged only with misgivings were it not for the splendid Late Norman and Transitional interior. But first, before you go inside, notice the rare surviving oculus window (more like a gun-port) on the west face of the tower, now rather oddly placed over a twelfth-century door which has been given a new head in the fourteenth century. On entering, go straight to the chancel before turning to look back into the body of the nave. What you will see, nicely framed by the Gothic arch of the Early English chancel, is a fine ornate tower arch at the west end of the nave, with a contemporary Norman north arcade, identical in treatment, to the right, and a Transitional south arcade (much plainer but still with rounded arches) to the left. This seen, there is not much else left of interest in the church. But the effect is not one you will forget in a hurry. This is Anglo-Norman building on a very human scale: well worth the pause, however brief.

**Nassington   This unusually large village church owes something of its importance to the fact that Nassington was chosen, early in the twelfth century, to be the seat and centre of jurisdiction of a prebendary of Lincoln, which was how it remained until the nineteenth century. However, the scale of the nave was set much earlier, in the tenth century or even before. Look back, when you enter the church, at the west wall of the nave, at the top of which, just below the roof, you will see a triangular-headed window, characteristically Saxon, over a blocked round-headed opening, marked out as a recess in the plaster. Compare these with the similar (but more elaborate) features at Deerhurst, in Gloucestershire. We are in a Saxon minster or monastic church, once fitted with the internal galleries of such a building. In the north aisle, an Anglo-Saxon cross-shaft, carved with a crucifixion scene on one face and typical interlace on the other, similarly recalls Nassington's earlier status as one of the major centres of pre-Conquest Christian worship in the locality. Under the Saxon openings in the west wall, a heavy and rather brutal-looking Late Norman tower arch contrasts with the exceptionally handsome thirteenth-century arcades, similarly cut into earlier walls when first the north and then the south aisles were added. Much remodelling occurred in the chancel in the nineteenth century, so interest concentrates in the nave and its aisles, particularly notable for their fine surviving wall-paintings, dated variously to the fourteenth and fifteenth centuries. Over the chancel arch, the upper part of a large Doom can still be made out quite well, with the Christ figure (hand raised in blessing) at the centre: a yawning Hell-Mouth would once have awaited the Damned at the lower right-hand corner. Other paintings include a large St George and the Dragon, centrally placed over the north arcade, with a Wheel of Fortune on the north aisle wall, over a St Michael (weighing a soul in his balance). The roofs of the nave and aisle are late-medieval, rugged but handsome, and there is a well-placed octagonal font of the fourteenth century, adding its bit to the general composition of this impressive church, best seen from the chancel arch.

Across the road and on the corner to the south-west, the prebendal house (now a farmhouse) incorporates a thirteenth-century hall, with the usual opposing entrances (east and west) and with an attached solar block at its south end. Further to the north, another house contains many fifteenth-century features, including a large door opening and mullioned windows, with a nice little oriel in the north wall. This stonework, which is of good quality, is said locally to have been brought here from neighbouring Fotheringhay.

Northborough On a dangerous corner of the busy A15 (Sleaford–Peterborough), the extraordinary fourteenth-century manor-house at Northborough may at first slip by unnoticed. But turn east at the corner and park by the church. This also, though kept locked, is worth inspection; together, church and manor-house make a group of some considerable importance, even if you can do nothing with either except view it from the churchyard or the road.

Certainly, manor-houses of this date and completeness are very rare. Seventeenth-century extensions to the main residential block set off, rather than hide, the medieval work, marked especially by the two tall traceried windows of the great hall. Notice the intact west gable, with contemporary chimney, of the early-fourteenth-century hall. And view the whole, as it was always intended to be seen, through the impressive gatehouse, now standing incongruously against the tarmac of the modern A15. This prominent gatehouse entry to the private courtyard of the lord's personal quarters is characteristic of the manor-houses of the period. By the early fourteenth century, the more random planning of the Anglo-Norman manor-house had settled down to a standard courtyard house such as the one we see here at Northborough. While in no real sense a defendable building, Northborough Manor at least had the advantage of privacy for the lord, with some of the qualities of protection too, as it presented its most formidable front to the road.

Northborough Manor's medieval buildings date to the 1330s, and it was at just this time also that work began on an ambitious rebuilding of the parish church, of which only the south transept was completed. Probably conceived as a chantry chapel of the Delamare family, which financed the rebuilding, this south transept is on a far grander scale than the body of the church itself, embattled and decorated with much costly sculptured ornament. As you can see from the arch at the north end of the transept's west wall, rising without apparent purpose above the roof of the earlier south aisle, further work was intended on the enlargement of this aisle, being the next stage in a projected total rebuilding of the church. No doubt, it was the Black Death and subsequent economic difficulties which frustrated an enterprise only possible in conditions of boom. Northborough Church, as we see it now, stands frozen at this crucial point of change.

Oakham This attractive little market town has always been the judicial and administrative centre of the county of Rutland, one consequence of which has been

45 The hall, seen through the gate passage, of the manor-house at Northborough, dating to the 1330s

the survival here of England's most remarkable late-twelfth-century domestic building, the castle hall, still in use as a courthouse. Oakham Castle is a large banked enclosure, formerly moated and with a circuit wall and mural towers of which fragments have survived. Almost facing the gate but slightly to the west of it, the castle hall is of unique importance as the earliest ground-floor baronial aisled hall of its kind. Dull on the exterior, with out-of-character dormer windows and a re-sited south door, the hall is of splendid internal proportions. Its arcades, built to

the order of Walkelin de Ferrers in the 1180s, are in the classical tradition favoured in the late twelfth century. They have carved capitals similar to those used by William of Sens in his rebuilding (after 1175) of the choir of Canterbury Cathedral, and are thought to be the work of a mason of the Canterbury school. In the east wall of the hall, doors (now blocked) led through to the service quarters – buttery, pantry, and kitchen. To the west, behind the magistrate's bench, a solar block, beyond the surviving west gable, would have housed the private accommodation of the lord. Notice especially the high quality of the stonework in the hall, recently cleaned and restored. Until the late twelfth century, an aisled hall of this size would have been built almost invariably of timber. At Oakham, Walkelin's great hall stands at the beginning of a very long tradition of domestic building in stone, during which in due course the arcades would be lost as techniques were developed to roof a broader span. It is a transitional building, from timber into stone, and transitional too in the details of its architecture, with twin pointed windows on the external faces while internally every arch remains round.

After the castle hall, the church at Oakham is bound to be something of a disappointment. It has a pretty approach through the L-shaped market square, centrally colonized by shops in the broader wing of the L, with a roofed market cross round the corner to the west. Externally too, Oakham Church is attractive, the tower and spire being especially impressive. But the interior, like that of so many other great urban churches, has been largely spoilt by the activity of nineteenth-century restorers, being now notable chiefly for its fourteenth-century arcades (approximately the same date as the Decorated steeple) and the spacious effect of its broad double transepts. If you have time to spare, keep it for Flore's House (34 High Street), a fourteenth-century stone merchant's house with central hall (still retaining its east door) and gable end against the street to the north. Few of its kind (and no other in Oakham) have survived.

*Oundle   In this pretty, rather randomly planned little town – its main street broadening out into a market-place 'colonized' by the early-nineteenth-century town hall – the best domestic building is the Talbot Hotel, dated 1626, with handsome bay windows very much of the period and a façade just irregular enough to give it interest. Otherwise, the centre of Oundle has not been helped by the expanding empire of its school. Tightly packed around by school buildings, the church nevertheless is nicely set, its beautiful fourteenth-century tower and spire (one of the most graceful in England) rising to dominate the surrounding countryside. Another good feature of the exterior of Oundle Church is the grand south porch. It was built in 1485 for Robert Wyatt and for Joan, his wife, in another of those gestures of burgess support for the town church so characteristic of the later Middle Ages. Internally, there is less to admire. Oundle has been horribly stripped and re-pointed, the consequence being that even its great scale is lost in the gloom of the restorations. Notice, though, the pretty Perpendicular pulpit – its recent re-painting, for all its garish quality, is probably as authentic as may be – and admire too the fine late-fifteenth-century brass lectern, one of the more handsome examples of a class of medieval church furnishing that invariably looks too good to be true. Of the screens, the parclose screens between the chancel and its chapels are of the same period as the pulpit and lectern, as is also the surviving base of the rood screen. The other furnishings are grimly Victorian.

**Peakirk   What chiefly justifies the diversion to this attractive but otherwise less than remarkable little church is the survival here of fourteenth-century wall-paintings of unusual interest in the illustration of contemporary tastes. At Peakirk, there is a nice Norman south door, characteristically ornate, with good nave arcades (Late Norman to the north; Early English to the south), and a fine chancel arch (note the classicizing capitals) of c. 1200, exceptionally tall for a church of this scale. Peakirk's lectern, too, with its rare fourteenth-century carved shaft, is certainly worth attention. But you will scarcely need telling, once you have entered the church, what it is that has brought you there most particularly. Prominently placed over the north arcade, where departing parishioners in need of such comfort could view it from the south door as they left, is a great St Christopher, patron saint of travellers, breaking the

46 A handsome late-fifteenth-century brass eagle lectern, preserved at Oundle Church

47 Two cadavers, dripping with slugs and other symbols of corruption, from a Three Living and Three Dead morality painting in the north aisle of Peakirk Church, dating probably to the period of the Black Death

continuity of an elaborate contemporary Passion cycle, no doubt invoked by generations of preachers to hammer home the message of their sermons. The cycle starts (top left) with a Last Supper, of which only the table with its load of food and eating utensils survives. Other scenes include the Betrayal, the Crucifixion, the Deposition, the Entombment (badly damaged), and the Resurrection, each of which would have been copied by the fresco-painter, more or less exactly, from a contemporary illuminated manuscript, perhaps in the library of Peterborough Abbey. More unusual, and worth very special attention, are the two morality paintings, sometimes called 'warning pictures', behind the arcade in the north aisle. The best known of these is a splendidly gruesome Three Living and Three Dead (one of the Dead is missing), where three kings are confronted by cadavers infested with moths (symbols of corruption) and dripping with slugs and worms. Appropriately enough, this version

of the legend was painted at about the time of the first onset of bubonic plague in the Black Death of 1348–9. Next to it, over the north door, two women are shown with their heads close together in an attitude of scurrilous gossip; behind them, a devil has his feet on their shoulders and his hands on their heads, as a Warning to Gossips and Scandalmongers. Peakirk's wall-paintings, restored by Mr E. Clive Rouse in 1950, are fully described, with interesting parallels, in his paper for the *Archaeological Journal*, 110 (1953). The date he assigns to the Passion Cycle is *c*. 1325, with the Three Living and Three Dead a little later, nearer the middle of the century.

Preston Much of the attraction of this pretty little church results from its siting on the western edge of one of the loveliest villages in Rutland. Beyond stretches open country, onto which the churchyard backs; to the east, the long village street (now just off the busy A6003, to which it runs parallel) is lined with golden-brown ironstone houses. Temptingly, the Fox and Hounds, a sixteenth-century pub, offers food and drink to the traveller.

The church itself is neat and compact, with a good west tower and spire, and with a particularly successful grouping externally of south chancel window and priest's door (with window over), both of a decorative and unusual form. Inside on the same wall, you will find a handsome fourteenth-century single sedile, next to the priest's door and undoubtedly the best individual feature of the church. It is a fine example of the Decorated style, as applied to church furnishings of this kind. In the nave, the twelfth-century arcades are pleasing, the northern (with splendid zigzag ornament) being some decades earlier than the south.

Rockingham   For the medievalist, Rockingham is a sad disappointment. At the foot of the hill, Rockingham's houses (laid out along the line of the main road like a model estate village) are attractive enough. However, both castle and church, on the scarp to the south, are largely Victorian, the former owing its present 'medieval' outline to the mid-century architect Anthony Salvin. To be sure, Salvin was a highly talented exponent of the fashionable antiquarianism of his time. His work is always interesting and may very well prove to your taste. If you are at Rockingham in the summer months – the castle opens at Easter – you should pause to savour Salvin's gifts. Nevertheless, to those who prefer the narrower path of medieval studies, it may well come as a relief to know that the best authentic feature of Rockingham's defences is also the most visible from the road. Stop the car long enough to take in the general appearance at least of Rockingham's great gatehouse, one of the most perfect examples (with its boldly projecting twin drum towers) of the highly sophisticated gatehouse architecture of the late thirteenth

century. It is fully the equal of anything you may find in the king's contemporary fortresses in North Wales. Like those, it owes much to the French.

*Seaton   Between Harringworth and Seaton, the Welland Viaduct (built in the late 1870s and one of the triumphs of Victorian railway engineering) nicely enlivens your route. But Seaton anyway is a church worth pausing at, in particular for its Late Norman and Transitional interior. Before entering, take time to admire the twelfth-century south door. It has finely carved capitals and is as richly ornate as the contemporary chancel arch within. Not much later, but very different in feeling, are the nave arcades, with their distinctly classical effect. They belong to the last classicizing mood of Romanesque in the North, and are immediately succeeded at Seaton by the paired Gothic lancets of the chancel. In this chancel, on the south wall, an ornate stepped set of piscina and sedilia belongs in date to the later thirteenth century. They are handsome enough, as is the chancel itself (with the exception of its Victorian east window). But what you will remember of Seaton is that telling contrast, with so few years intervening, between the exuberant stone-carving of the Anglo-Norman masons and the quite different discipline of the southern-biased Angevins who succeeded them. In a small country church, the French fashions are yet faithfully observed.

***Stamford   Most visitors will find their satisfaction in Stamford today in its eighteenth-century pattern-book architecture. And in truth it is the ingenuity of the Georgian mason, assembling the elements of his façades from such texts of the trade as Halfpenny's *The Art of Sound Building* (1725) or Langley's *The Builder's Chest Book* (1727), that has given Stamford its entirely individual allure. Nevertheless, that hard local building stone which was to serve the eighteenth-century mason so well had already been at least as useful to the craftsmen who preceded him, so that Stamford now presents a composite picture, outwardly Georgian in the main but with bones that are likely to prove medieval and that may not infrequently poke through. Take, for example, the famous George Hotel, a former posting-house on the great trunk road to the North. Here, almost half of the main buildings of the hotel, on the south side away from the river, reoccupy the site of one of Stamford's greater medieval houses, of which a number of traces still remain. Burghley Hospital, just across the road to the north, is now for the most part an early-seventeenth-century almshouse, re-founded for that purpose by the great Sir William Cecil, Elizabeth's Lord High Treasurer, but again on much earlier roots. Throughout the modern town, medieval vaulted basements underlie buildings which, above ground, are Tudor or later. And then, of course, there are the major standing monuments of our period. No fewer than five of Stamford's medieval parish churches are still, if precariously, in use. On Broad Street, one of the noblest Georgian thoroughfares in England, Browne's Hospital (1475) preserves its fine façade and late-medieval internal arrangements – common dormitory below, chapel and 'audit chamber' above, the whole approached through a fashionably crenellated porch. It was William Browne, founder of the hospital, who contributed also to the rebuilding of All Saints, where he and his kin lie buried. Indeed, before 1500 All Saints had become as much the tomb-church of the Browne wool-merchant dynasty as St Martin's would be, from a century later, for the lordly Cecils of Burghley.

Stamford is so rich in material of all ages that you will not do it justice without a guide. But, guide-book in hand, note especially at the churches the remarkable Early English external arcade at All Saints and the Browne brasses collected within; the unforgettable west tower (Early English below, with a Decorated spire) and Perpendicular Corpus Christi north chapel of St Mary's, the latter with its splendid painted ceiling

(recently restored) donated by William Hickman, alderman, in 1467; the castellated capitals (already seen at St Mary's) and the magnificent late-medieval timber roofs at St John Baptist; the fifteenth-century stained glass (brought there from Tattershall) and the assembled Cecil monuments, the grandest of which is to Lord Burghley himself, at St Martin's, in Stamford Baron. Among abundance like this, individual features – the fine parclose screens at St John Baptist for one, the handsome pre-Reformation Phillips memorial (1506) at St Mary's for another – may well receive less attention than they truly deserve. But Stamford anyway is a town for which an appreciation of the atmosphere its many vistas create is at least as important as the recognition of its treasures one by one. Keep an eye out, though, as you pass down St Paul's Street, for the Brazenose Gate (mid-thirteenth-century) and the Whitefriars Gate (half-a-century later), the only relic of a Carmelite community. On the castle site, a good triple arcade is all that remains of the castle hall, plundered by archaeologists and developers in their turn. Once noted for its religious houses, Stamford is now left with little more of this important slice of its past than the Norman north arcade and ambitious west façade (with a lovely vesica preserved in the gable) of St Leonard's, at the extreme east end of Priory Road, once one of Durham's more distant and troublesome dependencies. To the south, behind its great wall, stretches Burghley Park, with Burghley House not a monument to be neglected if it is open. But be warned: Burghley might well absorb the lion's share of an already over-stretched visit; nor would you be viewing it on your own.

Stoke Dry This delightful and unusual little church is nicely sited to the west of the A6003, on the hillside overlooking a large reservoir. It has a charming interior, given a very individual character by the short three-bay nave, and has many features of interest. Entry is by a little north porch, very rustic in style and doll's-house in effect, with a priest's chamber over the door lit by its own diminutive embattled oriel window. In the nave, some fifteenth-century poppy-head bench-ends survive, while it is to this period also that the timber rood-screen belongs, battered by the post-Reformation iconoclasts yet retaining still the original coving that formerly supported a rood loft. Behind the screen, the chancel arch, with its grotesquely carved shafts of Anglo-Norman workmanship, is individually the most important feature of the church. Notice the richness of the carving along the full length of each shaft, continuing also on a surviving capital to the north. On the south shaft, a bell-ringer is represented; on the north, a dragon, a lion, a human figure, and an eagle; on the capital, a winged man in ecclesiastical vestments. At Stoke Dry, there are many surviving paintings, recently restored, including some post-Reformation texts and emblems over the nave arcades. In the south chapel, walled off from the aisle on this side to make a separate chantry chapel, there is a fine thirteenth-century St Christopher (with the Christ Child on his shoulder) and a St Edmund (shot through with arrows). Other somewhat later paintings in the chancel include a St Andrew (crucified) and a Virgin and Child. Of the monuments at Stoke Dry, the most interesting is the effigy and tomb-chest of Everard Digby (d. 1540) in the south chapel. Even at this date, it has many Renaissance characteristics, demonstrating how quickly these new fashions were spreading. A clumsy monument in the later taste to Kenelm Digby (d. 1590) and his lady, with their eleven children against the tomb-chest, takes up a large part of the chancel east wall. It shows some of the ill-effects of the Northern Renaissance, especially in country areas where the new motifs were only imperfectly understood, comparing very unfavourably with the large late-medieval incised slab to Jaquetta Digby (d. 1496), preserved at the end of the south aisle.

***Tickencote   Do not allow yourself to be turned away by the charmless exterior of this highly important little church. In the early 1790s, Tickencote was extensively restored, and it is to this period that the curious nave belongs (put together in what then passed for 'Norman'), together with the present south tower. Today, Tickencote recalls the worst in municipal cemetery architecture, being even then of an unusually eccentric variety. Persevere, though, and the magnificent chancel arch will delight and surprise even those who already know it well from illustrations. Tickencote's chancel arch, in five richly carved orders, is one of the most extraordinary products of that tradition of stone-carving which peaked in the mid-twelfth century. It is crude and somewhat barbaric in form, with two of its orders given over to the sinister beak-heads favoured by masons of the period. But it forms, nevertheless, a very splendid frame for the almost equal exuberance of the carved and vaulted chancel behind it. Sexpartite vaulting of this kind, it has often been pointed out, is unknown in England (except at Tickencote) before its use in the rebuilding of the burnt-out choir at Canterbury in the mid-1170s. Direct French influence is the only explanation, once again establishing the close contacts with the Continent that characterized the Anglo-Norman aristocracy of the time. Tickencote's chancel and its arch are what we have come here to see. But spare a little time also for two other features of interest – the oak knight effigy in the tomb recess south of the altar (rare in this material and probably no later than the early fourteenth century) and the handsome arcaded font, reduced to insignificance by its unfortunate placing next to the great chancel arch but nevertheless an important piece, the bowl of which may be dated to the late twelfth century.

Uppingham   In a small country town, the presence of a great school can be something of an irritant, and at Uppingham (as at Oundle and, to a lesser extent, at Oakham) there is no way of being rid of it. If you are interested in Victorian public-school-making in the grand manner, Uppingham School

48 The mid-twelfth-century chancel arch, in five richly carved orders, of the chancel arch at Tickencote

49 An early-fourteenth-century oak knight effigy in the chancel at Tickencote

deserves a visit. Otherwise, keep to the east of the main road (A6003) which bisects the town. There is a little market square, adjoining the road, particularly attractive at its southern end, where the church porch peers out between early buildings. It is by far the best feature of the town. Good though it is on the exterior – the fourteenth-century tower and spire being especially fine – Uppingham Church is not worth entering. It was ruined by a thorough-going Victorian restoration which coincided with the growth of the school. Opposite it, on the north side of the square, the Falcon Hotel similarly suffered from nineteenth-century prosperity, having a forbidding Victorian façade. However, at the back its long wings stretch away from the street front in the typical late-medieval manner, making the best use of restricted urban plots, while next on the east is one of the best of Uppingham's early-modern houses, worth a stroll down the adjoining open passage to see its back.

Warmington The thirteenth-century steeple at Warmington, tower and spire together, make an especially satisfying whole. And this is a village anyway for dawdling, obviously looked after and loved. Yet as you step inside its church, steady yourself for the shock. A vault of timber sits darkly on the nave, resting on the shafts of a late-thirteenth-century rebuilding which should have been completed in stone. Like Northborough, at no great distance to the north-east, Warmington stands as a monument to unfulfilled ambition, soaring beyond available resources. Yet the check came comparatively late in the day, and many of the more handsome features of the church had already been acquired by that period. Note, for example, the generous late-thirteenth-century clerestory (part of the over-ambitious rebuilding), the great west door of a century earlier, and the two fine porches (especially grand on the south) built at a date in between. The work at thirteenth-century Warmington was of very high quality – there is a good corbel of the period, one of a set of the Seven Deadly Sins, built into the east chancel wall, north of the altar – and this may well be the reason it never got further than it did. In any event, little happened to the building after 1300. Some of the fenestration at the east end is Perpendicular, but the most interesting additions of the later Middle Ages are to be found, rather, in Warmington's furnishings. Although too lavishly repainted, both the pretty little pulpit and the lower part of the rood screen are fifteenth-century. There are some original Perpendicular bench-ends in the north-west quarter of the nave, on which the other benches in the church have since quite successfully been modelled. Finally, in the easternmost bay of the north aisle, a sixteenth-century parclose screen, shutting off a chapel, displays in splendid confusion the mingling of Renaissance and Gothic decorative motifs as one style took over from the other. There are few better individual demonstrations of the contradictory pressures of contemporary fashion on the crafts.

HOTELS AND ITINERARIES

Without much doubt, the **George** at Stamford is the best place to stay for this tour. It is a large hotel, sophisticated and professional. In the winter, brisk fires burn in the grates; in the summer, there are pleasant gardens and a flowered court, catching some of the flavour of Normandy. The short break holiday is well developed here, at all but the highest of high seasons. Moreover, should you find it a hardship, financially or otherwise, to eat your way through a four-course meal in the main restaurant, there is always food available at the bars. The George is a hotel where, in contrast to many, the management would seem to have gone out of its way to discover what best suits its guests. And if the frame of the building is more obviously eighteenth-century than earlier, you can tell yourself at least that it re-occupies the site of one of medieval Stamford's premier merchant houses, some fragments of which are still visible, in particular in the area of the main bar.

Under the same management, the **Haycock** at Wansford is a late-seventeenth-century building in a pleasant village now off the line of the main road and next to the magnificent multi-arched Wansford Bridge, the greater part of which dates about a century earlier, built on a core that is certainly medieval. The Haycock has its own fine garden and much period charm. However, the Great North Road, immediately to the east, still holds Wansford in its thrall, and as an alternative to the George, my preference would be for the **Talbot**, in the little town of Oundle. The Talbot again is a substantial hotel, much larger than it looks; in the yard at the back, new bedrooms have been carved out of former stabling and stores. However, the best architectural features of the Talbot are concentrated at the front, behind a charming bay-windowed façade of 1626, including panelled rooms and a handsome contemporary oak staircase. Pause at the Talbot whether you stay there or not. I have little doubt that one day you will return.

At Uppingham, the **Falcon** occupies the best site in the town, facing south across its charming market square. Here a Victorian façade hides much earlier work, of the sixteenth century or before, in two backward-trailing wings which fill up their plots in a typically late-medieval manner. Try to forget what happens in the front, and you may picture yourself in two burgess houses, chopped up inside by a succession of fire-doors and mercilessly modernized in other ways, but unchanged in basic structure for many centuries. The Falcon is not a top-class hotel, and its dining-room seemed to me at the time especially dismal. But there are good restaurants in Uppingham to provide an alternative, and your night will be comfortable enough.

*   *   *

There is so much to see in this rich stretch of country that you are bound to face problems of selection, not the least of which will centre on the time you can rightly give to **Stamford**. This in itself would be reason enough to stay in the town, for much of its atmosphere can be captured best on a relatively late-night stroll. But what to do with Burghley House, if you are at Stamford in the summer and have not been to Burghley before? My own instinct would be to save it for another time, but the agony of decision rests with you.

50 The inner court at Kirby Hall, retaining conventional planning with the great hall on the right but showing the new symmetry in an attempt to balance the fenestration left of the central porch; note the use here of giant pilasters as a decorative device in the classical taste, hitherto unparalleled in England

After this, other choices can seem straightforward. In the immediate vicinity of Stamford, to the north and west, you must see the chancel arch at **Tickencote** and should spare time, if you can, for **Ketton**'s steeple; **Empingham** and **Little Casterton** are less important, though the latter would be lovely for a picnic. To the east, **Northborough**, **Peakirk**, and **Barnack** are all almost equally worth visiting, with Barnack taking the prize. Further south, **Castor** and **Longthorpe Tower** may seem a diversion, but both have features of great importance. However, remember that the custodian at Longthorpe must have his lunch; there is a good pub at Castor, a little west of the church, where you might linger to allow him to finish it. Going west again, **Elton** and **Nassington** are good country churches, but it is for **Warmington** and for **Fotheringhay**, in particular, that you must save your time as the day closes. Go to Warmington first and then come to Fotheringhay from the south. Your first sight of its great collegiate church, rising above and behind the river meadows, is likely to prove unforgettable.

Oundle lies on the margin between the two divisions of the tour, and might well be missed out (as could **Glapthorn** to the north) unless you have opted for the Falcon. It will be a shorter day on the western tour, but you must keep an hour at least for **Kirby Hall** and **Oakham** at either end. Other high points here are the churches, each very individual, at **Brooke** and **Stoke Dry**, and the almshouses (formerly the bishop's country palace) next to the great church at **Lyddington**. Village churches like **Preston** and **Morcott**, **Seaton**, **Harringworth**, and **Gretton** are all worth seeing, but not if time, for any reason, is running short. Remember that neither Oakham nor Kirby Hall can be rushed.

In this tour, Stamford is an obvious priority. Tickencote and Barnack, Peakirk, Longthorpe and Castor, Kirby Hall and Lyddington, Stoke Dry, Brooke and Oakham, are none of them buildings you should miss. But give me Brooke and Stoke Dry for private preference, with a special diversion to see the wall-paintings at Peakirk. They would justify the tour on their own.

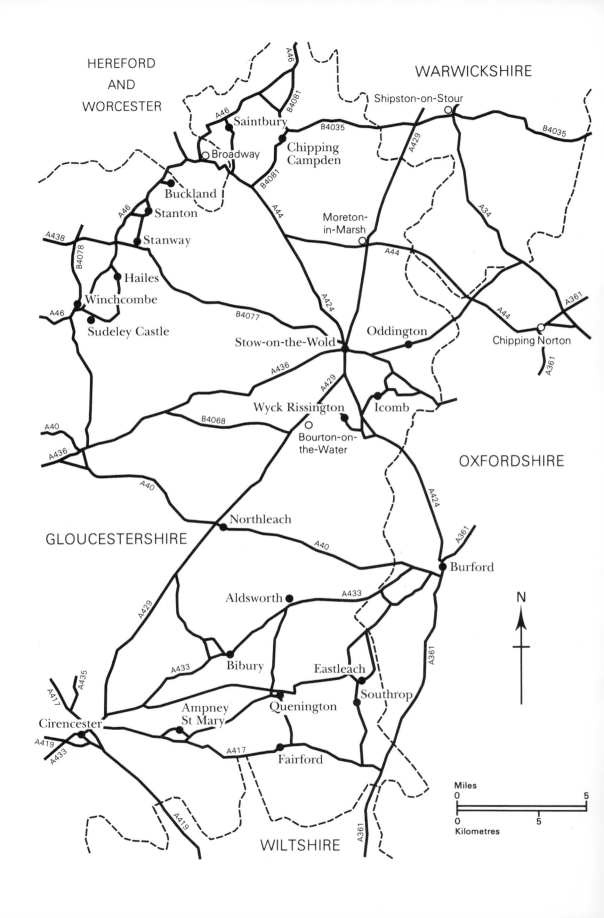

Chapter 5

The Cotswolds

Few Cotswold houses are as old as they look. It is an illusion, furthermore, that we welcome. Nevertheless, this has had the effect of making the landscape, ancient and venerable though it genuinely is, unusually difficult to unpick. Well-intentioned restorers have had their way with too many Cotswold churches. In the villages, the recent modernization of the more covetable properties has been taken well beyond mere restoration. Consider a small but important Cotswold town like **Stow-on-the-Wold**, once crucial to the economy of the region. Today, Stow is attractive still; it has an air of antiquity, being a well-known focus of tourism. But its church has been ruined by an over-energetic restoration; its domestic buildings, although certainly pretty enough to draw the crowds, are almost all of the seventeenth century or later; its great market-place — quite the best and the most authentic medieval survival in the town — has now been put to use as a car-park.

Lock the car and leave it; then ponder how this prosperity began. At Stow, the royal grant of market (awarded initially to Evesham Abbey, its entrepreneurial landowner) is one of the earliest, datable to 1107. It signals the arrival of a period of urban expansion, familiar throughout the twelfth-century West, which we can recognize more clearly at **Burford** (Oxfordshire), even earlier than Stow, or at **Chipping Campden**, much more prosperous of course in the later Middle Ages but founded towards the end of the same century. Both Burford and Chipping Campden have their medieval buildings, being luckier than Stow in this respect. However, what is especially interesting about all three is the physical evidence they preserve of their dependence from the start on their markets. Stow's great void at the centre was there to accommodate the trade, in weekly markets and in two annual fairs, for which the monks of Evesham had established their new settlement. Burford, although as well situated as Stow on an important junction of the ways, had grown with less system, with the result that it was the main street (exceptionally broad and handsome to this day) that had to do duty as a market-place. When Chipping Campden was

51 The house of William Grevel (d.1401), most notable of Chipping Campden's many prosperous wool-merchants

founded, much later in the twelfth century, some of the best qualities of both plans were re-used there. Notice the way that the High Street at Campden swells to give room for the market-place. If the plantation were successful – as indeed it was – settlement would spread out in both directions, north and south, along the road. If it failed, the seigneur lost little in the process, for he had had few expenses in the laying-out of a market and had ventured even less on burgess plots.

Hugh de Gonneville was lord of the manor in the 1170s, when Chipping Campden came into being. And by the time he and his contemporaries, all over the country, came to embark on such speculations, they knew the price they would have to pay in burgess privileges. In the very early twelfth century, when the men of Burford had claimed it, burgage tenure – in effect, a right of freehold, or unfettered transferability of lands – was exceptional. In securing Henry I's grant of market for Stow-on-the-Wold, the monks of Evesham had been trail-blazers back in 1107. Before 1200, almost every new town would enjoy these privileges, usually accompanied by the right to conduct its own courts, and any community still denied them felt aggrieved. **Cirencester's** sad story of bullying by its abbot is not the only such tale to have survived to us. The men of Bury and St Albans, similarly growing in wealth and self-confidence under the tutelage of a great abbey, were as restive (and as luckless) in their bondage. But what these chronicles of oppression so clearly display to us is the value men set on their freedoms. Cirencester had missed out on that sequence of developments, one privilege arising from another, by which the typical borough of the later Middle Ages had separated itself from the countryside. Repeatedly, Cirencester's militants fought for what they believed they had lost. Sometimes, as John Tame would do to the great good fortune of **Fairford**, they simply took their wealth and their energies elsewhere.

John Tame may have been a progressive in many respects, but his concern for Fairford parish church was an ancient one; he rebuilt it primarily as a mausoleum. Other Cotswold wool-merchants – William Grevel (d. 1401) at **Chipping Campden**, John Fortey (d. 1458) at **Northleach** – had already anticipated their deaths in much the same way, while there is scarcely a church anywhere in the region which does not carry the mark of this characteristic late-medieval preoccupation. The aristocracy, long before, had set the pattern. **Hailes Abbey**, founded by Richard of Cornwall in 1246 and given its famous relic (the 'Holy Blood of Hailes') by Richard's son, Edmund of Almaine, was initially the fulfilment of a vow, dragged from the earl when especially frightened by the violence of a storm at sea. Yet soon enough, in reward for Richard's considerable investment, the abbey was to become his memorial as well. What you will notice at Hailes and at its adjoining parish church is the insistent heraldry of its decorative work – the floor-tiles in the abbey, the wall-paintings at the church – most prominent being the eagle of Richard as King of the Romans (to which title he was elected in 1257), the paly of Richard's second wife, Sanchia of Provence (sister of Henry III's queen, Eleanor of Provence), and the castle emblematic of Eleanor of Castile (Richard's niece by marriage and next queen of England after her namesake). These purely secular concerns, centering on the after-life of the founder and his kin, would not have been admitted to a Cistercian house of an earlier and stricter generation. To the first Cistercians, relics themselves had been anathema, and the elaborate stonework of the church at Hailes, especially as rebuilt to accommodate the Holy Blood, would certainly have been deplored and rejected. Yet even had they wished it, Richard was too powerful a patron to refuse. His father, King John, had founded another Cistercian house at Beaulieu, from which Hailes itself was settled; Henry III, Richard's brother, endowed Netley; Edward I, his nephew, founded Vale Royal. Perhaps not unwillingly, for they stood to gain much materially by their pliancy, the Cistercians had become the guardians of the Plantagenet soul.

Just a few miles to the south of Hailes Abbey, the great castle at **Sudeley** – more a country mansion than a fortress – is yet another example of man's obsessive desire for a memorial. Sudeley, as rebuilt by Ralph Boteler in the mid-fifteenth century, was the intended last abode of a war captain of distinction who had also served as Treasurer to Henry VI. One of Sudeley's towers, the Portmare Tower, got its name (so the story goes) from a ransomed French admiral. And Boteler, whose companions-at-arms included other great builders (Sir John Fastolf of Caister, Sir Roger Fiennes of Herstmonceux, Sir Andrew Ogard of Rye), was certainly not alone in deploying his fortune in this way. Sudeley, only lightly defended but equipped nevertheless with impressive gatehouses and with a secure inner court dominated by a strong tower at one corner, is a classic example of the great houses built by successful returned soldiers of the period. The Hundred Years War, fought almost entirely in France with only the occasional sea-borne raid to trouble England, was the source of great profit to individuals. In Ralph Lord Sudeley's case, the profit drained away in the loss of his Sudeley estates. But before this happened, he had built the castle for which now he is chiefly remembered. Characteristically too, for a man of his temperament and generation, he had put up a church in the shadow of his castle, no doubt intending it as his mortuary chapel. In a gesture of loyalty to his Lancastrian patrons, Henry VI and Margaret of Anjou, he had ordered the heads of his king and queen to be carved on the stops of the hood-mould over the west door, where everybody entering the chapel would see them.

While at Sudeley, Ralph Boteler had been associated with another act of piety, this time on behalf of the neighbouring market town. The men of **Winchcombe**, having lost their parish church in an earlier collapse, had found themselves sharing, over a couple of generations, the abbey church of the Benedictines in their borough. Neither party had welcomed the arrangement, and by the 1460s, all had united in a cooperative effort to rebuild the parish church, of which the chancel was assigned to the abbot as rector, while everything else was recognized as the responsibility of the parish. Winchcombe's merchants had recently prospered in the wool trade; collectively, they were able to assemble a large sum of money. But their project, which included a noble west tower, was over-ambitious, and even they could not have found the funds to complete their church had they not had Ralph Lord Sudeley to help them. What resulted was the only major Cotswold church to have been built from scratch in a single concerted campaign. Sadly, the product of their efforts is rather boring.

Other great churches in the region – **Chipping Campden** and **North-leach**, **Fairford** and **Cirencester** – offer more variety, even Fairford having an earlier tower-base at its centre. Nevertheless, the huge spaces of these buildings, the uniformity of their furnishings, and the symmetry of their arcades, have cost them a good deal of their charm. Like Winchcombe, they are usually at their best on the outside. Here, of course, it is the lesser

Cotswold churches that have the advantage. Inside and out, the two **Eastleach** churches, facing each other across the meadows, will seem to you equally memorable. Yet the little parish church at **Hailes,** with the counter-attraction of the abbey next door, would be easy to pass by without a second glance, which makes it so much more of a discovery. Not unlike Hailes, both in its modest exterior and in the treasures within, is the isolated country church at **Oddington**, near Stow, which to me is the prize of the Cotswolds. Oddington itself is not a village of great character. For such, you would do better at **Icomb** or at **Stanton**, both to be lingered in and cherished. But the village at Oddington has moved away from the church, leaving it now on a farm track only, every man's pastoral idyll. There is nothing symmetrical about this old church; even its great Doom, confronting the astonished visitor on the north wall as he enters, is wrongly (or at best exceptionally) placed. In plan, Oddington is an improvisation. A second church has been built next to the first, the former chancel adapted to carry a tower, the naves linked by a common arcade. In the seventeenth century a Jacobean parson was to build himself a pulpit here, comically lofty and pompously canopied, from which to thunder at the yokels below. Yet put together these elements and what emerges from the mixture is something unique and irreplaceable in our heritage. If we require to be reminded how lucky we are to have a past, here it is. Give more generously than I did to Oddington's repair fund. God knows, and so do we, that the church is in dire need of it.

*Aldsworth** Above and behind Manor Farm, itself a pleasant and well-kept seventeenth-century building, Aldsworth Church is nicely placed away from the village on a site of comfortable isolation. It was one of the churches dependent on Bibury, being an element of the abbot of Oseney's Gloucestershire 'peculiar', and this has left its mark in the heraldry of the Late Perpendicular north aisle (including the Oseney Abbey arms) which is now the building's best feature. Both the north aisle and the interesting north porch are datable to about 1500. Externally, the aisle is exceptionally handsome for a church of this situation and scale. Grotesque figures support the parapet, and there is a finely finished canopied niche on the north-east angle, no doubt intended to hold a figure of St Catherine, to whom the new work was evidently dedicated. St Catherine's wheel decorates the base of the pedestal on which another image of the saint must have stood, under a tall canopied niche in the east wall of the aisle. Other empty statue niches of the same period occur in the north and south walls of the church, which is otherwise internally of little interest. In the porch, a prominent niche on the east wall preserves the fittings for lights placed there by the pious, with a flue for carrying off the smoke. The maintenance of lights, towards which a cow or a sheep might be donated to the church glebe, was one of the most common provisions in late-medieval rural wills, having of course a memorial purpose. Here, in the porch at Aldsworth, there is a rare survival of these arrangements.

*Ampney St Mary** On the main road (A417) between Fairford and Cirencester,

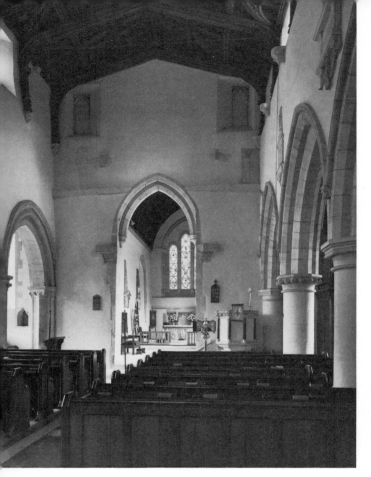

52 Bibury Church, a former Anglo-Saxon minster still showing the characteristics of the earlier building in the unusual height of its nave, as well as in individual features like the jambs and imposts of the narrow chancel arch

this simple and isolated little country church makes an instructive contrast with its greater urban equivalents. Time stopped at Ampney in the fourteenth century, and it is to this period that its best features belong. Over the north door, the strange carved lintel (a Lion of Righteousness) is twelfth-century, and the little round-headed window to the west of the south door may be earlier. The font, chevron-decorated, is also Norman. But note especially the rare stone chancel screen, with surviving bench-end on the south side, and the good Decorated west window of the nave, flooding the interior with light. Then turn your attention to the principal feature

of the church, its wall-paintings. These are badly damaged on the north wall, with little left of the St Christopher or St George that once took their place in what is still recognizably a total scheme. On the south wall, however, there is a fourteenth-century Christ of the Trades which is one of the better survivals in England of this strange and interesting subject, intended to be a warning to sabbath-breakers by whom Christ, in the painting, is injured.

** **Bibury** This lovely village, complete with seventeenth-century mill (now a craft museum) and contemporary row of weavers' cottages (Arlington Row) picturesquely spanning the meadow, is a little too well known to tourists these days. It is no place for a Bank Holiday weekend. However, its parish church, off the main track, certainly merits a visit, not least for its attractive setting next to Sir Thomas Sackville's great country house (Bibury Court), externally mainly of 1633 and run, enticingly enough, as a hotel. Bibury Church has been important since the Anglo-Saxon period, to which several features, including most obviously the jambs and imposts of its chancel arch, still belong. Clearly, it was already a large church in the eleventh century, on which several lesser local churches (among them Aldsworth) were dependent. Moreover, this status was preserved throughout the Middle Ages by its transfer (with dependencies) to Oseney in 1130, to become a major element in the founding endowment of this wealthy Augustinian priory, shortly afterwards promoted to abbey. It was the canons of Oseney who undertook a major extension of the church, enlarging the nave westwards and adding a north aisle, towards the end of the twelfth century, of which the handsome Late Norman arcade had to be cut through the original Saxon outer wall. If you want to follow these alterations in detail, buy the excellent guide-book to the church. But notice especially the early south porch, datable to c. 1200, the unusual contemporary font (square with Transitional arcades on each side), and the exceptionally fine and spacious Early English chancel, with its remarkable collection of aumbries for the storage of church plate and relics. In some respects, the church and its churchyard have been too well cared for, thus losing some of their charm. But you must think of Bibury as one of those rare survivals where the evolution from Anglo-Saxon minster to post-Conquest head-church, a 'peculiar' of Oseney, was achieved with exceptional smoothness. Bibury, indeed, lays out before us a slice of the past which is usually impenetrably obscure, taking us back to the missionary days of England's Dark Age conversion.

Buckland The parish church at Buckland is nicely situated on a rise at the east end of the village, with the medieval rectory (hall still intact) to the west across the road, and with Buckland Manor (sixteenth-century at core) immediately to the south. Inside especially, Buckland Church is a building of great interest, preserving features through the blitz of a Victorian restoration which, when it came to church furnishings, was undoubtedly more sensitive than most. Sadly, the walls lost their plaster at the time. Nevertheless, Buckland retains a warmth and a well-furnished look which it owes especially to its fine seventeenth-century west gallery, and to the contemporary pulpit, panelling, and side-wall benches, some of these last still keeping their canopies. Good late-medieval features include the roofs of the nave and its aisles, with a few contemporary benches, an early-fifteenth-century font, and a little glass of the period, amongst it three panels of Seven Sacrament glass, restored and re-set in the east window. Most exceptionally, a large area of fifteenth-century tiled pavement has survived in its original arrangement in the south aisle. And notice also the way that the oak wainscoting in the chancel continues behind the present altar across the east end, being itself a survival from an earlier seating plan, typically Puritan, where side-wall benches surrounded on all sides the central communion table.

***Burford** Think of Burford first as one of our most ancient independent boroughs, with its own gild merchant acknowledged before 1107, and with free burgess status (not much later) both conceded and protected by the king. Armed with its privileges and ideally situated on an important crossing of the ways, Burford continued to flourish through the Middle Ages – and it still shows. Take a walk after dark down the broad and handsome High Street, towards the bridge over the Windrush at the bottom, and you will glimpse everywhere, behind Georgian and later façades, the beamed interiors of much earlier buildings, many of them going back to the fourteenth century or before. Gothic arches open into corridors that mark the limits of medieval burgess plots, extending back from their narrow street-fronts. Occasionally, as in the magnificent timber-framed town-house ('The Crypt Antiques') opposite Sheep Street, a fifteenth-century building still stands unaltered, being a useful reminder of the high standard of domestic comfort already achieved by the wealthy burgess of that day.

Towards the bottom of the hill, Church Lane runs eastwards, with the attractive bulk of the earl of Warwick's almshouses (preserving many original mid-fifteenth-century features) to serve as frame and introduction to the parish church. Here again we are at once reminded of Burford's commercial purpose, for the church is a patchwork of late-medieval expansions and improvements, the most important of which incorporated (to form a large Lady Chapel most unusually placed at the south-west angle of the building) the originally free-standing chapel of Burford's gild. A good guide-book and plan are essential aids to the proper understanding of this complex building. But notice especially the multiplicity of its chapels, filling in vacant corners so that even the exceptionally graceful south porch was not permitted to stand proud of the building. Under the easternmost arch of the north nave arcade, a fifteenth-century timber chantry chapel, enclosed in its screens, was subsequently preserved as a family pew and has since reverted to private worship. Opposite, set high over a charnel house, the Thomas Becket Chapel was the chantry of Thomas Spicer, prominent in Burford in the late fourteenth century. The St Catherine's Chapel to the north of the chancel, and the Holy Trinity Chapel to the south, both functioned as gild chapels and chantries. There is no missing, in the former, the grotesquely pompous monument of Sir Lawrence Tanfield (d. 1625), but observe the skeleton under the effigies (a return to medieval preoccupations) and take note too of the vaulted niche in the east wall of the chapel, probably built there originally to hold a reliquary. More of Sir Lawrence's day is the black letter inscription on the same wall of the south chapel, reminding us still that 'All transytory thynges shall fayle at the last', even as they failed Tanfield and his high-handed lady (builder of the monument) in their time.

***Chipping Campden This well-groomed town must be central to all recollections of the Cotswolds. Already recognized as a borough by the late twelfth century, Chipping Campden preserves many of the characteristics of the medieval town, including most notably the curved line of its High Street, which swells at the middle to accommodate a market, like a snake digesting a rabbit. As has happened so often elsewhere, the market-place has been largely built over at Campden, one of its 'colonizers' being Sir Baptist Hicks' handsome Market Hall of 1627. Moreover, through the town as a whole, few buildings (despite their sometimes contrived antique appearance) are older than the seventeenth century. Yet in William Grevel's house, north of the market, Campden retains what is undoubtedly the best example of a late-fourteenth-century stone burgess dwelling – albeit an unusually large one – to survive anywhere in England. Its finest feature now is the two-storeyed bay window, with six-light openings on each floor. But notice too the way that it is set, alongside the street, not back from it. Across the High Street,

the almost exactly contemporary Wool-staplers Hall (now a museum) presents its gable, more economically, to the road.

William Grevel (d. 1401) was a wool-merchant without equal. He could afford to purchase a large plot for his house, even in this favoured trading position, and is known to have given generously to the church. It is no longer thought that Grevel alone was responsible for the almost total reconstruction of this building. The nave arcade and clerestory, so closely paralleled at Northleach, seem to belong rather to the late fifteenth century. However, Grevel's brass is the finest in Chipping Campden Church, and there is little reason to doubt that it was his large bequest that set the scale for the subsequent campaign. Consider what resources this small community had to find for a building at least the size of a colonial cathedral. Nor was spaciousness the only effect Campden's burgesses sought at the time, for the triple sedilia in the chancel are of excellent quality, while the church preserves (most exceptionally) important examples of fifteenth-century needlework – a fine embroidered cope and set of altar frontals – themselves no doubt the product of contemporary piety, commissioned by Grevel's successors. After Grevel himself, the next most considerable Chipping Campden benefactor was Sir Baptist Hicks (d. 1629), who now lies grandly in the south chapel of the church, represented next to his wife in medieval-style effigy under a canopy of Renaissance magnificence. It was Sir Baptist, a London merchant who had made good, who built the fine almshouses just down the road from the church, giving during his long life a 'large portion' to charity, as his epitaph records to this day. We forgive him a monopoly of the floor-space in the chapel, which in others we would be more ready to condemn.

***Cirencester These days, there is not much of charm in Cirencester's too busy approaches. However, leave the car as close as you can to the centre of the town, and take your time over walking its streets.

53 The west tower and south porch (formerly an administrative building of the canons of the adjoining abbey) of the parish church at Cirencester; the porch dates to *c.* 1500, the tower being almost a century earlier

There is the elegant Georgian length of Cecily Hill, with the famous avenue beyond, ideal for walking the dog. And there are the narrow winding streets of the medieval town, of which Coxwell Street is the most picturesque, focusing at the market by the church door. Cirencester's market-place is still very obviously the centre of the town, dominated now (as it has been since *c.* 1500) by the extraordinary bulk of the church porch. Intended originally as an administrative building for the wealthy canons of Cirencester Abbey, the porch's upper chamber was used after 1539 as a town hall. Three centuries later, in 1836, its top storeys had to be taken

down and rebuilt, but the reconstruction was careful and the finely vaulted entrance passage remains absolutely authentic. It will lead you through into a building so full of points of interest that you will need to buy a guide-book as companion. But hesitate enough to take in first the great height and splendour of the west tower at Cirencester, built with the help of Henry IV in gratitude for the townspeople's loyalty during the Earls' Revolt of 1400; and notice too the vast scale and elaboration, inside and out, of the early-sixteenth-century nave, a project just as dear to those same burgesses' descendants and similarly politically inspired. Cirencester's long struggle with its notoriously oppressive landlords, the Augustinian abbots, is one of the saddest chronicles of democratic failure in medieval England. Yet if the rebellious townspeople failed to secure the independence in law to which they felt their wealth had entitled them, they could still cock a snook at the abbot in stone. Compare the splendour of their tower and nave with the meagre earlier chancel for which the abbot, as rector, was responsible. It is not difficult to see what they were doing. In other ways also, they laid out their money to obvious effect. The mid-fifteenth-century Holy Trinity Chapel, north of the nave, had associations with Cirencester's gild of weavers; in the south aisle, the Garstang Chapel was a wool-merchant's chantry, still enclosed by its original fifteenth-century carved screen; the beautiful stone pulpit, again of that date, is one of the finest in the country. This handsome church has had its bad times, not least at the hands of Sir George Gilbert Scott, some of whose less tasteful 'improvements' have only recently been unpicked from its fabric. But it is more than a building: it is a political statement, and should be seen and remembered as such.

Eastleach Those who can choose, come to Eastleach in daffodil time, for it is then that its two little churches, within hailing distance of each other across the stream, undoubtedly look their best, set in a carpet of rich green and yellow. Such proximity, of course, is highly exceptional, and what it must reflect is the building of private churches to serve individual estates, their boundaries determined by the Leach. Neither church, as one would expect in the circumstances, grew to any great size. However, it is their rustic character that contributes to their charm, and both have individual features of some interest. At Eastleach Turville, the church of St Andrew has a good Norman south door with zigzag work and with a Majesty (supported by angels) in the tympanum; inside, its great feature is the fine thirteenth-century chancel, with a particularly handsome triple lancet east window, exactly right for the period and of outstanding quality for such a very rural location. Across the Leach, St Michael and St Martin, in Eastleach Martin, has a very pretty west tower (with nice tower arch and Perpendicular west window) and a complete set of early pews (late-medieval at the back,

54 The waters of the Leach, separating within easy hailing distance the two churches at Eastleach Martin and Eastleach Turville

Jacobean towards the front). In the north transept, the three Decorated windows are of excellent quality, while the rather earlier chancel is of unusual size for a church otherwise modest in scale. But give most of your attention to the group as a whole, not to its individual components. On the right day, the two churches at Eastleach rank among medieval England's most enchanting survivals.

***Fairford** In this lovely little town, with its broad medieval market square fringed by early buildings, the parish church stands on the edge of open country, in a situation still as domestic and unspoilt as its 'founder', the wool-merchant John Tame (d. 1500), first intended it. Tame brought his great fortune to Fairford from the troubled monastic borough of Cirencester, and it was here that he invested a good part of his wealth in the almost total rebuilding of the parish church, subsequently completed by his son, Sir Edmund Tame (d. 1534). Both father and son are buried in the church, in positions of particular prominence, the first next to

the high altar, the second under a great marble slab in the floor of the Lady Chapel to the north. It is John Tame who bids us, at the foot of a fine brass to his wife Alice and himself: 'For Jesus love pray for me / I may not pray, nowe pray ye / with a pater noster and an ave / that my paynys relessid may be'. And Fairford remains very obviously a memorial to its rebuilder, the home of an expensive (if short-lived) chantry that Tame endowed for himself, and a powerful aid to the swift passage of his soul through the anticipated discomforts of Purgatory. As the parish church of an always small community, Fairford is of no great size, but it is exceptionally complete. Only the base of the great central tower survives from the earlier building, adding interest to an interior which might otherwise have seemed just a little monotonous in its repeated use of the Late Perpendicular four-centred arch, a shape we have since come to associate with the Tudors. Give some time to this interior, for its broad arcades, impressive clerestory, and fine contemporary timber roofs are an excellent guide to what good money could

55 Fairford Church, completely rebuilt at the expense of a wealthy wool-merchant, John Tame (d. 1500), and of his son, Sir Edmund Tame (d. 1534), for whom the church was to serve as a chantry

buy towards the end of the fifteenth century. But spare most of your attention for the remarkable church furnishings — the early-sixteenth-century carved screens and elaborate choir stalls (the latter probably imported by Sir Edmund Tame from elsewhere), the family brasses in the Lady Chapel and on the founder's tomb, and particularly, of course, the painted glass (the most complete of any parish church in the country). Fairford's glass, covering the whole range of the Christian faith from the Creation, through the Life and Passion of Christ, to the Last Judgment, is a unique survival, happily spared by the Protestant reformers and still largely intact to this day. In the great west window, the finest spread of all, the upper half is a Victorian reproduction. Nevertheless, there is so much here that remains original that it would be churlish to complain of what is not. John Tame's church has been kept entire, precisely as he planned it for his final repose. It is a monument as useful now as it was in 1500 and (to our good fortune) as well cared for.

***Hailes   Archaeology has recently cost us the trees that used to shade Hailes and give it character. However, the compensations are a site that is meticulously set out, a good museum, and an excellent up-to-date guide-book. Look first at the museum; it will tell you all you need to know about the abbey. But remember that the particular importance of Hailes is first that this Cistercian house was a royal foundation (Richard of Cornwall was the brother of Henry III) and second that it was established unusually late for that order. The consequence of both was that the monks brought here from Beaulieu in 1246 felt able to embark on a building programme of costly magnificence — look at the great thirteenth-century vaulting bosses now on display in the museum — which they could not have contemplated with a lesser founder or at an earlier, more austere time. Very rapidly, they found themselves in trouble. However, the gift of a phial of Christ's holy blood (thereafter known as

the 'Holy Blood of Hailes') restored their fortunes in the 1270s. And it was to accommodate this most precious of crowd-pulling relics that they rebuilt the east end of their already vast church, laying out there the *corona* of radiating chapels that you can still follow very clearly on the ground. Within the resulting ambulatory stood the famous shrine — its base has been preserved near the centre; nor were the monks to regret their investment. In the fifteenth century, when other monastic houses, forced by low agricultural prices to lease their estates, were in the grip of a deepening recession, the monks of Hailes promoted their relic and successfully built up its cult. Before the century was over, they had rebuilt their cloister, vaulting it grandly in stone. It is the cloister now, particularly on the western side where the abbot's lodgings came to be, that has left the most significant remains.

Ante-dating the abbey by a century or more, the parish church became the property of the Cistercians in 1246, again in contradiction of the earlier practice of their order. Do not neglect to go inside, for it is a building of great charm and human interest. The furnishings are for the most part seventeenth-century, retaining clear traces of the typical Puritan arrangements in the chancel when the altar was centrally placed. In addition, there is a fifteenth-century rood-screen, with benches of that date, and with both floor-tiles and glass from the abbey. But you will find the paintings of particular interest: a large St Christopher (staff in hand and with Christ Child on shoulder) on the north nave wall, a splendid hunting scene on the south; in the chancel, a heraldic decorative scheme commemorating the founder and his son (donor of the Holy Blood relic), dating to about 1300, with two female saints (perhaps St Catherine and St Margaret) in the window splays, scarcely faded by the passage of the years.

*Icomb   A visit to Icomb Church is a good excuse to escape the main roads and to linger a little in one of the Cotswolds'

56 The fine south porch at Northleach Church: high-quality work of the first half of the fifteenth century

lovelier villages. But Victorian restorers have again been let loose on the church, with the result that its interest is now limited to no more than two features. The first of these is the chancel – restored like the rest of the building but nevertheless remaining a very pure and perfect example of a chancel rebuilding of the thirteenth century, complete and nicely symmetrical. Notice the way a continuous roll moulding links the great triple lancets of the east window with the single lancets (opposite each other) on the north and south walls, to be broken only by the priest's door and contemporary piscina on the south. This is work of excellent quality, entirely charac-

teristic of the Early English period. Much later, an existing south transept was converted into a chantry chapel for Sir John Blaket (d. 1431). Sir John lies in effigy under an arched canopy on the south wall, in full armour and with his hands raised in prayer. A little window lights his figure on just about the line of his belt; below, angels and other figures stand against the tomb-chest.

***Northleach   In this pretty but rather touristy little town, still uncomfortably bisected by a busy main road (the A40 from Oxford to Cheltenham and Gloucester), the parish church rises with exceptional grandeur and lavish late-medieval display. Take a long look at it before you enter, for Northleach Church is at its best externally. At the west end, the great square tower dates to about 1400; a little later is the elegant south porch (one of the best of its kind) with contemporary images of Our Lady, the Trinity, John the Baptist, and Thomas Becket remaining most unusually in place; the handsome clerestory, Northleach's finest individual feature, is work of the 1460s, notable especially for its nine-light east window into which the gable of the chancel roof intrudes; in the south-east angle, the Bicknell Chapel, built as a chantry for the family of that name, is datable to the late 1480s. Together, the assemblage is highly successful; more so indeed than the rather spare interior, too brilliantly lit to seem anything but cold, and largely stripped of its original furnishings. Notice the marked contrast in scale between the nave and the chancel: another example of a rector, in this case the abbot of Gloucester, being left well behind by his parishioners. And observe how closely the nave arcade resembles, in its curiously hollowed-out piers and capitals, the arcade in the rival 'wool church' at Chipping Campden, almost certainly the later of the two. Northleach's spacious nave, although probably begun some years before John Fortey's death in 1458, was finished on the proceeds of this rich wool-merchant's legacy, enough to pay for its extraordinary clerestory. It is to this period also that the attractive Perpendicular stone pulpit belongs, with the painted reredos (another comparatively rare survival) and accompanying piscina at the east end of the south aisle, west of the Bicknell chantry chapel. But most important at Northleach is its collection of memorial brasses, celebrating the wealth of the wool-merchants of the town, among them John Fortey (one foot on a sheep, the other on a wool-pack, surrounded by medallions in which the Fortey wool-mark is prominently displayed). John Fortey, in his pointed shoes and belted fur-lined gown, is richly dressed in the style of his period, and the Northleach brasses have

their value still as closely datable guides to the extravagance of contemporary high fashion. These Cotswold wool-men and their wives travelled constantly to London; they went to Flanders and to Calais in the normal course of business; when at home, it pleased them to be seen as up-to-date. Their vanities touch a chord in us now that their piety has long since ceased to reach.

***Oddington   When, in 1852, Oddington's parishioners built themselves a new church nearer their centre of population, they left the old in neglected isolation and thereby did us all subsequently a great service. This marvellous building has been left largely untouched since that time. Walk into it now, through the wide south door, and you will find yourself entering a slice of history such as you will normally experience only in France. In heavy rain, water drips steadily through the roof; in sunshine, light floods an interior which, with its flagstone floor and ancient dusty furnishings, has all the crumbling charm of the South. Oddington is two churches, built next to each other and linked by the broad arches of the thirteenth-century arcade cut through the north wall of the original building at the time of its contemporary enlargement. Very probably, the extension of the first stone church on the site had to do with the archbishop of York's use of the adjoining manor (now wholly vanished) as an occasional residence, to which Henry III also was a visitor. In the mid-thirteenth century, perhaps to accommodate these great households at worship in the church, a much larger nave and chancel were built up against the old, while retaining the former nave as a spacious south aisle and strengthening the Norman chancel to support a tower. At the present east end, the small three-light window is of an unusual form, with flanking statue niches to north and south. But by far the most interesting feature of Oddington's interior is the one you will see first as you enter it. On the north wall, facing the south door in what is a most exceptional position for such a subject, is a great late-fourteenth-century

Doom, or Last Judgment, with Christ in the centre and with the Elect and the Damned, most explicitly painted, to either side. Other paintings in the church include the remains of a double-tier cycle in the south-east chapel, under the tower, the whole set off nicely by a William IV royal arms up over the chancel arch in contrasting style, just where a Doom more appropriately might have been. A simple but handsome fifteenth-century roof still covers the nave, and climb up, if you can, into the lofty Jacobean pulpit, on a single turned pedestal and complete with its sounding-board, the best vantage-point to view the interior. No Jacobean preacher would have tolerated that Last Judgment on his right as an aid. Yet it would have been precisely to serve the instructional purposes of his medieval predecessors that Oddington's great Doom was first painted. A parishioner seated captive in the body of the nave could do little to evade the thunder of his divine. On the wall beside him, his options most graphically were laid out.

*Quenington A late-nineteenth-century restoration of this church has almost destroyed its character. However, the setting (next to the preceptory of the Knights Hospitallers) is interesting, and the superb twelfth-century doors, both north and south, would by themselves fully justify a visit. Both doors appear to date to the mid-century, although the fine Harrowing of Hell tympanum of the north door is earlier. On the south door, the Coronation of the Virgin tympanum, crude but entirely delightful, is of a piece with the rest of the decorative carving, which, between the two doorways, incorporates almost every ornamental convention known to Anglo-Norman masons of the period. You need not bother to go inside, unless you feel you owe it to the parish as a courtesy.

Next to the church, Quenington Court has been built on the site of the Hospitaller preceptory, of which the handsome gate-house (dating to the late thirteenth or early fourteenth century) has survived. It is a charming fragment, easily inspected from

the road, of one of the more valuable Hospitaller estate-centres, founded here in the 1190s and suppressed, with the other surviving preceptories of the order, at the general dissolution in 1540. Just before the Black Death, there had been three knights resident at Quenington, where other Hospitaller preceptories more typically had two. They were attended by a chaplain of their own and assisted by a large complement of farm-workers and household servants.

*Saintbury What draws us to Saintbury is an unforgettable site, its church pressed against the hillside with fine views in every direction but the south. Saintbury Church, visible for miles around, is placed at the top end of a village of great charm, straggling down its street towards the main road. For those short of breath or less than sure-footed, the final climb to the church is not recommended. However, persistence is rewarded by a pleasant building and by a setting that is by far its best feature. Externally, the fourteenth-century steeple is a pretty addition (unusually placed over the south transept) to a much earlier nave, of which the Norman north and south doors still survive. Within, a nice set of late-eighteenth-century box pews in the Gothick taste, well shaped round the font towards the west, gives the nave a pleasantly furnished look, while some of the original late-medieval pews have been preserved, unexpectedly, in the north transept. In the broad, light chancel, some medieval glass (including two saints under canopies) survives in the present east window, and there is a nice double-headed piscina, probably of about 1300; the painted texts are of the seventeenth century. The nave roof is late-medieval; that of the chancel, eighteenth-century but good. Altogether, a satisfying church but not one to be visited for itself.

*Southrop The church at Southrop's great glory is its magnificent Norman font, which makes it all the more unfortunate that the font should be so ill-placed, cramped against the north door of the building. Take time over it, though, for it is certainly well worth the trouble. Round the bowl, the arches of an elaborate arcade hold the figures of armed Virtues, triumphing over the opposite Vices at their feet; with them, Moses is flanked by Ecclesia and Synagogue, while over the whole, acanthus ornament is framed in a belt-like beaded interlace. Dating to the mid-twelfth century or a little later, this is one of the finest fonts of that period in England. Nothing else in the church is of the same quality or interest, although internally the Early English chancel has a pleasing simplicity, nicely framed by the chancel arch and characteristically supplied with an over-

57 Detail of the Norman font at Southrop, showing armed Virtues triumphing over the Vices at their feet

abundance of aumbries. Adjoining the church, Southrop Manor is said to contain twelfth-century work, nothing of which is visible on the outside.

**Stanton   This is not a village to miss, being one of the prettier assemblages of Cotswold houses, sympathetically restored earlier this century and since very carefully maintained. The church, too, is an interesting example of how intelligent restoration can put back the atmosphere into an early building, re-creating the feel of the Middle Ages. Much of Stanton's woodwork, including the west gallery and elaborate rood-screen (complete with rood-beam and figures), is by Sir Ninian Comper and is of the period of the First World War. However, it makes a fine setting for genuine medieval features, including a good Perpendicular font and an unusually early miniature pulpit, dating to the late fourteenth century, north of the chancel arch. A few of the medieval poppy-head benches have survived, the other benches at Stanton (characteristically for this restorer) being copied from the fifteenth-century model. There are traces of fourteenth-century wall-paintings on the north wall of the north transept, with some panels of fifteenth-century glass from Hailes Abbey re-set in the chancel's east window, and a nice squint (with unusual architectural detail) linking the chancel and south transept. But Stanton is a church for mood-making, not for the relentless pursuit of individually interesting features. As you go out, take note again of the nice little two-storeyed porch, with Perpendicular windows of an attractive, almost square-headed form to right and left. Enough said: now take a walk through the village.

*Stanway   This is a sad church, grotesquely over-restored in 1896, of which the only remaining feature of interest is the carved Norman corbel table circling the outer walls of the chancel. Stay in the churchyard, and use the time instead to take a good look at Stanway House, east of the church on the site of the abbot of Tewkesbury's manor-house, and at the abbot's great barn to the north-west. For our purposes, the most interesting feature of Stanway House is its splendid early-seventeenth-century gatehouse – the last in a long line stretching back through the Middle Ages – with its thoroughly classical entrance arch and pretty gables, each of them topped by the scallop-shell badge of the Tracy family, acquirers of the estate at the Dissolution. Neither house nor barn are regularly open to the public. However, the gatehouse at least can be studied from the road, and enough can be seen of the barn from the churchyard to obtain an idea of its scale. Datable to about 1300, the abbot's barn at Stanway fits squarely into that peak period of agricultural investment when the monks still controlled their own estates. Have another look at it from the main entrance of the estate, on the road north towards Stanton. It has the fine tall gables and projecting porch typical of the more ambitious buildings of its class. As in their case also, it was too useful still in the mid-sixteenth century to be demolished by Stanway's new owners.

*Stow-on-the-Wold Although rather touristy these days and not, on the surface, very medieval, Stow-on-the-Wold retains the great market-place (only partly colonized even now by the Victorian St Edward's Hall) to which it owed its commercial growth. Stow was founded by the abbot of Evesham, obtaining its royal grant of market as early as 1107. The enterprise was well timed to exploit the steady economic expansion of the twelfth and thirteenth centuries, for the new settlement was ideally placed on an important road junction and in a region famed throughout Europe for its wool. Sadly, the great church at Stow, which might have given us such a good record of this growth, has been spoilt by over-zealous nineteenth-century restorations. As with the market-place, all we are left with is a sense of scale, considerably enhanced by the best feature of the church, the double arches of the arcade linking the north aisle and north transept.

Note too the handsome tracery of the fourteenth-century west window, and the good contemporary piscina at the extreme east end of the south chancel wall. But otherwise close your eyes to the hideous church furnishings and gaudy glass of Stow's misguided restorers, and hurry out to get the feel of the market-place where the regular trading fairs of May and October, once the economic life-blood of the community, have now been replaced by parked cars.

**Sudeley For the medievalist, a visit to Sudeley these days is a sad experience. Energetic exploitation of the tourist potential of the house and its grounds has indeed, as Sudeley's publicity boasts, provided something for everybody. But at what high cost! If you have children with you, prepare yourself for a long visit; you will not get away with less than a full afternoon. Otherwise, what remains of the medieval house can be inspected relatively quickly. The first thing you will see (on the left, as you approach what is now the castle's main entrance) is the mid-fifteenth-century barn, built by Ralph Boteler, Baron Sudeley from 1441, a successful war captain and for three years (1443-6) Treasurer of England. It was Boteler who began the rebuilding of Sudeley, laying it out in the fashion of his day as an ambitious double-courtyard mansion, only lightly defended, with an inner and an outer gatehouse (the latter still surviving in the present north range) and with the usual strong tower (now, of all things, a museum of toys) in the south-west corner of the inner court, rather strangely placed between the kitchen and the hall. Boteler, as an old Lancastrian supporter, ceased to prosper when the Yorkist interest triumphed in 1460, and in 1469 Sudeley became the property of the crown. Granted shortly afterwards to the king's brother, Richard of Gloucester (later Richard III), it was probably during the royal duke's tenure that the private apartments at Sudeley acquired what is now their most spectacular feature, the ruined 'presence chamber' at first-floor level in the inner

58 Sudeley Castle from the Great Tower: on the right, Richard of Gloucester's ruined Presence Chamber; on the left, Edmund Brydges's outer court, remodelled in the late sixteenth century

court's east range, with its soaring multi-light windows – an apartment fit for a prince. It was in the later sixteenth century, under Edmund Brydges, second Lord Chandos (to whose family Sudeley had come by gift of Mary Tudor), that the outer court at Sudeley was largely remodelled in its present shape, with lodgings below and residential apartments above, outwardly more like a college. It was at that time that the outer gatehouse was cut down to scale, although other defensive features of Boteler's original mansion, including the three still remaining angle towers of the inner court (the Portmare Tower, Garderobe Tower, and Great, or 'Dungeon', Tower), were preserved. One other important surviving element of Boteler's scheme is the church of St Mary, immediately to the east of the outer court, prettily embattled and a very fine example of the contemporary taste in memorial chapels.

Externally, it is substantially as Boteler conceived it in c. 1460. But spare yourself the trouble of going inside unless you are interested in the work of George Gilbert Scott, who rebuilt the interior four centuries later, including with this an elaborate and inappropriately 'medieval' confection, the tomb of Katherine Parr.

Winchcombe Nothing is now left of Winchcombe Abbey, a great Benedictine house of pre-Conquest origin that was once sited immediately east of the fifteenth-century parish church. Yet Winchcombe is still very obviously a monastic borough, for the George Hotel, with its pretty galleried courtyard to the rear, is likely to have been built by the abbey as a pilgrims' hostel (it has Abbot Richard Kidderminster's initials carved in the spandrels of its great door), and at the church itself, the chancel was financed by Abbot William Winchcombe

(1454-74), one of Abbot Richard's more distinguished predecessors. Take your time over the George. Such survivals are rare and its late-medieval court, although much reduced in size, still retains enough of the gallery on one side to convey a good deal of the flavour of the period. Moreover the parish church, is must be said, is a disappointment. Handsome enough on the outside, it has that undivided barn-like interior with which Late Perpendicular churches, built in a single campaign, quite often came to be afflicted. And then, in 1872, one of the more energetic Victorian restorers was allowed to have his way with the building. But try, if you can, to re-live the time, probably in the mid-1460s, when the abbot of Winchcombe found the funds for a chancel, when his townspeople raised another large sum to begin on the nave, and when Ralph Lord Sudeley, their nearest great landowner, came to the rescue with a further subsidy. For some decades before this, on the decay and collapse of an earlier parish church, the burgesses of Winchcombe had found themselves sharing the church of the monks in an unpopular arrangement of which both sides were eager to be rid. With the Cotswold wool trade approaching its peak period in this quarter of the fifteenth century, the time had arrived to seek a remedy. At Winchcombe it was now possible to lay out a great church, quite as grand in prospect as the local competition at Northleach, for example, or Chipping Campden. But the single period of its building worked against it. Notice the way that the Perpendicular timber screen, still largely intact, fails to make more than a token division between the chancel and the rest of the church. It was a style well enough suited to King's College Chapel but less appropriate to the needs of a parish. Technique, among the master masons of the Cotswold churches, had triumphed over genuine sensibility, and Winchcombe was to be one of its victims.

*Wyck Rissington   There is not much in this little church untouched by the heavy hand of its restorers. But stop here all the same, for it is the remarkable east façade (not visible from the road) that you must see. Note Wyck Rissington's pretty west tower, with the unusual trefoil-headed openings of its parapet, but go first to the east end, where a highly original composition of paired lancets and diamond-shaped lights is meticulously framed by that characteristic signature of the Early English mason, the continuous roll moulding or string course. Inside, the same device links the features – for example, the priest's door and piscina – of as nice a little chancel of the third quarter of the thirteenth century as you are likely to find anywhere in England. Along the south wall, broken only by the priest's door, the original stone bench has survived, and the chancel is further remarkable for its numerous contemporary aumbries, three in the north wall and one in the south, recalling the same feature, again of that date, in the much grander chancel at Bibury. Under the tower, the exaggerated point of the thirteenth-century tower-arch adds some interest to a nave otherwise destroyed by Victorian refurbishings and extensions, the only other feature of the church worth remark being the survival, again in the chancel, of some early-fourteenth-century glass including (in the middle south window) a nice Crucifixion with a cross of an unusually vivid green.

HOTELS AND ITINERARIES

In a tourist area like the Cotswolds, there may be seasonal difficulties in booking into a hotel, but the agony is as much in the choice. You need have no anxieties, though, over the **Lygon Arms** at Broadway, very much the most sophisticated and most expensive of the hotels in the region, well up in the international class. The Lygon Arms is a handsome sixteenth-century building, sensitively modernized and extended, with a claim (not unfounded) to be 'England's most famous Inn'. Stay there if you can: you will not forget the experience. However, one night at the Lygon Arms will set you back as much as two at the attractive **Broadway Hotel** (another ancient building) just down the road. If Broadway is to be your base, this might need thinking about.

There are good reasons, too, for not settling on Broadway in the first place. At the Lygon Arms, and particularly in the fine modern extension at the back, you can feel protected against the traffic. Nevertheless, the A44 is a continuously noisy road, and Broadway itself, at almost all seasons, is the victim of its good tourist image. Chipping Campden, of course, is much the same. But at least here there is no busy road to bisect the community – Chipping Campden, mercifully, is not on the way to anywhere important – and you can enjoy the calm of a small country town hardly changed in its essentials since the Middle Ages. One of Campden's nicer hotels, in the traditional English style (which naturally has nothing to do with the cooking), is the **Noel Arms**: very clean, very comfortable, and fortunately modernized in such a way as not to conceal its early features. You will not see much here of the fourteenth century, of which the hotel's publicity boasts. But with William Grevel's house a little up the High Street, there is perhaps less reason to invite the Middle Ages into one's bedroom; those carefully picked-out beams in the hall and corridors will have to do.

Very like the Noel Arms – slightly less quiet but rather nicer – is the **Bull** at Fairford, again an early building which has been skilfully converted in all but its unauthentic scraping-back to the stone. After Broadway's **Lygon Arms**, this would be my choice for the tour. However, there could be much to be said also for that splendid (and perfectly situated) early-seventeenth-century mansion, built for Sir Thomas Sackville in 1633 and now run as the **Bibury Court Hotel**. Successive conversions have largely destroyed the original interior here, and there is a touch of the morgue about the dining-room. But the façade is still beautiful and the gardens lovely. And how nice it is that somebody else should be ready to look after such a house for our own occasional enjoyment!

A little of the personal feel of Bibury Court may be experienced too at the **Bay Tree** at Burford, for which I confess a private affection that goes back a great many years. The Bay Tree, gathering moss gently with its owners (as with most of its present clientele), is part-hotel, part-finishing-school for the daughters of our well-off county families. You can get a good jam sponge in the Bay Tree's restaurant – none better; and very prettily served. But the wise tourist books in there only for lunch; the bedrooms are just a little too rustic.

*   *   *

59 The early-seventeenth-century gatehouse of Stanway House: a pretty pot-pourri of Renaissance motifs, and one of the last of its kind

If you stay at Burford, at Fairford, or at Bibury, there is an obvious group-ing of churches in this area, with **Oddington** and **Stow-on-the-Wold** as its northern limits, and with **Cirencester** and **Northleach** on the west. You should avoid Cirencester on a busy weekday, if you can. And this may persuade you to take the northern sector first, from **Winchcombe** along the edge of the Cotswolds to **Chipping Campden**. Here the only seasonal constraint is **Sudeley Castle**, open daily from March through October. But Sudeley to me is a flawed pearl; I would not deny myself a winter break to accommodate it.

Sudeley will mop up your time, if you let it. But hoard an hour especially for **Hailes**, just up the road from **Winchcombe**. Here, Cistercian abbey and parish church together make a group that is both unusual and reward-ing. A little to the north again, **Stanway** has its gatehouse and medieval

60 Seventeenth-century weavers' cottages at Bibury, known as Arlington Row and still, for their date, very medieval in appearance

barn, while the village at **Stanton**, only a couple of miles beyond, is all that you could wish of the Cotswolds. **Buckland** and **Saintbury** are both worth seeing, but Broadway has little these days for the dedicated medievalist, and you can by-pass it quite happily unless you are staying there. Of course, **Chipping Campden** must be visited. Plan to spend time there, for there is much to see; without it, no Cotswold journey is complete.

It may be that you will have time to spare; in which case, make for **Oddington** while there is still a reasonable chance that the church remains open. **Icomb, Wyck Rissington**, and **Stow-on-the-Wold** could each be visited without much loss if the church were locked by the time you got there; their principal attractions are external. However, if you miss Oddington this time, you will have to come back. In my view, it is the pivot of the tour.

To the south again, **Burford** is as interesting for its late-medieval townscape as for its church, and you will need to walk the long main street to enjoy it. At **Northleach**, however, it is the church that you will want to visit, and the same is true of **Fairford** and **Bibury**, to both of which you should give high priority. **Cirencester** is magnificent but daunting to get at, unless you happen to reach it on a Sunday afternoon. **Aldsworth** and **Quenington**, **Southrop** and **Ampney St Mary**, are all worth a pause. However, if time is short, sacrifice these for the two churches at **Eastleach**: just the place to sleep off a good lunch – perhaps that jam sponge from the Bay Tree at Burford.

You may not share my preference for Oddington above all. But do at least visit it, and take in also the other prime sites – Burford and Chipping Campden, Cirencester and Eastleach, Fairford, Hailes, and Northleach; none of these ought really to be missed. In the second rank, to my mind, are Bibury and Buckland, Stanton, Sudeley, and Winchcombe, with a much larger group falling below these in the third. Yet the joy of the Cotswolds, as I am sure you will agree, is in the landscape more than in the buildings. Whatever you do, don't let your map-reading get in the way of it.

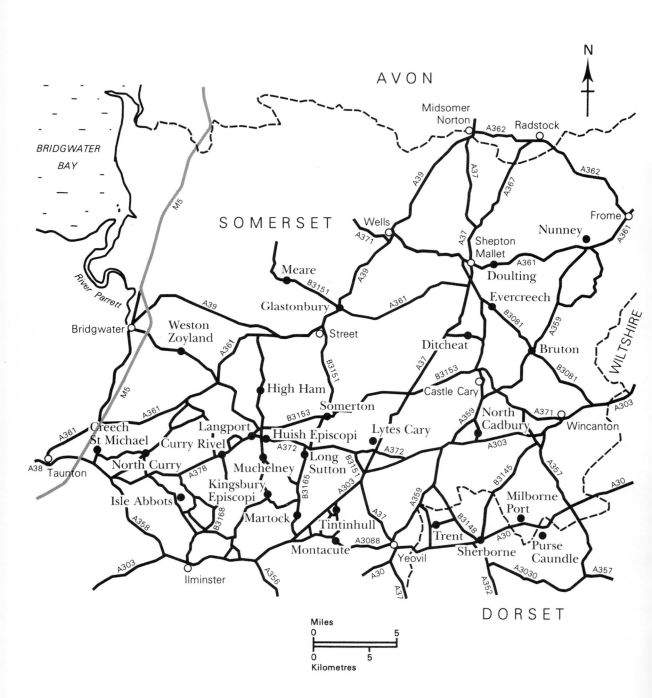

Chapter 6

West Dorset, Somerset, and the Levels

In this land of sharp contrasts – the marshy plain of the Somerset Levels on the one hand, natural eminences like Glastonbury Tor on the other – legends may linger but authentic relics of a pre-Conquest presence are now faint. This is Arthur's country at Glastonbury and South Cadbury, Alfred's on the land-bound Isle of Athelney. But it is names, not buildings, that recall this past. What we see instead is a landscape both drained and built over in such a way as to conceal its originally dominant characteristics. Even its points of emphasis have changed. Little towns like **Langport** and **Milborne Port** still embrace the roads which gave them their significance at the time of the Wessex kings. But they are a pale shadow now of the commercial communities which the Anglo-Saxon 'port' in their names yet recalls. Milborne Port's loss was **Sherborne**'s gain. However, it must have been apparent even before the Conquest that Sherborne's great abbey would suck trade in towards itself. Close though they are to each other, both towns were to be equipped with ambitious stone churches, scarcely smaller than their later replacements, some decades before the arrival of the Normans. Such churches were rare in eleventh-century England, a sure badge of privilege and status. Yet early in the next century, at both centres again, rebuilding was actively under way.

Sherborne's reconstruction, in abbey church and castle, was the work of Roger of Salisbury (d. 1139), one of the wealthiest ecclesiastics and most notable builders of his day. And it is difficult not to see, in the transformations of his time, some impatience with the habits of the past. At **Glastonbury**, another pre-Conquest Benedictine house, claiming an antiquity even greater than Sherborne's, the hostility of its first Norman abbot to the ancient customs of the community led to riot and bloodshed and to the packing-off of Abbot Thurstan back to Caen. Already though, from his appointment in the late 1070s, Thurstan had begun on the rebuilding of Glastonbury's church, which was to be transformed again in the time of Abbot Herlewin early in the twelfth century, taking its final shape (as

127

61 The abbey church at Glastonbury from the east, looking down its great length towards the twelfth-century Lady Chapel at the west end

we see it today) after the conflagration of 1184 had cleared the site of everything previously upon it.

The Arthurian traditions still alive at Glastonbury were important already in the late twelfth century. Arthur himself had become, by this date, a major figure of literary romance. And it was the 'discovery' of his bones in deliberate excavations at Glastonbury, ordered by the abbot himself in 1191, that materially assisted the rebuilding of the monastery, attracting the donations of faithful and curious. After this, Glastonbury's status as a pilgrimage centre was to remain secure throughout the Middle Ages, to be buttressed, early in the sixteenth century, by the development, or revival, of fresh cults. But Glastonbury, even without this, was an exceptionally wealthy house, leaving its mark in many ways on the region.

One of the places we can still see this is at **Meare**, just a few miles to the north-west of Glastonbury itself, where the abbot maintained a favourite country retreat. Since the draining of the broad lake from which it took its name, Meare has changed greatly in character. Nevertheless, what remains here is a group of buildings, not as charming as they used to be when water lapped their fences, but representative of the monastic economy. Glastonbury owned the parish church at Meare, being instrumental in its rebuilding in the fifteenth century. Next to it, the abbot's manor-house is a fourteenth-century building, much of it preserved in the present farmhouse; it has two great chambers at first-floor level, one of them the hall, with accommodation also for such members of his suite as the abbot brought with him to the countryside. Away in the field to the east, Glastonbury's fish-house is a unique survival, stranded now amongst acres of dry pasture, like a fish landed gasping on the shore. It is a utilitarian building, equipped with workshops on the ground-floor. But the living-quarters above are of excellent quality, appropriate to the status of that important official, the keeper of the Glastonbury fisheries.

In historical myth, the monks' reputation for looking after their men does not stand high. Yet the fish-house at Meare is some evidence to the contrary, and we have also in our region another important monument which helps show them in quite a different light. One of the most covetable houses in **Muchelney** today is the former vicarage, just across the green from the pleasant but comparatively modest parish church. It is a comfort-able thatched building, with a central hall (originally open to the roof) and with chambers at each end, now maintained by the National Trust. A reconstruction in the fifteenth century, including the insertion of new windows, has left Muchelney's vicarage looking younger than it is. How-ever, the original building, of which the arched door is a reminder, prob-ably dates back to the early fourteenth century, closely following the provisions negotiated in 1308 for a properly instituted vicar in the parish. As part of a bargain which included their own formal appropriation of the parish church and its tithes, the monks of Muchelney (a Benedictine house almost as venerable as Glastonbury) agreed to supply the vicar with a suitable dwelling and to feed him daily, should he wish it, from their own kitchen: he was to draw bread and two gallons of good ale daily from the cellarer; on Sundays and Tuesdays he could have meat, with fish or eggs for the rest of the week in accordance with the custom of the com-munity; he was entitled to a small salary and to oblations.

Muchelney's vicarage and the smaller but still commodious Chantry House at **Trent** should be enough to persuade us of the high standard of accommodation enjoyed by at least some of the secular clergy before the Middle Ages were out. But this was a prosperous region – especially so in the fifteenth century when other areas were doing less well – and we should be careful how we use it as a model. Other indications of pros-perity are not hard to find, being especially obvious, of course, in Somer-set's great churches and their towers, but evident also in the increasing comforts now required in their dwellings by contemporary landowners. The 'rising gentry' of Tudor and Stuart England are familiar to most of us these days; in our own region, the Nappers of **Tintinhull**, absorbing the estates of Montacute Priory, are a splendid example of the class. How-ever, what is not so often appreciated is that the rise had been launched long before. The Lytes of **Lytes Cary** and the Longs of **Purse Caundle** were each doing well enough by the mid-fifteenth century to contemplate expensive building works. Modifications and extensions in the following century would conceal or disguise these earlier efforts. Nevertheless, the fact that both manor-houses remain medieval at core is a tribute to the care of their first builders. At Lytes Cary, in particular, the noble fifteenth-century hall, with its fine arch-braced roof and grand contemporary side-wall fireplace, is an especially handsome apartment. When the Lytes assembled their broad acres in the following generations, they felt little need to improve on it.

Where they did make changes, these were to be part of the severing of old traditions that signalled the end of the Middle Ages. John Lyte, rebuilder of Lytes Cary in the 1530s, was a conservative in many ways: an upholder of values from the past. There was a strong antiquarian streak in his ancient family, which would surface again in the next two generations with John's son and grandson, Henry and Thomas, both of them preoccupied with heraldry and with pedigrees (going back, in one instance, to the Trojans). At Lytes Cary, there is heraldic glass of John's time preserved in the windows of the hall; a frieze of coats of arms was an element in Thomas's remodelling of the chapel. Nevertheless, John found the large 'chivalric' hall of his fifteenth-century great-grandfather (another Thomas) too spacious and draughty for his own family's regular needs. He kept the hall for special occasions, but added a private parlour in a new oriel bay, screened off and separately heated. Coinciding with this work, a total reconstruction of the former solar range gave John and his family a set of apartments which was at once comfortable and very up to date. Both Great Parlour below and Great Chamber above are equipped with handsome stone-panelled bay windows; in the latter, too, the fine plaster ceiling (with the arms of Henry VIII prominently displayed) is one of the first of its kind. In quarters of this splendour, there is more than one parallel with the lodgings, only a little earlier in date, that Abbot Thomas Broke (1505–22) had only just completed for himself at nearby **Muchelney**. Both have fine chambers, well lit and well heated; both present a façade to the outer world which is more Renaissance than medieval in its symmetry.

The eventual working through of many of these new ideas may be studied conveniently at **Montacute**. The west front at Montacute is a late-eighteenth-century pot-pourri, put together from Tudor elements imported from Clifton Maybank, and now almost totally a sham. However, Montacute seen from the east, with its Flemish gables, its pediments and shell-headed niches, its classical entablatures, its obelisks and Roman-dressed statuary, and above all its meticulous symmetry, is precisely as its original builder, Sir Edward Phelips (d. 1614), first conceived it. Internally, too, there is much of interest. By Sir Edward's day, the need for a great hall, even in a mansion of this size, had diminished just short of extinction. There it is still, just through the front door on the right. But the screen is ornamental and the apartment only modest: the hall is much nearer to its present purpose as a formal passage to the private family quarters beyond. These apartments are numerous, warmly panelled, fully glazed, and individually heated, each with a good fireplace of its own. Even the Great Chamber, on the first floor of the north wing, has become ceremonial in purpose, the family retreating from that contact with its servants which communal living in the medieval hall had been intended, very deliberately, to foster. Along the top of the house, a fresh element has been added, unknown to builders and their patrons in the Middle Ages but not unlike a cloister in intention. The Long Gallery at Montacute is longer than any other that survives. But it belongs to a whole class of such apartments, favoured by the wealthy of Queen Elizabeth's day and used by them for indoor exercise and for personal display when the weather made their gardens inaccessible. A characteristic obsession of the time, perhaps true in general of any period of significant change, was a preoccupation (seen already among the Lytes of Lytes Cary) with the things of the past. Montacute itself is full of classical echoes, and in its Long Gallery there hangs today a set of royal portraits (contemporary with the building although actually from Hornby Castle) celebrating the monarchs of Old England. Such historical reminders were common in these circumstances, and Montacute, almost certainly, would have had a set of monarchs of its own. In their absence, of course, there were the Nine Worthies of its statuary – including those heroes of chivalry, Hector and Alexander, Arthur, Charlemagne, and Godfrey of Bouillon – snug in their niches on the east façade, to be viewed by the company from the garden. Many who took their promenades in Sir Edward's gallery or in his garden would have been brought up on stories of the suppression and pillage of the religious houses, with all the traumas of King Henry's break from Rome. They lived themselves in an atmosphere of religious dissent and of accelerating political change. No doubt they drew as much comfort from their contemplation of the great figures of their past as we do from walking in their footsteps.

Bruton The first thing you will recognize of medieval Bruton is the former abbey dovecot, roofless now but spectacularly sited on a neighbouring eminence, like a windmill ripe-for-tilting in Spain. Of the abbey itself, a jumped-up Augustinian priory promoted to its new status in 1511, there are few other major survivals, the most obvious today being a heavily buttressed stretch of the original precinct wall, on the south side of the street known as Plox. On the other side of the same street, spanning the River Brue, the nice little late-medieval packhorse bridge is among the better survivals of its kind, while a short way up Plox, towards the west, Old House preserves the buildings of a sixteenth-century school, founded with the cooperation of the abbot of Bruton as early as 1519. Down Plox again to the east, Bruton has one of the grander of Somerset's urban churches, although time has not been especially kind to it. The Late Perpendicular west tower, with its canopied niches and finely judged fenestration, is undoubtedly the best feature of the present building, completely dwarfing an earlier fourteenth-century tower against the north aisle. Inside, too, the decorative niches are repeated again (as at Martock) in the shafts of the handsome nave arcade, the whole supporting a fine Somerset roof, unusually steep so as to cope with the great width of the nave. Sadly, though, the walls have been scraped, this being among the many 'improvements' of a Late Victorian restoration which heaped insult on injury with a nasty tiled floor and with one of the most obtrusive piped heating systems imaginable. The east end of the church, rebuilt in the mid-eighteenth century, is magnificent but wholly inappropriate, being conceived in the gaudiest Rococo. It is entered now through a modern screen in the Georgian taste, and preserves its complete set of contemporary chancel furnishings – very fine but again out of place to any but the most agile and eclectic of church enthusiasts. Slightly bridging the gulf, the recessed monument in the north wall is of Sir Maurice Berkeley (d. 1581) and his two wives, the second of whom survived him by four years. Sir Maurice, a prominent courtier of Henry VIII's reign, had come into possession of Bruton Abbey and its lands following the suppression of the religious houses. His monument, as one might expect of a man of his position, is Renaissance in flavour, making prominent use of the newly fashionable classical motifs; its siting (north of the high altar) is still, however, wholly medieval.

*Creech St Michael In its somewhat unpromising surroundings, the church at Creech St Michael comes as a particularly agreeable surprise. It has a pleasant domestic interior, made so by its handsome wagon-roofs in nave and chancel, the former nicely set off by its carved wall-plate. At the west end, an attractive timber gallery, with central royal arms, adds to this effect, dating to the early eighteenth century. On the nave walls, and again highly decorative in the same domestic vein, are substantial remains of seventeenth-century black-letter texts in the usual ornamental surrounds. Notice the characteristic fifteenth-century emphasis on statue niches, on the west façade but also throughout the interior – neatly built into the north arcade, against the chancel arch, and framed in the panelling of the elegant arch which leads into the little south chapel. Despite its many Perpendicular additions, Creech St Michael is basically a thirteenth-century church, with a north tower of this date (heightened in the fifteenth century) and with other early features (the south door and piscina) surviving through the late-medieval remodelling. You will not regret the diversion it must cost you.

**Curry Rivel Do not allow yourself to be put off from a distance by the west tower of this church: it had to be rebuilt (though faithfully enough) in 1860, and still looks raw and Victorian. In other respects, both the church and its setting (away from the main road and north of the village green) are most attractive. Note, as you enter, the heraldic frieze over the arch of the south porch, dating it to the late fifteenth century. And it is to this period too that the adjoining aisle, south chapel, and rebuilt chancel belong, all with richly traceried windows – spectacular from the outside, rather too heavy within. In this well-looked-after church, the delicate nave arcades and very broad chancel arch give a spacious feel to the interior, only partly spoilt by a heavily Victorian nave roof. The aisle roofs, fortunately, are original and good. In addition, there is a fine set of fifteenth-century bench-ends, some with poppy-heads, and excellent Perpendicular parclose screens in the north and south aisles, with their coving still in place. Much earlier is the most unusual feature of the church, being the curious set of late-thirteenth-century tomb recesses, all under elaborate if mutilated canopies, in the north wall of the north-east chapel – the only part of the church not rebuilt in the fifteenth century. In the centre, the largest of these recesses holds a contemporary knight effigy (left hand on sword and shield on that arm); the smaller recesses, each with its damaged effigy, were probably built for the knight's children. On the south wall of the same chapel, an elaborate piscina in the characteristic late-thirteenth-century style confirms the date of what must be among the earlier of such family mortuary chapels. In the early seventeenth century, it was to be the chancel at Curry Rivel that would be made to serve the same purpose. The Jennings brothers, Marmaduke (d. 1625) and Robert (d. 1630), lie in effigy on their tomb-chest, behind a contemporary iron railing and under a pompous canopy of rustic 'classical' taste. The total effect is both ridiculous and lovable.

Ditcheat A short diversion will take you to Ditcheat, and it is certainly well worth the trouble. Unfortunately, despite the handsome early-seventeenth-century manor-house immediately north of the churchyard, the setting of Ditcheat Church is uninteresting. Nevertheless, in this county of Perpendicular west towers, the central tower of Ditcheat already holds some promise, fully justified by an unusual and characterful interior. Hidden by a pier of the north arcade but nevertheless one of the first things you will see as you enter the south door, is a great St Christopher, gaudily painted in rustic style and datable to c. 1500: it is one of the largest and most complete survivals of its kind. The crossing (but not the upper part of the tower) is late-thirteenth-century, and it is to this date also that all but the clerestory stage of the spacious chancel belongs, with its particularly fine and original fenestration and with the characteristic continuous roll-moulding of the period still preserved along the south

wall, where it rises over the piscina, sinks below the single sedile, and ascends again over the priest's door. Most of the rest of the church is Late Perpendicular, in which style the chancel was heightened and the nave rebuilt, a particularly elegant late-fifteenth-century fan-vault being inserted rather incongruously in the crossing. There are good contemporary timber roofs to the nave and transepts, the former on boldly sculptured corbels, while prettily facing each other under the west arch of the crossing are a nice Jacobean pulpit and reader's desk, of about the same date as the next-door manor-house. North of the high altar, a priest effigy in the floor is datable to the early fourteenth century. This is a notably pleasant church interior, made the more so by handsome timberwork, by clean stone, and by brilliantly whitewashed walls. If anybody still believes in scraping back to the stone, let him come to Ditcheat before doing so.

Doulting Although still in use, the great fifteenth-century stone barn at Doulting, with its prominent gables, multiple buttresses, and magnificent twin transeptal porches, is easily visible from the road. Ignore the church, which has been much restored, and turn south instead at the Abbey Barn Inn; you will see the barn almost immediately on your right. Doulting, manor and church together, had been an important possession of the wealthy Benedictines of Glastonbury since before the Norman Conquest, their first claim to it dating back to the early eighth century. By the fourteenth century, they were farming 357 acres of arable at Doulting, with 30 acres of meadow, and another 118 acres of rough pasture. Depressed farm prices in the later Middle Ages cost Glastonbury a good deal of the value of its Doulting estate. Nevertheless, the abbey's interests here, in tithes as well as produce, were still important enough in the fifteenth century to justify expensive investment in a new barn. In the next century, they were sufficiently attractive for Jack Horner, former steward of the abbey and now of nursery-rhyme fame, to pull Doulting out as one of the plums in his pie. Before the Dissolution, in a self-interested deal typical of his class and his period, Jack Horner had negotiated a lease for himself of the tithes and the tithe-barn at Doulting. The lease was confirmed in March 1540, no doubt in recognition of Horner's services to the crown in betraying his late master, the abbot.

*Evercreech   The slender west tower of this middling-sized village church is one of its nicest features. Inside, too, the tower is rewarding, for its arch into the nave is pan-elled with exceptional elaboration. But it is not this that you will remember of Ever-creech. Instead, the memory you will carry away is of an interior made cramped and domestic by the 'Gothick' galleries, built in 1843 and tucked behind the arcades of the nave. Above those, too, the fine Somerset roof has been richly re-painted (most recently in the mid-1960s). Like the tower, the roof is one of the best of its kind, yet fails to register as such in this setting.

***Glastonbury   No short account can do justice to this great concentration of med-ieval monuments. Buy Dr Ralegh Radford's excellent pictorial guide: he was the exca-vator of Glastonbury and knows it best. Then allow yourself plenty of time to absorb the many things you see. Starting with the town itself, notice the way it bends like a boomerang round the abbey ruins, demonstrating the initial near-total dependence of this little urban community on the Benedictine monks who lived in its midst. Outside the abbey gate on the west of the precinct, a modern market cross marks the site of the medieval market-place. By the later Middle Ages, partly as a result of the activity of this market, the prosperity of the burgesses of Glastonbury had grown, permitting them to build, in their major parish church of St John Bapt-ist, one of the grandest urban churches in the county. Its remarkable late-fifteenth-century west tower, with its pinnacled crown of pierced ornamental battlements, is the first thing you will see of the town.

In the chancel of St John Baptist, built into the arcade north and south of the high altar, are the tombs of important benefac-tors, Richard Atwell (d. 1476) and Joan (d. 1485), his wife. And it is very evident that it was on the proceeds of the local cloth industry, in which the Atwells made their fortune, that both Glastonbury and its abbey flourished in the later Middle Ages. In St John Baptist itself, the nave arcades are especially lofty, the roofs are original and good, the panelled tower arch and internal vault are both particularly fine. In the south transept, the good alabaster effigy of John Cammell (d. 1487), with shield-bearing angels and camels against the tomb-chest, reminds us – as everything about Glastonbury is bound to do – of the local dominance of the great abbey, of which Cammell himself was once treasurer. Indeed, the other church in the town, St Benedict's (to the south), is thought to have been rebuilt, in west tower and nave, with the assistance of Glastonbury's penultimate abbot, Richard Bere (1493–1524), never able to resist such an opportunity. It is a plain little church, but pleasant and well kept, with a nice tower and with good sym-metrical arcades: worth a brief visit, if time permits.

It was Abbot Bere, again, who put a handsome new front on the Tribunal, the abbey's fifteenth-century court-house in the High Street, now restored as nearly as possible to its original condition and open daily as a little museum. Notice the fine fire-places and generous windows here, and compare them with those at the George and Pilgrims Hotel, just down the street to the west, re-faced in the time of Abbot Selwood (1456–93) with stone panelling as lavish as any in Somerset. You may not be staying at the George and Pilgrims, but treat your-self at least to a drink there. The fireplace, the beams, and the very splendid bay window of the ground-floor bar are still those of half a millennium ago. Together, they make up a late-medieval interior for which there are now few parallels.

Prepare yourself for the pleasant shock of a total change of scale by visiting the

diminutive St Mary's Almshouses, towards
the south end of Magdalene Street on the
other side from the abbey, before entering
the monastic precinct itself. St Mary's preserves the chapel and at least the outline
of the former hall of a thirteenth-century
hospital of conventional plan, like the
chancel and nave of a church. In its final
late-medieval form, the infirmary hall was
converted into two cottage wings, each
being a row of separate lodgings, the northern of which has been preserved. It is a
charming and highly evocative spot, no
longer in use for its original purpose but
perfectly adapted, even today, for the
modest needs of the aged and infirm.

There was nothing modest about the
great house of Benedictines over the way.
The former porter's lodge (if this was its
purpose), next to the main gate of the
abbey, is domestic enough; once inside,
everything changes. The first building you
will see — and the most complete survival,
apart from the abbot's kitchen — is the
remarkably lavish twelfth-century Lady
Chapel, built in a single brief campaign
immediately following the disastrous fire of
1184. Here the decorative angle-turrets,
two of which survive, are an especially
memorable feature. But the building is
important, too, as a closely datable Transitional structure, having Early Gothic vaulting (now largely destroyed) springing from
a Romanesque arcade. The crypt and galilee
are later, and what you should try to do
is to see the Lady Chapel without these
additions: a jewel of its period, built in this
way as a shrine to the saints and as a
repository for Glastonbury's relics. The
chapel was dedicated in 1186; five years
later, the monks of Glastonbury made the
miraculous discovery of the bodies of King
Arthur and of Guinevere, his queen, which
was to give them the relics they needed to
attract the donations of the faithful and to
assist in the rebuilding of their church. The
site of Arthur's shrine, to which his bones
were translated in 1278, is still marked out
in the grass of the former choir. Take yourself up to the east end of the church, and
look back down its great length. Difficult

62 The fifteenth-century panelled stone
front of the George and Pilgrims at
Glastonbury

though it may be to imagine it now, this
was one of the longest churches of
Christendom. Typically, Abbot Bere, by
the addition of his Edgar Chapel (another
crowd-pulling device) in the early sixteenth century, made it even longer than
before.

Of the other Glastonbury Abbey buildings, the only complete survivals are the
late-medieval stone barn, now housing the
Somerset Rural Life Museum, outside the
precinct to the south-east, and the abbot's
kitchen, being part of the expansion of the
abbot's lodgings which occurred in the
later fourteenth century. Probably, it will
be this kitchen that will remain with you
longest as a memory of Glastonbury. It is
a remarkable structure, without question
one of the finest of its kind in Europe, with

great central louvre and fireplaces (each with its short chimney) at the angles. Although quiet now, it would have been the scene of demonic activity when the abbot, as he was frequently expected to do, had important guests to dinner. Better than any account-book, it tells us of a life-style dominated at this period by display and conspicuous waste.

High Ham The road to High Ham would not be anybody's choice as a through-way. So much the better, for it is a pleasant country route – one of the best – and the church in the middle is most rewarding. High Ham Church, set behind its green, needs to be approached from the south. At its west end, a modest tower (basically fourteenth-century) is all that survives of an earlier church otherwise completely rebuilt in the 1470s: nave and chancel together. One survival from this reconstruction is an entire set of roofs (nave and aisles, chancel and south porch); another is the major part of the furnishings – benches in the nave and a fine contemporary rood screen, intact in all but its figures, having coving, loft, and doors still in place; a third is a little of the fifteenth-century glass, preserved in the head of the east window. Now that the rest of the glass is clear, High Ham has become an exceptionally light church, visitable until late in the evening. It is spacious, nicely set, and well finished with tall symmetrical nave arcades and a handsome panelled chancel arch only partly obscured by the screen. This is Late Perpendicular at the domestic scale which seems often to have suited it best.

*Huish Episcopi** Nobody could visit this church today without being struck by the magnificence of its great west tower, lavishly decorated with quatrefoil friezes, with pinnacled angle buttresses, with canopied niches, and with an over-sailing parapet of particular elaboration and splendour. After this, the rest of the church must inevitably appear rather dull. Unfortunately, too, the church interior has been mishandled by its Victorian restorers. Spare

64 The great west tower at Huish Episcopi, one of the finest and the most elaborate of such towers in Somerset

time, though, to enjoy the handsome Burne-Jones window (1899) in the south chapel, and look from there north at a very different window, facing you across the nave, the tracery of which is an excellent example of the extraordinary inventiveness of the fourteenth-century mason, working within the Decorated tradition. To appreciate fully this interesting – if mutilated – interior, with its set of oddly flattened fourteenth-century arches, stand back under the lofty panelled tower arch at the extreme west end of the nave. From here, you will have a view also of the nice late-medieval wagon-roof, alas robbed of its authenticity by Victorian stencilling. In this church, one of the most evocative survivals is the richly decorated Late Norman south door. It is still fire-reddened in a very obvious way, as it has been, probably, since before 1232, at which time the building was re-dedicated. Other traces of the same fire have been found elsewhere in the church, but what is puzzling about the

◀ 63 The abbot's kitchen at Glastonbury, equipped with fireplaces at each of its angles and dominated by its great central louvre

door is that no attempt was made, in several subsequent rebuildings, to replace it. Perhaps our sense of the past is of greater antiquity than we might think?

**Isle Abbots　Although remote and not especially easy to find, this beautiful church is well worth the considerable diversion it will take you to get there. From the road, the west tower (work of *c.* 1500) is exceptionally handsome, even in this county of beautiful towers; note the finely proportioned windows, the many canopied niches with original figures still intact, the elegant buttresses and pierced and pinnacled parapet. Both the south porch and the north aisle are of this date too, being of at least equivalent quality. But there is no need to linger outside this church, for the interior is still more rewarding. Here the chancel, two centuries earlier than the late-medieval remodelling, holds an elaborate piscina and unusual three-seat sedilia (tub-seated in the Victorian club manner), both framed under the continuous roll moulding of the period. The chancel arch is a Perpendicular rebuilding, panelled in the Somerset style. And notice too how the continuous moulding of the early-fourteenth-century chancel has been adopted again as a decorative device by the builder of the much later north aisle, thus enhancing the harmony of a particularly light and elegant interior. Both the wagon-roof of the nave and the panelled north aisle roof are original, as is the rood screen and a complete set of benches with ends in the architectural style. Between chancel and north aisle, an impressive squint cuts through the rood-loft stair, adding another feature of interest to a church interior which, with its handsome stone floor and green-house fenestration in the Perpendicular north aisle, is one of the most satisfying mixtures in Somerset.

*Kingsbury Episcopi　The crazy lean of a great stone chimney, perpetually threatening to crush the sixteenth-century cottage to which it belongs, adds spice to the approaches of this handsome church, nicely set on the eastern edge of the village.

Chiefly remarkable here is the fine west tower, one of the most ornate in Somerset. Note the use of decorative friezes and the many statue niches, several still having the original figures in place. Inside, the tower is impressive too, for buttresses have been brought forward into the body of the church, making a double-thickness tower arch, panelled in the Somerset manner and further decorated on the east faces of the buttresses with two pairs of canopied niches, as at Martock. Another good feature of the church is its grand Perpendicular chancel, with an embattled vestry (cf. Langport) built out to the east and with great windows immediately to the north and south of the high altar, more than compensating in light for the restriction of the east window to allow for a vestry beyond. In the Early English manner, a continuous string course has been used here to link the features of the chancel; the rood screen, in all but its upper part, is original; in the chancel windows, especially those of the north chapel, some fifteenth-century glass remains in place.

**Langport　Like Milborne Port, this interesting little town has a longer history than its present condition might lead us at first to assume. Langport's situation at an important junction of the ways is no help to its tranquillity these days: the town is cruelly quartered by busy roads. But it was these roads, with the control of the crossing over the River Parrett and the navigable qualities of the Parrett itself, that brought Langport to prominence in the first place. The 'port' in the town's name still recalls its Anglo-Saxon role as a trading centre; it was here that one of the forts named in the early-tenth-century Burghal Hidage was established; not much later, there was a mint in the town, and there is no doubt of Langport's borough status in Domesday. After this, its later history was uneven, one of its curiosities being the continuing dependency of the borough's church on neighbouring Huish Episcopi, of which it remained a chapelry, without independent parochial status, until as late as 1882. Just to the east of the church, the survival of Langport's still impressive east gate, with the so-called Hanging Chapel preserved over it, provides us with an intriguing reminder of civic life in the Late Middle Ages: it was here, in their own chapel, that the portreeve (ancient title), bailiffs, and commonalty would have met, to do business and for sessions of the court. These days, sadly, the chapel is inaccessible as the Portcullis Lodge of Freemasons. Nor is the church, being the only other important medieval monument in the town, of much interest. Scarcely a bow-shot from the much grander mother-church at Huish Episcopi, its principal features now are the chancel (with embattled vestry to the east) and south chapel, both of them dating to the early sixteenth century and associated with the chantry foundation of John Heyron (d. 1501), a wealthy portreeve of Langport. Note here the fine large windows and good contemporary roofs, the easternmost bay (over the high altar) being especially intricately panelled. And look also at the glass in the east window, restored but genuinely late-medieval, with the figure of the Virgin (to whom Heyron's chantry was dedicated) in the middle, surrounded and supported by her saints. Elsewhere in the church, Victorian glass deepens the gloom of a building already made depressing by a particularly tasteless nineteenth-century refurnishing. Escape to the churchyard where, on the south, there is a very fine prospect towards Muchelney.

*Long Sutton** What ought to be an interesting and impressive church somehow fails to be so, nor is this the fault entirely of an open and rather featureless setting. Certainly, the west tower is handsome; it may date a little before the rest of the church, which was rebuilt in the early 1490s. But the building has been cherished rather too well for its health. The churchyard, with war memorial and roadside boundary wall, is suburban. Inside, the walls have been horribly scraped, while one's immediate reaction to the gaudily

painted pulpit and rood screen is not, to put it mildly, very favourable. In this, of course, one would be wrong, historically if not aesthetically, for the colours of the re-paintings are authentic enough and it was thus that the medieval congregation would have seen them. Try to ignore the scraping; swallow your revulsion at the paintwork; what you will then see is a remarkable mid-fifteenth-century carved pulpit (the figures in the niches are modern) with, behind it, a complete set of rood and parclose screens stretching the full width of the church and demonstrating how such a building of the Late Middle Ages was intended to be divided at that time. Look up then at the fine late-fifteenth-century tie-beam roof, with the usual greater elaboration of panelling at the east end of the nave, over and in front of the rood. In the chancel, too, the wagon-roof is original and has only recently been magnificently restored. Here the contemporary piscina, triple sedilia, and priest's south door make a good set, and there are nice panelled arches into the two chancel chapels. Under the lofty panelled tower arch and lierne vault, a handsome Perpendicular octagonal font is yet another good original feature. But the cheap pews, the Victorian tiles, and the nasty gaudy glass – dear me!

***Lytes Cary** A modern lodge and hill-top setting (most unusual for a medieval secular building) make an unpromising beginning. Nevertheless, this delectable house must not be missed. It has been extended in several campaigns, the latest early this century. Fortunately, though, the separate stages are easily unpicked, and what we have here quite obviously is a mid-fourteenth-century chapel, originally free-standing, with a great hall of a century later, and a residential wing adjoining them both and dating to the early sixteenth century. Throughout all this time, and indeed until the mid-eighteenth century, Lytes Cary was the home of the Lyte family, a Somerset clan whose dynastic alliances brought them a wide spread of acres. As you see it now, it is a careful restoration by Sir Walter Jenner, whose bequest of the property to the National Trust was moved, he said in nicely medieval vein, by the desire to 'perpetuate the memory' of himself and his kin. In some respects, Sir Walter's attentions have left Lytes Cary more useful as a guide to early-twentieth-century monied antiquarian taste than to anything genuinely earlier. Nevertheless, if you strip Lytes Cary mentally of its valuable (but variously dated) antiques, you may well picture the hall as built originally by Thomas Lyte, soon after his inheritance of the property in 1453, for the great timbered roof and broad side-wall fireplace at least are his, making an apartment of some style and splendour. Other works followed here at the time of his great-grandson, John Lyte, builder of the fine porch and oriel bay that now ornament the east front. And it was John, too, who rebuilt the solar range at the south end of the hall, with Great Parlour on the ground floor and Great Chamber above, and with a number of other lesser apartments. Note the handsome arches, in Somerset stone panelling, which open into John Lyte's new staircase at the south-west end of the hall and into his private dining-chamber, opposite on the ground floor of the oriel. Originally separated from the hall by a timber screen, this little chamber, with its separate fireplace, is important evidence of the developing taste of the day for family privacy away from the hall. In the reconstructed solar wing, the splendid panelled bays are still medieval in flavour, but the roof of the great chamber is a fine coved plaster ceiling, datable to 1533 and one of the earliest of its kind, while the symmetrical arrangement of the bays and the adjoining windows suggests the new standards of the Renaissance. The heraldic glass now in the hall windows is also of John Lyte's day. A century later, the genealogical enthusiasms of the Lyte family surfaced again in Thomas Lyte's charming heraldic frieze in the chapel at Lytes Cary, made interesting too by the rustic screen of his time and by a nice set of contemporary altar-rails.

Martock This handsome church benefits much from its setting and you should come here, if you can, from the south. In front of it, Martock's main street takes a right-angled bend to the east; to the left, Church House is a fine stone building much earlier than the date (1661) it now carries; to the right, facing the chancel, the Treasurer's House was once the rectory, taking its present name from the Treasurer of Wells. Set back from the road, with one arch of its great double gate still intact, the Treasurer's House has a thirteenth-century solar block running east to west, with an early-fourteenth-century hall projecting north towards the road. It pairs interestingly with the church, not least for the point it makes about the resources the medieval rectors of Martock took out of the church, while giving back comparatively little in exchange. Observe the marked difference in scale between Martock's chancel and its great nave for which the townspeople, not the Treasurer, were responsible. True, the five lancets of the thirteenth-century chancel's east window are handsome enough; against the chancel also there are embattled north and south chapels, the first of which (dedicated to St Thomas) may have been financed, in part or in whole, as the chantry of John Harris, rector and Treasurer of Wells. Nevertheless the real glory of Martock is undoubtedly its nave, with the west tower and south porch of the same period. In comparison, the chancel seems diminutive. Study the roof especially; its date is given (convincingly enough) as 1513, and it rests on a clerestory of appropriate quality, lavishly decorated with vaulted and canopied niches (empty, but painted internally with seventeenth-century renderings of the Twelve Apostles) and splendidly lighting the timberwork above. This roof, recently fully restored, is one of the best in Somerset. But more individual are the decorative niches at Martock, repeated on either side of the great tower arch and again on the chancel arch, facing into the body of the nave. There are some things about Martock which fail to appeal; the church furnishings are dull, there has been some unattractive scraping back to the stone, and many signs remain of an over-vigorous late-nineteenth-century restoration. However, stop here to sense the scale of the late-medieval rebuilding, to examine the fine roof (with angelic host well lit by the generous clerestory below), and to appreciate the still-medieval authenticity of its setting. There are few groups in Somerset as complete.

*****Meare** This intriguing and very complete little group makes more sense if it is remembered that Meare formerly stood on the edge of a great shallow lake, drained comparatively recently and once richly stocked with fish. Coming into the village from the east, the abbot of Glastonbury's fish-house, alone in its field, is the first medieval building you will see. Of two storeys, with a comfortable lodging above and workshops below, the fish-house dates to the early fourteenth century, being now preserved and maintained as an ancient monument. On the far side of the same field, to the west, the abbot's manor-house has been remodelled in the seventeenth century, but retains on its south façade (east of the porch) the blocked arches of the three great windows of a first-floor hall; another large chamber survives in the back wing, running north at the west end of the building, but little early work is now visible in that quarter from the adjoining churchyard. Both manor-house and fish-house are contemporary, and it is to the early fourteenth century again that the tower and chancel of the parish church belong, the nave and its aisles being later. In this charmingly light and spacious village church, Abbot Selwood's modifications of the later fifteenth century are most prominent. There is a nice stone pulpit in the Perpendicular style, with a goblet-shaped font of that curiously classical form seen also at Weston Zoyland. A good, if rather plain, Somerset roof survives in the nave, dating to Abbot Selwood's rebuilding; in the chancel, an earlier and much steeper-pitched roof, heavily raftered, has a distinctly domestic look, most unusual in churches of this county. Other features of the church include the splendid ironwork, probably fourteenth-century, of the south door; also an early poor-box, now placed on a late-medieval carved pedestal.

***Milborne Port** The A30 has not been kind to Milborne Port, nor has this little Somerset town (on its limb of the county projecting south into Dorset) kept the importance it once had in the earlier Middle Ages. Many might prefer, with some reason, to travel on without pausing to Sherborne in one direction, or to Purse Caundle, almost equidistant in the other. However, for the whole-hearted church enthusiast, Milborne Port has something rather special to offer. Its chancel, its central crossing, and its south transept all belong to the immediate post-Conquest period, with at least a suggestion (in the pilaster-strip treatment of the south chancel wall) of earlier Anglo-Saxon work on quite a considerable scale. Milborne Port, as the 'port' of its name still reminds us, was a pre-Conquest trading centre of some standing, although it was soon to be overshadowed by neighbouring Sherborne. It should be no surprise, therefore, to find it well equipped with a stone church, elements of which have survived successive rebuildings, the most complete in the late 1860s. Do not linger in the nave or north aisle: both are distressingly Victorian. Go instead straight to the crossing and, turning your back on the north transept (again Victorian), study the early Norman capitals of the crossing itself, the Norman west window in the south transept, and the remains of contemporary work now exposed in the lofty chancel, characteristically Anglo-Saxon in its proportions. Outside, the south door (although rebuilt in the nineteenth century) preserves its original carved tympanum, while next to it, the diamond-work on the stair turret likewise establishes its Early Norman date. Inside again, there is a pretty Perpendicular chancel screen, complete with its doors; on either side of the altar, two life-sized statue niches, defaced at the

65 The hall at Montacute House, with its Renaissance stone screen at the lower end yet preserving the medieval tradition

heads, carry traces of the medieval paint-work and are now furnished with statues of the Virgin Mary and St John the Evangelist, in accord no doubt with their original purpose but in the modern 'brutal' tradition.

***Montacute** Sir Edward Phelip's great house at Montacute was built at the very end of the sixteenth century out of the profits of a successful legal career which was subsequently to branch into politics. However, despite the date, Montacute House retains many medieval features, as well as illustrating (in the most agreeable way) the new fashions and standards of its own period. Buy the excellent guide-book to this meticulously cared for National Trust property: you will find in it everything, and perhaps more than, you want. But you will not wish to keep your head in the guide-book throughout your visit, and what you need to note especially are the following: the fanciful Elizabethan garden approach with its corner pavilions, balustrades, obelisks, and turrets; the great ornamental east façade (always intended to be the glory of the building), symmetrical in the new manner and equipped with Flemish gables, with pediments, shell-headed niches, and with statues (ludicrous but charming) of the Nine Worthies in Roman dress; the hall with its ornamental stone screen at the entrance end, just where a medieval builder would have placed it; the medieval-style stone stair rising, not like a Jacobean timber stair round an open well, but on every side of a central masonry pier; the internal porch, ornamental chimneypiece, decorative plaster frieze, and heraldic glass (some of this also in the hall) of Sir Edward Phelips's Great Chamber on the first floor, now the library; and the magnificent Long Gallery on the second floor, with tall oriel windows as viewpoints at either end, unparalleled at houses of medieval date but well suited to the Elizabethan promenade. At Montacute, the hall (so important to previous generations) has been reduced in scale, although still traditionally equipped. The Great Chamber remains as a formal apartment, but the emphasis is already shifting to more comfortable private quarters, panelled and glazed, each room with its individual fire-place. The irregular but functional diversity of the medieval country house has been replaced by strict symmetry, even where this (as in the case of the hall) may seriously limit the internal design. And yet, both inside and out, Montacute is as full of conceits and of pattern-book Renaissance detail as any great house of the period. This splendid embodiment of the Elizabethan *zeitgeist* is not on any account to be missed.

Certainly, you can save time for it by ignoring the parish church, notable only for its assembled Phelips monuments in the north chapel and for the odd little lobby, with stone panelling in the Somerset manner, linking this chapel with the porch. However, immediately beyond the church (to the south-west) you can glimpse from the road the formidable early-sixteenth-century gatehouse which is all that remains of Montacute Priory, once one of the better-off Cluniac houses. It is worth parking the car to walk up there.

*** Muchelney

This magical place is not easy to appreciate at first glance. Round it, the low-lying country still has a marshy look; it was subject to frequent flooding throughout the Middle Ages, leaving Muchelney in most winters as an island. Today, so much has gone of the abbey and its buildings that the surviving fragments are barely intelligible, at least until you are well and truly in amongst them. Persevere; there is a great deal to see, starting with the abbot's house at the south-west angle of the former cloister, only recently rebuilt at the time of the Dissolution and subsequently retained as a farmhouse. Restorations here have left us with a building of unusual purity and much period charm, stripped of its post-Dissolution accretions. You will need to buy a guide to appreciate the plan of the abbot's lodgings and to see how these relate to the adjoining cloister. But notice especially the fine-quality guest provision in the first-floor chamber at the west end of the building, the great stone stair leading up to the abbot's own quarters futher east, the very splendid windows (with some early-sixteenth-century glass intact) and remarkable chimney-piece of the abbot's parlour at the head of these stairs, and the suite of private chambers (one with its original barrel-roof) up another short flight of steps, above the cloister. Below the parlour, a large ante-room has a fine panelled door north into a surviving fragment of the south cloister walk, with another door opening east into the former refectory. The cloister vault has gone, but enough remains to show that this also was a contemporary rebuilding, again of high quality and no doubt attributable to a revival of the abbey's fortunes in the early sixteenth century when the community's assets were reviewed under Thomas Broke (1505-22), builder of the new suite of lodgings. Stand back as far as the site will allow you, and look at the south façade of Abbot Broke's personal quarters. So symmetrical are the upper windows and other details of this front that they have something of the character of late-Georgian 'Gothick', more exactly suggesting the arrival of Renaissance standards in the planning of this pre-Reformation building. To the right of this façade, the surviving stone panelling was once internal, decorating the north wall of the monks' refectory which originally lay parallel to the cloister. With the reredorter to the south-east (drain-openings still intact at its base), these are the only standing remains of a Benedictine house of great antiquity and of more than average wealth. On the ground, the church (incorporating as a crypt the remains of the much smaller Anglo-Saxon building) will not impress you: it is, after all, only half the length of Glastonbury. But now compare it with the parish church, just a few feet to the north. From the air, the difference in scale is especially striking; on the ground it is almost as obvious.

The abbots of Muchelney were rectors of the parish. In the early years, they had probably found room in their church for the parishioners. However, the sharing of churches between monks and laymen was always stressful, and it may not have been too long before the two communities were separated. Certainly, the present parish church is not the first on its site. It is a Perpendicular building with a pretty but unremarkable west tower. Note the way the main façade of this church faces north: it could hardly have done otherwise, with the abbey church so close to the south. Its two-storeyed north porch, nicely finished with a good internal star-vault, is one of the building's better features; behind the panelled tower arch, the excellent fan-vault is similarly worth inspection. Otherwise, though, the major interest of Muchelney's parish church centres now on the wagon-roof of its nave, charmingly painted in a naïve country style of the early seventeenth century, with angels (bearing texts) among clouds. The medieval encaustic floor-tiles, set in a raised square behind the handsome Perpendicular font, are earlier than the font itself and have been brought there from the abbey site next door.

To the north again, across a small green on which the medieval parish cross (authentic in all but its head) still stands, Muchelney's third monument – and in many ways its most perfect – is the fourteenth-century priest's house, built for the vicar (or so it is presumed) soon after a vicarage was first ordained here in 1308. Improvements to the house in the late fifteenth century have since given it the square-headed windows that are now such a feature of the hall and its adjoining chambers. However, the arch of the north door is of fourteenth-century type, giving admission to a cottage which, in all major particulars, is the same as it was when first built. Internally, a central hall (with screens-passage to the west, next to the door) had the usual two-storeyed solar block at its upper (eastern) end. At the lower end, another chamber was sited over a service room, probably partitioned, which would have done duty as a buttery and kitchen. Covetable enough even today, Muchelney's priest-house is the property now of the National Trust, although visitable only by appointment. Few comparable examples have survived to modern times of the kind of accommodation thought appropriate in its day for the household of a parish priest and his clerks.

***North Cadbury** Church and manor-house together make a noble group: one of the nicest such pairings in England. You will wish to linger here in the well-kept churchyard. From its vantage-point, certainly, you will be able to inspect the late-sixteenth-century mansion built next door by Sir Francis Hastings (d. 1610), author and politician, before his uncongenial Puritan opinions brought him into trouble with the Crown. Unfortunately, the house itself is private property.

Adjoining it on the east, the parish church is unexpectedly spacious for such a rural spot, with fine symmetrical porches to north and south, giving a splendid transverse view if both doors (as may often be the case during the summer months) are open. Only the late-fourteenth-century tower here is modest. Just a few years later, the whole of the rest of the church was rebuilt in the grandest manner, the intention of the 'foundress', Lady Elizabeth Botreaux (d. 1431), being to establish a collegiate chantry at North Cadbury. There is no evidence that the college ever reached its full strength. However, Cadbury was still described as a college at its formal dissolution in 1548, and it is plain from the imposing scale of the chancel and from the stalls once fitted there (three misericords from these are now on display at the east end of the south aisle) that the church was well equipped for the purpose. Lady Botreaux, wearing the fashionable horned head-dress for her period, lies in effigy on a tomb-chest next to her husband, William Lord Botreaux, whom she survived a full forty years. Sadly, both this tomb and a pair of seventeenth-century monuments (one of them, probably, of Sir Francis) have been crammed inappropriately behind the tower arch, robbing the foundress of her due. Look back down the church towards the east end and you will appreciate the scale of her enterprise. A grand five-bay nave

66 Muchelney's priest-house, or vicarage, dating originally to the early fourteenth century but remodelled a century or so later, to which period the windows belong

opens into the great chancel, not as long but as broad and as high. On either side of the altar, splendid canopied niches once held life-sized figures. There is a fine Somerset tie-beam roof in the nave, with original roofs also in the north and south aisles, each elaborately panelled in the east bay. The carved poppy-head bench-ends are sixteenth-century work, one of them dated 1538; and note the way the chancel windows are set, high over what would have been the choir-stalls below. In the west window, behind the well-set Perpendicular font, contemporary glass includes the figures of eight saints, among them (top left) the martyred Apollonia, deaconess of Alexandria, patron saint of all sufferers from toothache.

*North Curry On the north edge of this pretty and well-cared-for village, the parish church of North Curry must make one of the most memorable settings in England for a wedding. Little Georgian houses, with much display of roses and mown grass, line its approaches; in front of the church itself, a manicured churchyard sets off the straight path that connects modern lych gate with spectacular triple-niched Perpendicular porch. With its fine clerestory, its pierced or crenellated parapets, and its great octagonal tower on the crossing, North Curry is a church to savour from the outside – much better out than in. Sadly, Victorian restorers have had their way with the interior, which, although it remains both handsome and spacious, has lost any sense of antiquity. Of the church roofs, only the north aisle retains its fifteenth-century timberwork. The chancel floor, in gaudy Victorian tiles, is a particularly stomach-turning feature, as are the walls scraped back to the stone. There is little left of interest in the church furnishings. However, an ancient chest is thought to be of the twelfth century; it is now at the west end of the church. At the east end of the north aisle, a fourteenth-century tomb-

67 Angle towers at Nunney, a castle built in the French style by Sir John de la Mare in the 1370s and probably based on his own experiences in the wars

chest carries a cadaver effigy, unusually placed thus and probably imported from a larger monument elsewhere.

***Nunney** Tucked down in its hollow, well north of the main road, Nunney is an island of unspoilt charm: an unexpected and very English retreat. Not that the castle at Nunney itself appears English, being much nearer in type to those tower-houses, more familiar in fourteenth-century France, which its ageing builder, an ex-soldier of the Hundred Years War, had come to know in the course of his campaigns. Sir John de la Mare, by the time he obtained a royal licence in 1373 to fortify his family home at Nunney, had long since given up the wars. However, it is clear that he felt the urge (as did others of his kind) to surround

himself with reminders of past victories. Nunney is a pseudo-fortress: difficult to defend even before artillery, impossible after the advent of the siege-gun. At its only time of trial, in 1645, it was to fall within two days. Yet we must try to see it, as Sir John himself would have done, essentially as a castle of chivalry. Nunney is a celebration not of strength but of status: a just reward, appropriately decked out in the trappings of war, for a lifetime spent in the field.

Some of the Frenchness of Nunney is now lost in its decay. But the castle's water defences are characteristic of contemporary France, as are even more obviously the prominent machicolations under the roof-line, which would have supported a continuous fighting platform. Picture Nunney also with conical roofs on its turrets and with a steep central roof (again very French and perhaps even including dormer windows) over the main body of the building. The entrance on the north side, formerly approached over a drawbridge, is original and noticeably lightly defended. On the ground floor, a great fireplace in the south wall opposite the door establishes that this was the kitchen, with above it, on the next floor, the service rooms (buttery, pantry, and servants' quarters) usually attached to one end of the hall. Over these again was the hall itself, and it is from here that the stonework changes quality as we reach the personal quarters of the lord. Notice the much larger windows (fitted with window-seats) at this level; the great fireplace on the south wall; the provision for a private parlour in the south-west tower, at the high-table end of the hall. Other private chambers in the floor above were similarly reserved for the use of the family; they included bedchambers, garderobes, and a family chapel (over the parlour).

To the south of Nunney Castle, on the hillside overlooking it, the parish church is pretty enough as a feature of the landscape but is a sad disappointment within. There are de la Mare, Poulet, and Prater monuments in the north chapel, representative of the three families who held the castle until the end of the seventeenth century. But the modern ceiling in the nave is a nasty shock. One can only hope that it is temporary.

Purse Caundle   Just off the A30 to the south, this pleasant house, in its lovely garden, is well worth the short stop it may cost you. Dating basically to the later fifteenth century, it has a central hall with solar wing to the south, subsequently extended in two further building campaigns, the first in the mid-sixteenth century, the second early in the seventeenth. The east, or road, front is the earliest, being almost exclusively of the first two periods. So even if you fail to gain admission to the house, there is still plenty to see from your car. Notice the pretty fifteenth-century oriel window on the south-east gable, corbelled out over the road. Towards the northern end of the same façade, an oriel bay at the north-east corner of the hall has been modified substantially in the sixteenth century, and this is the date also of alterations in the hall which reversed it internally, so that the screens passage (serving the porch and east door) is now at the south end of the hall, not the north. Features of special interest at Purse Caundle are the fifteenth-century tie-beam roof of the hall and the contemporary wagon-roofs in the first-floor drawing-room and in the chamber over the oriel bay. Fifteenth-century moulded beams occur in the earlier parts of the north and south ranges, with a door of this period in the south wall of the porch, and with sixteenth-century fireplaces in the hall and in its oriel bay. The impressive west window of the hall, on the far side from the road, is not original. However, a good part of the charm of this house is to be found precisely in its mixing of periods, and you will get as much satisfaction from the deliberate symmetry of the south garden front, characteristically seventeenth-century, as from the equally typical confusion of the medieval and mid-Tudor east façade.

A little further down the road to the south, the parish church has a north chancel chapel probably built by William Long (d. 1524) as a chantry for himself and his family. The Longs had been lords of Purse Caundle since Richard Long's purchase of the manor in 1428. William Long's canopied tomb is placed between his north chapel and the high altar, in the traditional position for such a monument. It is the only thing worth looking at in a church which, although of uniform Perpendicular style, was substantially rebuilt in the nineteenth century.

Sherborne   There is so much to see at Sherborne that it makes sense to concentrate on what is most important, coming back another day for the remainder. You could start – chronologically, this certainly works best – at Sherborne Old Castle, at the south-east angle of the town. Most striking here is the scale of the great earthworks, of geometric polygonal plan, which defended Bishop Roger's country palace. Roger of Salisbury (d. 1139) was Henry I's justiciar: after the king himself, the most powerful man in Anglo-Norman England, and certainly one of the wealthiest. He was a famous builder, at Sherborne as elsewhere, being something of an innovator in castle-design at a time when experiment was common. Sherborne Castle, like the bishop's other major fortress at Old Sarum, was supplied with an encircling ring of massive earthworks, with strongly fortified gates characterized by narrow gate passages, and with a tower-keep as a place of last resort in an emergency. But both Sherborne and Old Sarum were also episcopal palaces. Central to Sherborne's fortified enclosure is a complex of buildings, constructed round a central court, with the remains of the tower-keep at the south-west angle. Under the tower, two barrel-vaults survive, supported by a monolithic central column at the south end; they give some impression of the strength of a building now much reduced in scale and overshadowed by the work, more domestic in character, of the chapel range north of the court. Notice the high quality of the

68 Early fan-vaulting in the nave at Sherborne, dating to the later fifteenth century before the perfecting of the vaulting tradition when the fans, as at King's College Chapel (Cambridge), met at the middle

fenestration and of the surviving fragments of decorative arcading, tokens of Bishop Roger's great wealth. To the east of the court was a kitchen range, with the hall probably to the south, the whole comprising an arrangement of buildings uniquely well ordered for its period. In the defensive circuit, the lower part of the south-west gatehouse (now the main approach) is of Bishop Roger's time, but the great north gate, with its extraordinary stepped barbican, is more likely to be a thirteenth-century modification of the bishop's original defended passage. Another gate survives at the north-east angle. To the south, the curtain wall has largely gone,

leaving a convenient platform to view Sherborne New Castle, over its ornamental lake in the middle distance. You should find time for this house if you possibly can. Its central core, built by Sir Walter Raleigh in the 1590s after he had been given the Sherborne estate by Queen Elizabeth, is a good example of Tudor taste in a characteristically bizarre and extravagant vein.

It was Bishop Roger again who was responsible for the first reconstruction of the abbey church at Sherborne, already a large and impressive Anglo-Saxon building when he began work on it. Today, one of the only obvious reminders of the pre-Conquest church is a round-headed door, very Saxon in flavour, at the west end of the present north aisle: it used to be the entrance to a north-west transept which was an element in the great west-work of the early church. Bishop Roger's own church took its scale from the Saxon building, but has itself left little behind. Its most striking survival is the huge tower arch, incongruously spanning a broad and handsome nave which, in every other respect, is Perpendicular. Indeed, it is this final rebuilding of Sherborne — a work that took almost a century to complete — that is certain to stick in your memory. Reconstruction began on the choir under Abbot Brunying (1415-36), but slowed down in the mid-century partly as a result of the riot and fire of 1437 (notice the walls of the choir, fire-reddened even today), and was not completed until the abbacy of Peter Ramsam (1475-1504), to whom the nave and its fine vault are attributable. An interesting characteristic of the fan-vaults at Sherborne, betraying their comparatively early date, is the failure of the fans to meet at the middle — as they do, for example, at the later King's College Chapel (Cambridge) — being separated instead by a complex lattice of thin vaulting-ribs like the lierne vaults employed in the aisles. Abbot Ramsam's concern in the work is everywhere celebrated by representations, on shields and vaulting bosses, of his personal rebus, the ram. And certainly, as the abbey's finances picked up towards the end of the century, he spared no expense in the rebuilding. Particularly handsome is the use everywhere of decorative stone panelling of the very highest quality, giving a luxuriously textured casing to the rather heavy nave arcades (where it probably hides earlier work) and framing the glorious clerestory. It is little wonder that the townspeople of Sherborne, like those of Great Malvern in a similar situation, purchased the abbey church in 1540 from Sir John Horsey, former steward of the Benedictines, to whom it had been granted with other monastic properties at the suppression of the previous year. They would have done it, probably, with particular satisfaction, remedying an exclusion which, a century before, had been the cause of great bitterness and violence.

Their own former parish church, built in the fourteenth century at the west end of the abbey church to rid the monks of lay disturbance in their nave, was demolished soon after the purchase of 1540, and has left few traces. Beyond it, however, the buildings of Sherborne School preserve quite substantial remains of the dissolved monastery: in particular, of the abbot's lodgings at the north-west angle of the cloister, and of the guest hall in the west cloister range. North of the school and beyond the original domestic buildings of the abbey, part of the monastic barn has survived in a private house known as 'Abbey Grange', retaining its great porches but otherwise much cut down and transformed. More recognizably monastic, and certainly more accessible, is the Conduit on Cheap Street, looking these days like a market cross but once (before its post-Dissolution re-siting) the claustral washplace, next to the refectory door, of the monks. Notice the way that the original mullions and sills have been removed in four of the openings to make an open arcade; internally, on the central boss of a nice lierne vault, angels support the arms of the dissolved abbey.

It is the Conduit that gives a good medieval flavour to Sherborne's principal shopping street, and there are of course other contemporary touches – windows, doors, gables, and passage-ways – up and down the length of the town. Most important, though, as a complete survival is the fifteenth-century almshouse of SS. John the Baptist and John the Evangelist, refounded in 1438 and rebuilt over the next decade on a site to the south-west of the abbey church. A considerable extension northwards in the mid-nineteenth century has partly disguised the nature of the original work here. Nevertheless, the existing south range remains much as it was first intended, with a chapel at the east end (retaining a fifteenth-century Rhineland triptych behind the altar) and with dormitories and a refectory in the main block to the west. Sherborne's almshouse was for women as well as men, and it is this that explains its unusual two-storeyed plan – women above and men below – with shared ground-floor refectory at the west end. Almshouse-rebuilding was a favourite activity of nineteenth-century philanthropists, and Sherborne's bede-house is a rare survival, very well worth a visit.

Somerton Apart from the parish church, there is not much that is medieval in Somerton today. Nevertheless, this is an attractive little town, especially if approached from the east, and you should allow enough time to enjoy it. On the north side of Somerton's colonized market-place, the church is nicely placed and very handsome both inside and out. It is the great chancel arch that gives the church interior its individual character, and this (like much of the rest of the church) is earlier than one has come to expect in Somerset, belonging to the first half of the fourteenth century. Stand back in the chancel and use its arch to frame the magnificent nave roof, an addition of the late fifteenth century and individually the best feature of the church. Note also the good Jacobean reredos and communion table (1626), with a pulpit of the same period and other contemporary chancel furnishings. Broad fourteenth-century arcades make this building seem especially spacious, and this would be a good church, undoubtedly, to worship in. What a joy furthermore, in a dull patch of the sermon, to be able to contemplate such a roof!

Tintinhull The church and manor of Tintinhull came to the monks of Montacute Priory in c. 1102 as an important element in their founding endowment. Formal appropriation of the church, delayed until 1528, is one of the latest recorded. Nevertheless, it is certain that it was the Cluniacs of Montacute who were chiefly responsible for financing the rebuilding of Tintinhull Church in the early thirteenth century, and this must explain the very striking uniformity of its interior. In particular, the single scheme can be recognized in the continuous roll-moulding, over doors and under windows, not confined (as is usual) to the chancel at Tintinhull, but prominent in the nave there as well. In the generously planned chancel, the work is of excellent quality. The east window is a nineteenth-century replacement. However, the fine piscina, although since restored, is of thirteenth-century date, while the symmetrically disposed windows of the north and south walls are characteristic of Early English building at its best. Notice the blocked window, west of the chancel arch, which shows how the nave, as originally planned, would have been lit by lancets similar to those in the chancel. As it is, the arch itself is a later addition, dating to the early fourteenth century, the tower likewise post-dating the nave. In the fifteenth century, larger Perpendicular windows were inserted in the nave walls and a south porch was added (1441-2), still retaining its original vault. Of the church furnishings, the bench-ends were supplied in 1511-12; the stone base of the rood screen remains intact; and the pulpit, fitted with sounding-board or tester, is Jacobean, dating to the early seventeenth century.

Next to the church, immediately to the south, is Tintinhull Court, formerly the rectorial manor of Montacute Priory. It preserves the medieval hall-centred plan in the main range of the present house, with some features (including an embattled projection) of c. 1500, but was extensively rebuilt and enlarged in the seventeenth and eighteenth centuries by its post-Reformation owners, the Napper family, purchasers of the rectory in 1559. In due course, as the family prospered, the Nappers bought up other former Montacute lands in the parish. They built the Dower House, north of the village green, and Tintinhull House, to the north-east, now the property of the National Trust. Both houses are of the seventeenth century, with later additions. Together, they make up as nice an example as one can hope to get of the rise of a local gentry family on the proceeds of a former monastic estate, not unlike (although on a smaller and more domestic scale) the Phelips family of Montacute itself.

Trent The charm of Trent, for all the individual merits of the parish church, lies rather in the buildings that surround it. Immediately on the left, as one comes in by the church path from the north-east, is the Chantry. Dating to the late fifteenth or early sixteenth centuries, it is a notably comfortable building, with fine sets of transomed windows and with the original chimney-stacks still in place. Very probably, as its name implies, this would have been the residence of the priest (or priests) serving chantries in the pre-Reformation church, one of them the mid-fifteenth-century chantry of John Franks, a native son of Trent, who made good in London at the law. Across the road to the east, Dairy Farm is another early-sixteenth-century building; its west gable-end has windows of this period visible from the road, although the south front is a seventeenth-century remodelling. And then again, beyond the church to the south-west, the surviving core of Church Farm is the former solar wing of a substantial late-fourteenth-century house, many of the features of which still remain there. Settled amongst all these, Trent Church seems especially well placed. It has an unusual plan, with an early-fourteenth-century tower and porch

69 The parish church at Weston Zoyland, remarkable for its fine roof and for an almost complete set of early-sixteenth-century pews; the rood-screen, while modern, is of good quality and authentic in flavour

sited adjoining each other on the south. The spire (rare in this part of the world) is a recent rebuilding, but a faithful one. Inside, there are many features of interest. In the nave and chancel, the curious vaults are an addition (not one of the happiest) of 1840. It was then, or a little later, that Trent acquired its lavishly carved pulpit: early-seventeenth-century Netherlandish work given to the church by its philanthropic incumbent, the Rev. Turner. The benches, however, are the original set, nicely varied

in theme and dating to the early sixteenth century. The font-cover, although small, is another interesting Perpendicular piece. And this is the date too of an exceptionally handsome rood screen, perhaps not original to the church but nevertheless illustrating with unusual clarity the late-medieval arrangement of rood-loft stairs and door. Among the monuments, a fourteenth-century knight effigy may be that of Sir Roger Wyke (d. about 1380); it is accompanied in the north chapel by a civilian effigy of a similar date, both under much later canopies. To enter this chapel, you must pass under an arch which is itself a monument to Ann Coker (d. 1633), wife of Thomas Gerard, one of the first of Dorset's more notable historians. On the soffit of the arch, above the inscription, are the family trees (forty shields in all) of the Coker and Gerard clans. It is a homely piece, designed by the antiquary himself.

Weston Zoyland You may have to go out of your way to visit Weston Zoyland, but you will not, I promise you, regret it. Neither the village nor its surrounding countryside are especially attractive; the church, on the other hand, is breathtaking. Look first at the great west tower – one of the most expensively ornate in Somerset. Matching it to the east, the rest of the church (with the exception of the chancel) was rebuilt in the same Late Perpendicular style, with characteristic display of battlements and buttresses, canopied niches and ornamental tracery, the whole fitting together most harmoniously in what must be everybody's favourite image of a parish church. Already handsome enough outside, Weston Zoyland is astonishing within. The first thing you will see as you enter the south door is a nave roof of exceptional richness, its tie-beams supporting kingposts in the usual Somerset manner, but everything carved in the most lavish fashion and superbly lit by the noblest of contemporary clerestories. There are other good roofs in the aisles and the south chapel; the benches are an almost complete set of the early sixteenth century, one at the front carrying the initials (RB) of Abbot Bere of Glastonbury (1493-1524); and the font is of that curious architectural form, bowl and stem circled by mouldings, seen also at the rebuilt Glastonbury church at Meare and distinctly classical in flavour. Take a good look at the rood screen. It is modern, of course, but it carries the loft and figures that would have been there on such a screen in the Late Middle Ages and which only exceptionally escaped the reformers. Opposite it, at the west end of the nave, a panelled tower arch soars into the roof, with a fine fan-vault supporting the bell stage behind it. This is a splendidly handsome and spacious church, well furnished and definitely worth visiting. However those (including myself) who have used it in the past as an example of rectorial meanness, pointing the contrast between the small-scale fourteenth-century chancel and the rest, may themselves have been less than generous. Abbot Richard Bere's initials occur again on one of the buttresses of the south chapel (a particularly rich piece of work), and it is clear that his treasury at Glastonbury contributed substantially to the new building at the church of St Mary, Weston Zoyland. Had the abbey survived in 1539, the chancel might indeed have had its turn.

HOTELS AND ITINERARIES

It makes good sense to establish one's base at a town where there is plenty to see. On this tour, Glastonbury and Sherborne share the honours: both have a hotel you will enjoy. At Glastonbury, there is no question that the **George and Pilgrims** will offer you all that you need. Dating back to the fifteenth century, it preserves many original features inside and out, including one of the loveliest late-medieval façades in England. The food is good and there is at least one other promising restaurant in Glastonbury (down Magdalene Street to the south) should you want variety. But the rooms may set you a problem. For one thing, the hotel is small; for another, you will have to make up your mind between one of the fine medieval rooms on the street front (handsome but inevitably noisy) and the more modest (but quieter and lighter) rooms in the late Georgian extension at the rear. Whatever you do, avoid the rooms in the middle. The clock of St John Baptist, you may be glad to know, does not chime all night.

No larger than the George and Pilgrims, but just as charming in quite a different style, is the **Eastbury Hotel** at Sherborne. Here a handsome Georgian façade hides earlier work more obvious in the cottage annexe to one side. One of the best features of the hotel is its lovely garden, so this (more than the thoroughly urban George and Pilgrims) would be the place to choose in the summer. The hotel, in Long Street near Sherborne Old Castle, is quietly placed and very relaxing. It is within easy walking distance of the town centre, just down the street to the west.

The little **King's Arms Inn** at Montacute would be my third choice for a base, and again there is a good restaurant in the market square to the east, which you could book in at for the second day of your visit. But with only a handful of bedrooms, you may find yourself excluded, in which case there are at least two further possibilities – the **George** at Castle Cary and the **Red Lion** at Somerton – both splendidly situated near the centre of the touring area, but neither to be recommended without reserve. The George may appear cramped in the summer months, when oak beams and heavy thatch are at their least appealing. The Red Lion has been modernized with little taste. Without question, you will be more comfortable in the well-situated eighteenth-century coaching inn of Somerton – a prettier town, anyway, than Castle Cary. Nevertheless, my preference remains for the late-medieval George, at any time except in the hot weather.

*   *   *

The regions east and west of Glastonbury offer a possible division, but there are a number of constraints here in opening hours which will certainly determine your itineraries. If you want to see **Montacute**, **Lytes Cary**, and **Purse Caundle**, you will have to make the tour in the summer: in any event, between April and October. Lytes Cary is open on Wednesday and Saturday afternoons; Purse Caundle on Thursdays, Sundays, and Bank Holidays; Montacute daily except Tuesdays, but not before 12.30 even then. Both **Glastonbury** and **Sherborne** could absorb a full morning, Montacute most of an afternoon. Obviously, you will find yourself having to be especially selective; either that, or come back another day for more.

From Glastonbury westwards, **Meare** looks like a diversion, but it will take you through some interesting country (a good way to get the feel

70 Lytes Cary: a comfortable manor-house of the late fifteenth and early sixteenth centuries (the wing on the right is later) for a family of prospering country squires

of the Levels) and has much to offer in its unique group of buildings. **Weston Zoyland** is again worth the detour. However, you may not have the time to take in **Creech St Michael**, **North Curry**, or **Isle Abbots**, on the western limits of the itinerary; in which case head south to **Curry Rivel** and **Langport** (again missing both out if time is short), stopping at least for the tower of **Huish Episcopi**, but reserving your best attentions for **Muchelney**. From there, it is a short trip south to **Martock**, taking in **Kingsbury Episcopi** if you can. A good map-reader will get you to **Tintinhull** easily enough, but you may be watching the time by that point, and it is **Montacute** really that you must visit. On the way back to Glastonbury, **Lytes Cary** is open till six in the evening (last admissions at half-past five), and this would be the right time of day to inspect it. From there to **Somerton** and home.

Eastwards, there are no problems with opening hours at **Doulting** or **Nunney**, so there is some point in starting in the north-east. After these, **Ditcheat** is more rewarding than **Evercreech**, if you have to make the choice, and **Bruton** has several points of interest, in addition to the noble parish church. Save as much time as you can for **North Cadbury** and **Trent**, both high priority and good spots for a picnic, and make sure you get to **Purse Caundle** before five. At **Sherborne**, the Old Castle need not take too much of your time, but try not to miss the abbey church: its extraordinary vaulting will be one of your more vivid memories of the whole trip.

Priorities, obviously, are Sherborne and Glastonbury, with Montacute and Lytes Cary, Nunney, Muchelney, North Cadbury and Trent. Following these, there is a large class of second-bests, of which Martock and Meare, Purse Caundle and Weston Zoyland are particular favourites, with remote High Ham put aside as a special treat, although sadly all too easy to miss. What you lose will depend on where you enter the tour and on the season in which you have to make it. Try the summer: it would be a crime to miss Montacute or Lytes Cary.

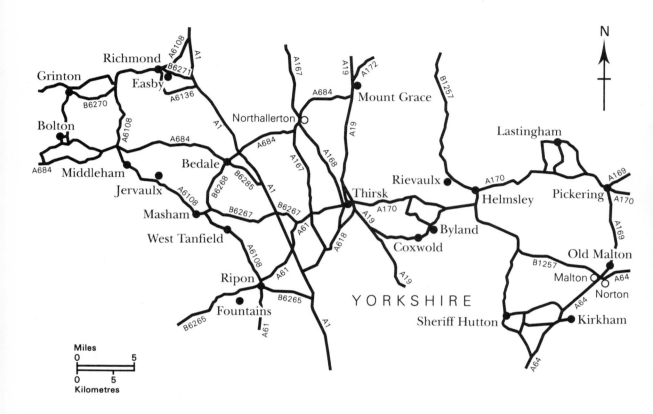

Chapter 7

North Yorkshire

Nobody knows how far William took his notorious harrying of the North. The Danes had been in Yorkshire for long years before him, and parts of the landscape may already have been laid waste. However, what is certain is that the Anglo-Saxons have left few traces here of what was once a flourishing northern kingdom. Under the crossing at **Ripon** still, St Wilfrid's crypt is one of our most precious and most evocative survivals of the seventh-century Anglo-Saxon Conversion. At **Easby** and at **Masham**, fine carved crosses have a Byzantine look, establishing the sophistication of Anglo-Saxon culture here in the early ninth century, shortly before the Viking onslaught swept the Church and its art clean away. The next crypt we have, at **Lastingham**, may belong in spirit with St Wilfrid's crypt and with the relic-bound traditions of the old Church. It was built to hold the relics of the great Wilfrid's contemporary, the lesser-known but still remarkable St Cedd. Yet it is a work of the post-Conquest ecclesiastical settlement, put there by monks who, just a few years later, would move on to York to found one of the greater Anglo-Norman Benedictine communities at St Mary's. This reorganization of the monastic church from its great centres at Durham, at Whitby, and at York, was as much a product of the recent invasion as were the castles now rising in the land. It is Anglo-Norman Yorkshire – nothing earlier – that we recognize.

One building, above all, captures the flavour of these events. **Richmond Castle**, almost as we see it now, was put up by Alan the Red, a kinsman of the Conqueror, to protect his men in hostile territory and to serve as a focus for his new estates. Like so many of the castles of the initial settlement period, it is an improvization, making use of a natural triangular platform well protected on the south by a sharp cliff descent to the Swale. The great keep at Richmond, of course, is later. However, it incorporates Alan's gatehouse at the apex of the triangle, and this, as were the thick curtain walls which still link with it from east and west, was already on a staggering scale. Nothing remotely like it had been seen in these lands

157

before. In the judgement of Orderic Vitalis, who ought to have known (for his father was a witness of these events), it was their castles that brought victory to the Normans.

Richmond belongs to that very small class of stone-built castles – Ludlow and Exeter are others – which dates back to the first generation of the Conquest. Generally speaking, the earthwork defences of the initial Norman military settlement have left few traces, nor would we expect them to have done so. At **Middleham**, held by the brother of Alan the Red, there are the remains of a motte-and-bailey earthwork castle just a little up the hill from the great stone fortress which had risen to replace it by the late twelfth century. More impressively, **Pickering** preserves the motte, classically upturned-basin in profile, which was certainly the first castle on its site. But Middleham is probably no earlier than 1086, which is the date of Ribald's acquisition of the estate from his brother. And there is no saying when the motte at Pickering was originally raised: its perfection of form suggests maturity, and it is unlikely to have been one of the earliest. Accordingly, what we are looking at in Yorkshire is a group of castles which, while it recalls the circumstances of the Norman Conquest, is generally much later in its emphasis. Richmond's magnificent rectangular keep, now the most spectacular surviving element of the great fortress, is a work of the 1160s and 1170s. It was at about this time too that Middleham acquired its keep and that at least some of the timber defences of the motte and bailey at Pickering were rebuilt more substantially in stone. A few years later again, the new fortress at **Helmsley**, dating to about 1200, was already showing in its plan some of the major innovations of castle architecture as this entered its most formative period. Helmsley's tower-keep, although in the old tradition, was now to be equipped with an experimental apsidal east front; drum towers protected the angles of the curtain and flanked the gate on the north; within half a century, sophisticated new barbicans had been added.

Helmsley was the castle of the de Roos lords, who had inherited the site from Walter l'Espec, one of the major figures of Anglo-Norman Yorkshire. We know more about Walter than almost any of his contemporaries, and the reason for this is the key role he played in the mid-twelfth-century monastic settlement of the county. It was Walter who gave the Cistercians their first northern site, three miles to the north-west, at the place they then christened **Rievaulx**. And it was Ailred, the third and most famous of Rievaulx's abbots, who later described him as an excellent soldier, quick of wit and wary in war, a big honest man, open of countenance, with black hair, a bushy beard, and a voice (so Ailred says) 'like a trumpet'. Walter had favoured the Augustinians before, and **Kirkham** was his earliest foundation. However, it is for Rievaulx especially that we now remember him, for it was from this tiny acorn that there grew the mighty oak of

71 The tower-keep at Helmsley Castle: early-thirteenth-century work with angle-turrets in the French tradition, added about a century later

the major Cistercian settlement of the North. On their way to Rievaulx, the party of monks had spent some time with the Benedictines at York. This was not an old community, having come to St Mary's not so long before from Lastingham. But it was already disaffected, to be upset still further by the example of the Cistercians, and to furnish from its number the original party that would set up house independently at **Fountains**. Rievaulx was founded in March 1132; Fountains in late December that same year, soon after which its community was welcomed by the Cistercians. Both had the personal backing of Bernard of Clairvaux, whose 'soldiers' thus colonized the North.

Over the next two decades, during which Cistercian expansion reached its peak, Rievaulx became the mother (or grandmother) of eleven separate houses, while Fountains acquired a family of twelve. Throughout the land, and even overseas to Scandinavia, they took the standards of abstinence and of purity of observance which made the Cistercians, in William of Malmesbury's view, a 'model for all monks, a mirror for the diligent, a spur to the indolent'. Moreover, we can still see some of this spirit in their earliest buildings. These men, as William said, 'love pure minds more than

72　The west end, with the remaining arc of its great rose window, of the abbey church at Byland

glittering vestments'. Look at the plain column-bases in the nave at Rievaulx, and you will see what he meant. But look further at the glorious choir and presbytery of the same abbey – Early English work of the very highest quality and decorative brilliance – and the short span of these standards becomes obvious. When **Byland**, the third of the great houses of North Yorkshire, came to be laid out on its final site in the 1170s, there was to be no further thought of austerity. While Rievaulx itself was being rebuilt and while Fountains was growing ever larger, the monks of Byland started a church so ambitious in its scale that it would take them more than a generation to complete it. Take note of the clustered columns of its arcades, of the elaborate multi-chapelled ambulatory of its east end, and of the great cathedral-like rose window (a broken half-circle now) at the west. None of this was wholly bad. It pleased lay patrons, did honour to God, and lifted the spirits of the monks. Yet it could not have happened while the great Bernard and his saints were still alive.

At almost all religious houses, whatever their allegiance, rebuilding programmes were actively under way in the thirteenth century. **Easby,** founded in 1151 and one of the earlier Premonstratensian abbeys, was never rich. Yet its buildings grew in elaboration throughout the thirteenth and early fourteenth centuries, adding to the beauty of a monastic complex that is still among the loveliest in England. Simultaneously, the Augustinian canons of Walter l'Espec's **Kirkham** were encouraged by the continued patronage of the de Roos lords of Helmsley to begin a campaign of expansion in their buildings which they were never, in the event, to complete. Kirkham's choir and presbytery (the site of the de Roos family burials) had been rebuilt on the grandest scale before work stopped; a new chapter-house of the same period still establishes the line of the pro-jected great cloister, subsequently abandoned by the canons; the priory gatehouse presents a fine show-front to the outside world, rich in de Roos heraldry and dating to the late thirteenth century. After this, the clouds gathered. Kirkham was already severely in debt early in the next century; it was bankrupt in the 1350s and in 1357 was all but disbanded. Kirkham's troubles were worse than many's, but they were not unique. Means and expectations no longer coincided. Monasticism in England had begun its long descent towards suppression.

This descent, not unnaturally, was uneven. At **Richmond,** the tower of the Greyfriars (a most exceptional survival) is still there to remind us of the continuing popularity of the Franciscan brothers throughout the later Middle Ages. They represented the most extrovert arm of the monastic church, and they had been preaching in Richmond's great sloping market-place since their first arrival there in 1257. At the other extreme, the Car-thusians of **Mount Grace** were the introverts. Here, against the western scarp of the Cleveland Hills, we have one of the most perfect manifestations of late-medieval piety, to which the best spirits of the Church had with-drawn. Mount Grace was founded in 1398 by Thomas de Holand, earl of Kent and duke of Surrey, and although experiencing a brief check on the death of its patron only two years later, was so much in tune with con-temporary religious sentiment that it soon revived and then continued to flourish. What Mount Grace could offer was withdrawal from the world and a retreat even from the customary companionship of the cloister. In this very holy place and in the privacy of his cell, the Carthusian monk could prepare himself for that individual confrontation with God which was the aim and object of every Christian mystic. It was after Mass one summer day, while continuing his meditations in the priory's little church, that Richard Methley obtained his own reward. God, he tells us, visited him 'in power', and 'I yearned with love so as almost to give up the ghost.'

How this could be I will tell you, my brethren, as best I can by the grace of God. Love and longing for the Beloved raised me in spirit into heaven, so that save for this mortal life nothing (so far as I know) would have been lacking to me of the glory of God Who sitteth on the throne. Then did I forget all pain and fear and deliberate thought of any thing, and even of the Creator. And as men who fear the peril of fire do not cry 'Fire hath come upon my house; come ye and help me', since in their strait and agony they can scarce speak a single word, but cry 'Fire, Fire, Fire!' or, if their fear be greater they cry 'Ah! Ah! Ah!', wishing to impart their peril in this single cry, so I, in my poor way. For first I oft commended my soul to God, saying: 'Into thy hands,' either in words or (as I think rather) in spirit. But as the pain of love grew more powerful I could scarcely have any thought at all, forming within my spirit these words: 'Love! Love! Love!' And at last, ceasing from this, I deemed that I would wholly yield up my soul, singing rather than crying, in spirit through joy: 'Ah! Ah! Ah!'

(Quoted here from David Knowles, *The Religious Orders in England*, ii:225)

**Bedale This pretty little town has a long north-south market street, cobbled on each side and lined with mainly Georgian houses. With many useful shops and with no trouble parking, it is a good place to stop to buy provisions. Bedale's parish church, too, is exceptionally interesting for North Yorkshire. Equipped with a powerful west tower, it is entered unusually by way of a south porch attached to this tower, bringing the visitor into the church at the best point to appreciate its spaciousness. A generous fifteenth-century clerestory floods the interior with light, and this impression is assisted by the huge east window (said to come from Jervaulx) of the already broad south aisle, giving that part of the church something of the character of a conservatory. Notice the curious experimental quality of the north arcade, dating to the early thirteenth century and varying in each of its piers. Behind it, there is a large fourteenth-century wall-painting of St George and the Dragon (very fierce and very complete), other paintings in the church including a contemporary Angel of the Annunciation to the right of the chancel arch, over which (to left and right) are handsome post-Reformation black-letter texts of the Creed and of the Lord's Prayer.

Bedale's monuments also are important. Most impressive are the fitz Alan effigies, to Sir Brian fitz Alan (d. 1306) and his lady, now placed to the north of the tower arch. Although damaged, enough remains of both effigies to illustrate the characteristically agitated style of the period (one of the most important in English monumental sculpture). Facing the fitz Alan monument on the south side of the arch are two knight effigies in the more reposeful manner of the later fourteenth century, and there is an interesting early-sixteenth-century carved marble grave slab in the north aisle floor – very elaborate and thought to be of Thomas Jackson, donor of the east window of this aisle – establishing how much better such things could be done in brass by the time that this memorial was fashioned.

***Bolton There is no better vantage point for a view over Wensleydale than the battlements of Richard le Scrope's castle at Bolton. This splendid building, in delicious decay, is one of the most important memorials of a chivalric life-style highly developed by the late fourteenth century. Richard le Scrope, first Baron Scrope of Bolton (d. 1403), had been Treasurer of England from 1371 to 1375; he was

Chancellor in 1378 when building at Bolton had already begun, and was a soldier of long standing and experience. Bolton itself was the child of his later years: a project to which he devoted the last two decades of his life, finishing it only in 1399 when death was just around the corner. George Jackson's excellent short guide still provides the best account of Lord Scrope's building. Buy it as you go in, but you may find the text over-detailed for the time you can afford, so look out for the following features in particular. First, as you will notice at once, Bolton is a castle with the merest handful of public rooms – the great hall on the first floor of the north range and the chapel on the second floor of the south range are the most important – set in a complex matrix of private suites and lodgings, each assigned to a different member of the lord's household. You will not wish to sort these out; and, indeed, you would find the utmost difficulty in doing so. However, consider the comfort of the apartments (with great fireplaces, individual garderobes, and bedchambers of their own) on display in the surviving south-west tower. Then take yourself to the roofless opposing tower in the south-east corner, and look up at the many levels of similar apartments, one fireplace stacked above another. Next to this tower, the original gate-passage was a simple vaulted corridor, protected by portcullises at either end, but otherwise only lightly defended. Yet stand under its inner arch and consider the problems that would immediately have met an intruder. Over the doors in each corner, there is a machicolated angle in the turret above; loops command the courtyard from the ground-floor store-rooms; the only way to ascend to the next level is by narrow stairs, where the advantage is all with the defenders. Bolton, in essence, is more country-house than fortress. But it is the work of an ex-soldier, and of one who intended to fill it with a lifetime's accumulation of the sort of treasures he had no wish to yield up to the Scots. Hence the contradictions in its design, for which the most important requirement was accommodation for a large

73 The south-east corner tower of Lord Scrope's late-fourteenth-century castle at Bolton, adjoining the main entrance passage

household but which must, at the same time, be secure. Compare Bolton with Sheriff Hutton or with the more fortress-like Bodiam, at the other end of the country, in Sussex. They are exact contemporaries; they were built for similar men; their purpose, of course, was identical, though the enemy at Bodiam was the French.

***Byland** Come to Byland from Coxwold and you will see it at its best, with the Hambleton Hills as a deep-green backdrop. Peaceful and isolated, this is not otherwise a very beautiful spot, at least if judged against Rievaulx or Fountains. Its importance lies rather in the comprehensive spread of its remains, giving us a model late Cistercian layout, begun in the 1170s and effectively finished shortly after 1200. For many years, since the inauguration of their community as a Savigniac house in the 1130s, the monks of Byland had moved from one site to another before a final resting-place was agreed. By the time this was done, there had been Cistercians at Rievaulx for more than a generation, a merger between the orders (Savigniac and Cistercian) had been arranged in 1147, and St Bernard was long since dead. All three circumstances are important for an appreciation of Byland: they moulded the buildings we now see. Immediately before you, as you enter the site, is Byland's most spectacular standing fragment – the Early English west front, with its cathedral-like rose window, which was the last part of the church to be completed. Behind this, the nave, choir, and presbytery stretch out to the east in a magnificent sweep, repeating in the plan of the elaborate east end the ambulatory and multiple chapels of post-Bernardine Citeaux. You may recall what this would have looked like when complete from your visit to Abbey Dore, on the Welsh border. However, there is enough here still, especially in the south transept, to establish both the scale and the quality of this late-twelfth-century building, rejecting (as the Savigniacs had always been inclined to do) the original severities of the Cistercian regime. Notice the surviving stretches of later-thirteenth-century tile mosaics, among the best-preserved in the country. Then take yourself systematically round the conventual buildings, appreciating the geometric regularity of their layout, and not forgetting to call in at the modern site museum, where several fine capitals from the church are now on display, establishing the high quality of the works. Among features of special interest are the fifteenth-century meat kitchen, next to the museum; the unusually sited reredorter and abbot's lodging, extending east from half-way down the dormitory range; the large kitchen (west of the refectory) and great length of the west range, both of them much grander than at Rievaulx. One rare survival for which you should remember Byland, and which no doubt reflects the relatively late date of its building, is the so-called 'lane' west of the cloister, which served the lay brothers as

a walk-place of their own. It reminds us how strictly the ranks were divided in a Cistercian community, architecturally as well as by function, and may help explain the later disaffection of the lay brethren.

Coxwold Prominently placed at the upper end of one of Yorkshire's prettiest villages, Coxwold Church is unusually well sited, with open countryside immediately to the south. Of course, nobody who comes to Coxwold today can miss its Laurence Sterne associations – Sterne was vicar here in the 1760s and wrote *Tristram Shandy* at Shandy Hall, a little way further up the hill. Accordingly, it is a particularly happy coincidence that many features of the church are themselves eighteenth-century, including much the greater part of its furnishings. Whereas the nave and the pretty octagonal west tower are Perpendicular, the chancel was rebuilt in 1777, some ten years after Sterne's death. In it, the exceptional projecting communion rail almost certainly goes back to before Sterne's time, and he would have preached from the handsome two-decker pulpit (cut down from three) which still survives next to the chancel arch. All in all, this is a complete Georgian church interior, very much as Sterne would have known it. It retains its box pews (again somewhat cut down), with the Hanoverian arms over the arch to the east, and the gallery still intact to the west. Behind and above all this are the elements of a fifteenth-century rebuilding. Late-medieval glass, for example, including several complete figures, survives in the heads of the nave windows; the octagonal tower is of an enterprising if somewhat rustic design; internally again, the nave roof is largely original. In the chancel, the gaudiest among several grand monuments is the early-seventeenth-century tomb of Sir William Bellasis (d. 1603), the first of a long family line to live at Newburgh Priory, a former Augustinian house (one of the richest prizes of the order) which had been awarded to Sir William's uncle, Anthony Bellasis, chaplain of Henry VIII. You will see on this tomb already the heraldry and the classical motifs with which the family continued to be obsessed.

***Easby** Just a mile or so down-river from Richmond (on the north bank of the Swale), this lovely place provides a picnic spot of special distinction, with everything to recommend it for the passage of a lazy summer afternoon. It was here in the 1150s that Roald, then Constable of Richmond Castle, brought Premonstratensian canons in one of the earlier episodes in the expansion of their order, subsequently very popular in England. As part of their founding endowment, the canons acquired the parish church of Easby, which they served from that time until the suppression of their house, and which remains within the limits of their precinct. Indeed, it is the parish church that is the first thing you will see of Easby once you are past the gatehouse on the left. Go at once inside, for though a modest enough building, the surviving thirteenth-century wall-paintings of its chancel are among the most complete in the country. On the north wall, between ornamental bands, a Creation cycle begins (on the west) with a Creation of Eve (emerging from Adam's side), followed by the Temptation, the Nakedness of Adam and Eve, the Expulsion from Eden, and the Curse of Toil (Adam delving while Eve spins); in the window splays, charming contemporary Labours of the Months represent sowing and pruning (for Spring) and digging and hawking (for Winter). On the south, a Life of Christ cycle opens (on the east) with the Annunciation and continues thereafter through the Nativity, the Annunciation to the Shepherds, the Adoration of the Magi, the Deposition, the Entombment, and the Holy Women (the two Maries) at the Sepulchre. Below, the contemporary triple sedilia, already a nice example of their kind, have paintings of archbishops (hands raised in blessing) behind the seats. Among other features of interest in the church are an Early Norman font (very handsome and antedating the arrival of the canons), some fourteenth-century glass preserved in the east window,

and a nice Perpendicular screen closing off the east end of the south aisle as a chapel. The Easby Cross, found in fragments here in the 1930s and now in the British Museum, is reproduced in plaster-cast, showing the high quality of the Byzantine-influenced carving on the cross-shaft. It dates to the early ninth century and is paralleled by the surviving shaft in Masham churchyard.

It is the placing of the parish church, cramping the abbey site on the south-east, that explains at least some of the peculiarities of Easby's later conventual plan. Buy a guide or study carefully the plan on display. What you will notice is that the canons' infirmary and the abbot's lodgings are here placed north of the abbey church, for there was no room for them in their usual position to the south-east. At the same time, the canons' dormitory and their guest accommodation intermeshes on the west side of the cloister, again partly for reasons of space on the site but also to take advantage of the mill-race by the Swale to flush the rere-dorter drain. It was in this range too that the warming-house was placed, at the north-west angle of the cloister under the north end of the dormitory, while the whole is characterized by surviving vaulting and other decorative thirteenth-century work of great expense and high quality. Like many communities of religious, the canons of Easby by the early fourteenth century were embarking on new programmes of improvements. Before 1350, they had extended their church with a grand new presbytery, still very obvious on the ground, with a sacristy to the south and a chapel (probably a family memorial chapel of some kind) against the west face of the north transept. Characteristically also for the period, they had reconstructed their refectory, south of the cloister, to make an exceptionally fine first-floor apartment, lit by a handsome set of windows. The refectory is the first building you will see after visiting the parish church: they have gables almost facing each other. It seals off the south end of the east cloister range, in which much of the chapter-house still

74 The nave arcades
at Fountains Abbey,
illustrating the
monumental austerity
of early Cistercian
work before the order
relaxed its first
prohibitions of
anything more
elaborate and
distracting

survives, setting the tone for a community more relaxed than the Cistercians but also more complex – and very well worth your study.

***Fountains** Like Venice, Fountains has never been known to disappoint its visitors. It is one of the most memorable survivals of medieval England, and you should give it plenty of your time. As you go in, though, stop for a moment in front of Fountains Hall, improbably placed against the cliff on the left. It was built by Sir Stephen Proctor early in the seventeenth century, being a fine example of the strict symmetry favoured in that period, along with its ingenuity and inventiveness. Immediately after this, the supreme experience of your visit will be the famous vista

of Fountains Abbey from the west. What we are looking at is a typical Cistercian site, not as steep-sided as Rievaulx but constrained by the limits of a narrow valley floor and, of course, exceedingly picturesque. Settled in 1132, Fountains was among the earliest of the English Cistercian houses, ending its days undoubtedly the richest. Prosperity came soon, with the result that the church was laid out on the grandest scale from the start, while the conventual buildings, within a generation, had to be extended to their present great size. Buy Mr Gilyard-Beer's excellent official guidebook: it is a model of its kind, and will make good reading at home as well as on the site. But while you are here, notice in particular the contrast in treatment between the austere nave, the five eastern-

75 The great vaulted undercroft of the west, or lay brothers', range at Fountains

most bays of which date back to the original building campaign, and the more decorative presbytery of the early-thirteenth-century reconstruction, capped on the east by the still more elaborate (and only slightly later) Chapel of the Nine Altars, a clear denial of the primitive rigour of the Order. The handsome tower on the north, another contradiction of earlier beliefs among the Cistercians, is as late as the early sixteenth century, being one of the many building works of the energetic Abbot Marmaduke Huby (d. 1526). However, restraint in building had gone long before, and the major extensions of the late twelfth and early thirteenth centuries (among them the chapter-house, the huge refectory, and the major part of the lay brothers' west range) were already expensively finished as well as large. Later remodellings at Fountains included successive rebuildings of the abbot's personal quarters (the last by Abbot Huby again), with extensions to the guest houses to the south-west of the great

cloister and significant modifications to the monks' infirmary to the south-east. But these are muddling on the ground, being better followed in plan or as Mr Gilyard-Beer has sorted them out in his guidebook. Store up instead as your major reward some impression of the scale and complexity of the monks' arrangements and of the unparalleled beauty of the tamed wastes that surrounded them. It was from such that generations of religious drew the holy joy which would prepare them for the company of the blessed.

*Grinton Too many Yorkshire churches have been spoilt by Victorian restorations. But Grinton is one of the exceptions. It is a wide, low and spacious church, with good stone floors and with much simple but original timbering in its roofs. Norman tower and chancel arches confirm the twelfth-century origins of the building. However, the present fabric is largely Perpendicular, as are a number of the more interesting church furnishings, including the font cover, the delicate parclose screens of the north and south chancel chapels, and much of the glass now collected together in the south-east window. The font itself is Norman. Grinton's dimensions somehow enable it to carry the burden of walls scraped back to the stone. Although hardly the 'Cathedral of the Dales', as it is sometimes known, Grinton is a mature and settled church, pleasantly domestic in contrast to the bleak slopes it adjoins.

***Helmsley There is no sense in wasting time on the parish church at Helmsley; it is almost entirely Victorian. Go instead to the beautifully sited and meticulously maintained castle here: it is of a most unusual but highly interesting and instructive plan. Although it probably replaces an earlier fortress, the estate centre of Walter l'Espec (founder of Kirkham and Rievaulx), there is nothing now at Helmsley Castle that need date before 1200. It was Robert de Roos (1186-1227) who, the Rievaulx Cartulary tells us, 'raised the Castle of Helmsley', and this certainly fits well with the round angle and gate towers of its inner curtain and with the experimental plan (apsidal on its outer face) of its tower-keep. Almost opposite the keep in the west curtain, there is another great tower of this period, although two successive re-fenestrations in the thirteenth and sixteenth centuries have made it look younger than it is. Helmsley's magnificent double-ditch defences must belong to the days of Robert de Roos, but the elaborate barbicans to north and south, defending the castle gates on those quarters, are characteristically mid-to-late-thirteenth-century work, and it was at this time also that the accommodation at Helmsley was improved, showing now especially in the works on the west tower, equipped with garderobes at one corner and with handsome two-light windows (most of them later obscured by their sixteenth-century replacements). Very little is left of the inner curtain. However, as further strengthened and raised in the early fourteenth century, it was certainly

substantial, while it was at this date too that the tower-keep was remodelled, acquiring the bold turrets (rather French in style) of which two have survived intact. The great hall, marked out on the ground in the south-west corner of the enclosure next to the west tower, is attributable again to this period of rebuilding, when the castle was strengthened and its accommodation extended, making it a fortress of the first rank, appropriate to the dignity of the long family line of the Ros (or Roos) lords of Helmsley. It was a descendant, the thirteenth Lord Ros, who was created earl of Rutland in 1525, and it was his grandson (the third Manners earl) who again remodelled the accommodation in the great west tower and made a fine suite of chambers in the range to its north, embellished with the plasterwork and panelling characteristic of his period (the 1570s) and furnished with a fine chimneypiece, handsomely inlaid. Helmsley, throughout the Middle Ages, was both sophisticated fortress and family home. For the first, look especially at the experimental tower-keep and at the extraordinary elaboration of the barbicans; for the second, inspect the west tower and the hall, kitchen, and service rooms to its south and east. As examples of not uncommon developments in castles, they are nevertheless very hard to beat.

***Jervaulx Garden, arboretum, and romantic ruin – Jervaulx Abbey has everything to offer. This tumbled, shaggy, overgrown place, still privately owned, has all the charm now lost in the gravel and greenswards of our national monuments. Bring a flask of tea and perch on a wall or on a column-base. Nobody will shout at you here, and this indeed is the way to enjoy Jervaulx, just as though you were a Regency Romantic. Such cheerful neglect, of course, has its disadvantages, and one of them must be the difficulties all feel in getting their bearings in this wilderness. Go straight to the church site or to the cloister immediately to its south. From there, it will be easy to locate the chapter-house (one of the more complete survivals) in the east claustral range. South of this again, the west wall of the monks' great dormitory, with its fine run of Early English lancet windows dating to *c.* 1200, has been preserved to full height, being the most obvious element in the abbey's ruins as you approach them over the fields. On the other side of the cloister, to the west, the lay brothers' range (the earliest building on the site, thought to have been erected first to give shelter to the men who worked on the completion of the church) is as long as the monks' dormitory; between them, south of the cloister, the north–south refectory is traceable still in the grass. The complications begin – as they usually do in Cistercian houses – at the south-east corner, behind the dormitory, where a jumble of ruins includes the remains of the monks' infirmary and the abbot's lodgings. Much of this work is late, dating to a reorganization of the routine of the community when, from the fourteenth century, regular meat-eating came to be permitted by the order. Even in their more austere days, the Cistercians had allowed their sick and dying to eat meat. Consequently, it became usual (as here) for the later much-enlarged misericord (where meat might be eaten) to be located next to the infirmary. At Jervaulx, it is the meat kitchen, with huge fireplaces in three of its walls, that is the most obvious reminder of this practice. Like a carcase of beef over one of its fires, St Bernard must have spun in his grave.

Kirkham If only Kirkham had a few great trees, it would be one of the most beautiful monastic sites in England. As it is, though, it is still easy to reconstruct the charm of Kirkham's riverside situation, on a bend of the Derwent to which Walter l'Espec (unaffected as yet by his later preference for the Cistercians) brought Augustinian canons in the late 1120s. There is very little now, except the modest size of the cloister, to remind us of this early community. What we see instead are the outlines of buildings undergoing a transformation round about 1300 when stopped abruptly by financial catastrophe. Walter

l'Espec's heirs, the de Roos lords of Helmsley, had contributed to Kirkham's prosperity in the later thirteenth century, making it the tomb-church of their clan. Probably for this reason, the choir and presbytery were rebuilt at just this time on a new and more lavish scale. At the same period, the chapter-house was rebuilt (again much larger) and the lower stages of a crossing tower were begun. But look down now from the east end of the church towards the river, and you will see where these schemes then aborted. By comparison with Kirkham's choir, the nave remained pathetically small and out of scale. The reconstruction of the chapter-house, on its new line east of the original cloister limits, was never followed by the enlargement of the cloister itself. Debts of over £1,000 (a great fortune in the money of the time) had accumulated by the early 1320s. Partly, these would have been the result of over-ambitious building. But the agricultural crisis of the previous decade had exacerbated Kirkham's problems, as had also the marauding of the Scots. Fortunately, before the recession set in at the priory, two important surviving works had been completed, being the principal ornaments of the site as we now know it. One of these is the exceedingly handsome laver, or wash-place, at the south-west corner of the cloister, with its beautiful late-thirteenth-century blind tracery. The second is the gatehouse, badly knocked about on its ambitious outer façade and certainly not helped by the graceless car-park it confronts, but recognizably still a work of the highest quality, as Early English turned the corner into Decorated. Notice the use of heraldry here to enrich the façade, anticipating the common practice of the Late Middle Ages and including, of course, the de Roos arms. The interdependence of monk and long-time patron is well illustrated at Kirkham, both here on the gatehouse and in the eastward extension of the church. A medieval monastic community, even had it wished to do so, would have experienced much difficulty in shaking off the claims of the great men, generations after the initial settlement, who continued to regard themselves as its 'founders'.

***Lastingham** Monastic life began at Lastingham as early as the mid-seventh century. However, it had come to an end before 900 as a result of the Danish invasions, and what we see at Lastingham today are survivals of a much later episode, dating to the arrival here in 1078 of Benedictine monks from Whitby, before their migration less than a decade later to York. In that short time, they had moved fast in the construction of a great church, of which the crypt, the apse, and the easternmost bay of the chancel still remain. First of all, descend into the crypt: it is splendidly untouched and complete, being the intended home of the relics of St Cedd, Lastingham's seventh-century founder, and entirely characteristic of the crypt-building tradition of the Anglo-Saxon Church, briefly continued by the Normans. Above it, the ambitious church planned by Stephen of Whitby and his companions in the late 1070s was never finished. The intention had been to continue the chancel by another large stage to the west: a second contemporary arch still crosses the nave to establish this. But the projected nave, barely begun when the church became parochial, was cut off at that point, and the greater part of the present church is thus no more than the original chancel. By great good fortune, this important building experienced a restoration of unusual sensitivity in 1879, to which the attractive stone vaults and the lancets of the clerestory all belong. The crypt entrance, the very grand pulpit, and the tiled floors are also of this date, and although the total effect is no longer medieval, it is nevertheless remarkably good. Lastingham is a pleasant village, being one of the prettiest in North Yorkshire, and its church (especially in east end and crypt) provides important evidence of the scale and the values of the immediately post-Conquest monastic settlement. A diversion here will be well worth its cost.

*Masham** This substantial but over-restored parish church would barely merit the pause were it not for its pleasant situation at the south-east corner of Masham's tranquil market square, with open fields immediately beyond. Once there, however, the church presents several points of interest. Notice first the great size of the Norman west tower, later finished off with a handsome Perpendicular octagonal bell-stage and pretty spire. Inside, this scale is continued in the exceptionally broad nave, no doubt reflecting the wealth of Masham as one of the richest of the prebends of York Minster. The chancel is gloomy and much Victorianized. However, it is from under the chancel arch that the church interior is best viewed, and you should find a moment too for the Wyvill monument at the east end of the north aisle, an early-seventeenth-century confection of classical motifs put up for his wife and himself by Sir Marmaduke Wyvill (d. 1617), both effigies propped stiffly on their elbows. In the churchyard, opposite the south porch, an early-ninth-century Saxon cross-shaft of heroic proportions retains worn but still recognizable figure-carving, including representations at the top of Christ and of the Twelve Apostles.

Middleham The castle at Middleham is something of a curiosity. It was the second castle to be put up in the town, the earthworks of the first (a conventional motte and bailey) being still visible up the hill to the south-west. In the 1170s, a massive stone keep was built on the present site, and it is this that remains the core of the present castle, wrapped around by a curtain wall of the thirteenth century within which lodgings and other additions were made by the Nevilles in the later Middle Ages. Stand back, before you enter, and study the gatehouse front. The machicolations over it and the sophisticated, sharply cut angle turrets are the best surviving indications of what the castle must have looked like as a Neville stronghold and as the regional centre of this exceptionally powerful clan. Equip the whole with battlements and machicolations, with turrets, flags, and stone soldier figures (fragments of these were found in excavations at Middleham), and what you have here is a flamboyant castle of late-medieval chivalry, quite unlike the powerful but sombre Angevin keep at its centre. Notice the domestic ranges against the north, west and south curtains, the many fireplaces indicating comfortable private apartments in these ranges, and the elaborate communal garderobe arrangements in the special tower, built for that purpose, on the west curtain. Then contrast these with the huge hall and chambers formerly on the first floor of the late-twelfth-century keep. By the time that the Nevilles made their own additions to the castle − for the most part, from the mid-fourteenth century onwards − new requirements of privacy and of domestic comfort (including warmth) had been recognized. At Middleham, the two traditions are seen side by side: a contrast as odd in military terms as it was in domestic, for the keep, now surrounded by its late-medieval towered curtain, was as much an anachronism as the accommodation it continued to house.

Down the hill and at some little distance from the castle, Middleham's parish church is a spacious largely fourteenth-century building, owing much to the Neville lordship in the borough. It would have been bigger still if Richard of Gloucester's project to found a memorial college here (approved in 1478) had come to anything substantial. But this was checked by Richard's death at Bosworth in 1485, and the church as we see it now, although certainly worth a visit, has nothing of the magnificence of Fotheringhay, that other longer-lasting Yorkist mausoleum. Restorations in the last century have not been kind to Middleham. Features of interest, though, include a handsome and very lofty Perpendicular font cover (repainted and restored) with, next to it, the grave slab of Abbot Thornton of Jervaulx, carved with his crozier and his rebus, the customary sixteenth-century pun on his name, represented by foliage (for thorns) and a large cask (or 'tun') at the base.

***Mount Grace** The peace of Mount Grace is now shockingly disturbed by constant traffic on the busy A19. Turning into it, you will be taking your life in your hands. Nevertheless, this is still a powerfully evocative spot: unique and worth every minute of the diversion. Certainly, it is the only English Carthusian site to remain sufficiently intact to demonstrate the routine of the monks. Here, round their great cloister, are the fifteen cells (later increased in number as the community acquired fresh funds) of Thomas de Holand's original community, founded in 1398. Each has its door and its food-hatch into the cloister. Yet each is essentially inward-looking: a place, above all, to be alone. Indeed, Carthusian monks seldom spoke to anybody and rarely left their cells. The church at Mount Grace is small, with a diminutive nave and larger (but still insignificant) choir. It was used only on special occasions. In contrast, the individual cells were both spacious and well equipped. Go first to the east side of the cloister, where the cells and their conduit house are especially well preserved. They are somehow more appealing than the total reconstruction, made earlier this century in the north range. Notice everywhere the meticulous planning, the elaborate arrangements for drainage at each cell, the fireplace to guard against the winter's chill, the garden for cultivation and enjoyment in the summertime.

The Carthusians were great readers, showing a special preference for the mystical texts which were enjoying a particular vogue in the later Middle Ages. At Mount Grace, Richard Methley was a home-grown mystic, and it is easy still to reconstruct the life he led there, sheltered from the world but enjoying its respect, embodying the best in late-medieval religion, with more than a flavour of that one-to-one relationship with God that would emerge as the root principle of Protestantism. Stay at Mount Grace as long as you can. It is not as impressive as Fountains, nor as beautiful as Rievaulx. Yet you are very close to God in its cloister.

76 The mutilated but still impressive west front of the Gilbertine church at Old Malton: high-quality Early English work with an inserted Perpendicular window over the west door

**Old Malton Coming south from Pickering on the A169, there is no need to enter Malton itself, for you will see Old Malton Church by the roadside on your left, almost immediately after crossing the Malton bypass (A64). The church is a remarkable fragment, being almost all that is left of an important Gilbertine priory, founded by Eustace fitzJohn in *c.* 1150 and endowed then and subsequently with the churches and hospitals, granges and other properties, that made it one of the wealthier houses of its order. What remains at Old Malton is the western portion of the canons' former nave, shorn of its aisles and retaining only one of its paired west towers, but still enough to demonstrate the considerable scale of the priory church completed here by about 1200. Demolition after the Dissolution was piecemeal, and it was not until the 1730s that the nave lost its clerestory and the roof was lowered, resulting in the blocking of the upper lights of the great Perpendicular window, itself a fifteenth-century insertion in the noble Early English west front. Inside, the effect of these alterations, of the fire of *c.* 1500, and of successive truncations of the fabric is peculiar. The south arcade, so far as it goes, is intact and of the late twelfth century. In the north arcade, however, a fire some decades before the suppression of the priory caused a rebuilding finished-off with Perpendicular panelling, inscribed and with the rebus of Prior Roger Shotton (an arrow shot through a barrel, or tun). Late Victorian refurnishing, quite well done for its date but nevertheless intrusive, has taken much of the character from the building. But look at the plan displayed in the church, and try to visualize the priory as complete. Bits and pieces still remain at the east end of the present church and where the cloister used to be, to the south. The total effect, in its day, would have been magnificent.

***Pickering** Castle and church are both worth a visit at Pickering, but whereas the church is central, the castle is set on the northern limits of the town: it is better to take the car to get up to it. No doubt, you will be stopping at the church first, and there is certainly much there of interest. Most obvious, from the moment you enter the building, are the famous wall-paintings in the nave, dating to the fifteenth century (although since much restored) and probably executed shortly after the completion of the new clerestory, which still assists us to study them. You will see, over the north arcade, a great St Christopher in the traditional placing, with a handsome St George and Dragon next on the west, and with four scenes (a Coronation of the Virgin, a Herod's Feast, and the Martyrdoms of St Edmund and St Thomas) to the east. Facing them on the opposite wall, a complex St Catherine cycle fills the large space west of the south transept arch; to the west again, the Seven Acts of Mercy run without pause into a Passion cycle, with a Burial of the Virgin above, and with a splendid Hell Mouth (Descent into Hell) and Resurrection below. Quite the best place to view these as a whole is from under the central opening of the chancel screen, while it is from here too that you can appreciate the difference (a text-book case) between the heavy north arcade of *c.* 1140 and the much lighter columned piers of the south arcade, dating to towards the end of the same century. Below

the chancel arch, on the north, the handsome knight effigy is probably a memorial to Sir William Brus, founder of a chantry at Pickering Church in the 1330s. The chancel itself is a spacious early-fourteenth-century rebuild, with piscina and triple sedilia of that date. To its south, the Bruce Chapel holds a good monument, with paired alabaster effigies, to Sir David de Rawcliffe (d. 1407) and to Margery his wife, both at one time in the service of John of Gaunt.

Sir David was master forester as well as constable of Pickering, and it is the hunting in the area, through the great Forest of Pickering, that probably explains the continued occupation of a castle which, very early in its life, had begun to look distinctly old-fashioned. Today, Pickering Castle preserves one of our most complete motte-and-bailey layouts, where a stone wall replaced the timber defences of the inner bailey in the 1180s, where a shell-keep was built on the motte some forty years later, and where the outer bailey (or barbican) was only walled in stone after the raids of the Scots in the early fourteenth century had persuaded the king of the need for such heavy investment. Compared with the baronial castle at Helmsley, just down the road to the west, Pickering remained very unsophisticated. But notice the careful design of the moat-bottom postern gate under Rosamund's Tower at the extreme north-east corner of the outer ward. Closed by a drawbridge of its own and commanded internally by the adjoining King's Tower on the motte, it gave Pickering's defenders a sally-port at just that point in the circuit where the outer moat was exceptionally deep. Whatever the constraints imposed on the designer by the shaky finances of the unlucky Edward II, he remained soldier enough to take advantage of a good situation when he saw it.

***Richmond** Cobbled streets and a great sloping market square make a delightful setting for the important castle which is Richmond's principal monument. It is not by any means a conventional castle, for what we have here is one of the first stone-walled fortresses of the Anglo-Norman settlement: a home and a retreat for the Breton soldiery of Alan the Red when everywhere the defeated English were restless and on the point of rebellion. The roughly triangular plan of Richmond Castle's great court, with the keep (formerly a gatehouse) at its apex and with a precipitous descent to the River Swale on the south, reflects the initial hasty fortification of a site already naturally strong. It was probably in Alan's time (1071-89) that the castle acquired its massive curtain wall, much of which still shows the distinctive herringbone masonry of the period. And it was not very much later that fine domestic quarters were added at the south-east corner of the enclosure, being the handsome first-floor hall (among the earliest and best of its kind) now known as Scolland's Hall, having taken its name from one of Alan's principal officials. Of the original gatehouse, only the inner arch now survives, leading into the ground-floor stage of the magnificent tower-keep, itself a work of the later twelfth century. When the keep was built, a new gateway was cut in the curtain wall to the east, protected by a barbican (now largely gone) to the north. With both original gate arches blocked, the door to the keep was at first-floor level, giving access to a large chamber with central pillar and with three substantial windows on the north. Notice the way the keep's builders have made use of the thickness of the wall to carry a stair up to the great hall above; they have done it again to create several wall-chambers, this being a characteristic expedient of builders of this date, as seen again at such keeps as Norwich (earlier in the century) and Dover (just a little later than Richmond and the most refined of the keeps of this class). Continue up to the roof of the keep, and use this viewpoint to look down on the castle court to the south and to appreciate the improvised simplicity of its plan. The outer bailey, east of Scolland's Hall and known as the Cock Pit, is a twelfth-century addition to the huge enclosure which, for the most part to this day, is as Alan the Red originally marked it out.

Look north from the keep's battlements and the town lies below you, with its wide market-place interrupted in the middle by an island of shops round a church. There is nothing much original at Holy Trinity now, so this is probably the best point from which to view it, especially as you can see from here also the more imposing parish church (tucked down the slope to the north-east) and the delicate crossing-tower (itself a rare survival) of the former Franciscan friary church, in municipal gardens to the north. The other friary buildings, apart from a reconstructed gateway, are now lost. At the parish church, a savage restoration by George Gilbert Scott has cost the building any charm it may originally have possessed. However, walking in Richmond is always a pleasure. You can take in the unique Georgian theatre on the way to the friary, and even the parish church, if approached from the north-west, has some features remaining to recommend it. Inside, too, there are at least two items of church furniture worth attention. The first you will notice is the handsome Perpendicular black marble font, with concave side-panels as at Ripon. Next, take a good look at the canopied choir stalls now in the chancel. Although (like everything else in the church) much restored, they are of high-quality sixteenth-century work, having been brought here from Easby Abbey shortly after its suppression. Below the seats, a good set of carved misericords is still in place, while on the cornice above an inscription lists the ten most common breaches of the monastic vows, once intended as a reminder to the canons of their weaknesses.

***Rievaulx The outstanding natural beauty of Rievaulx's setting has earned it the admiration of many. Shakespeare, one feels, must have had Rievaulx in mind when he wrote of his 'bare ruin'd choirs' (sonnet lxxiii). In the 1750s, the laying out of the Rievaulx Terrace, which you must certainly visit if you can, gave the guests of Thomas Duncombe a vantage point to view the ruins, shiveringly Romantic,

77 Rievaulx Abbey, seen from Thomas Duncombe's Terrace and one of the most remote and romantic of monastic ruins

down below. Steep wooded slopes on either side, a flat valley floor, and inaccessibility – these were the characteristics of a classic Cistercian site, chosen and settled by monks from Clairvaux at the bidding of St Bernard himself. When you enter the ruins, eschew the temptation to linger in the great presbytery and go instead directly to what is left of the nave. Here, in the austere stonework (the square unadorned column-bases) of the monks' first building, datable to within just a few years of their arrival in 1132, you will see what it meant to follow the Rule 'to the last jot', as St Bernard would have had it. Very quickly, other temptations intervened. The great cloister, dating to Abbot Ailred's day (1147–67), when Rievaulx had reached its

apogee already, is exceptionally spacious: it could have had few rivals in the North. A little later in the century, the chapter-house was extended with a fine apsidal end, most unusual in Cistercian houses and replacing the earlier simple square. By about 1200 the refectory was being rebuilt on an expensive vaulted basement; it was to be decorated internally with a handsome Early English arcade. And then, with only a generation at most to separate them, the reconstruction of Rievaulx's church was put in hand. It is the glorious choir and presbytery at Rievaulx, triple-tiered Early English work of the highest quality and of extraordinary ambition, that will remain most deeply bedded in your memory. But consider what it must have meant for a

78 The west front of Ripon
Cathedral, one of the triumphs
of the Early English style,
restored but kept authentic by
Sir George Gilbert Scott in the
nineteenth century

79 A fifteenth-century
Elephant and Castle bench-end
among the choir-stalls at Ripon

Cistercian community to engage in a work such as this. What price now austerity? With St Bernard long dead and with the rivalry of Byland, close at hand, to provoke them, the monks of Rievaulx began easing every rule in their book. Before long, they were to divide their great infirmary into private chambers, although this is now hidden by still further alterations as the abbot, shortly before the suppression of his house, took over the entire complex as his own. In this final generation, Rievaulx must have looked like a country house: its abbot the companion of the local gentry, its monks like the fellows of an Oxbridge college — over-privileged, self-indulgent, and inert. There are times when the apparatus of communal living may destroy or obscure its first purpose. At Rievaulx, beautiful though it is, we can recognize these stages one by one.

Ripon You may find yourself reacting against Ripon Cathedral's well-cared-for look: I did myself. But persevere. Sir George Gilbert Scott cleaned up the famous west front; however, he left it essentially intact. Inside, furnishings like the choir-stalls may look Victorian, but in truth they are restorations (faithful in most details) of what was put there in the late fifteenth century; indeed, the set of misericords from that period is among the best in the country. This is a complex building. Buy a guide or attach yourself to one of the parties led by Ripon's formidable lady custodians. There is much to be explained, starting with the lop-sided look of the tower arch, the result of a rebuilding left incomplete when the Reformation brought such works to an end. You will see this confronting you immediately you enter the cathedral, and of course it was the mid-fifteenth-century collapse of the central tower which accounted for a good many of the changes introduced after that date, inspiring a much more general rebuilding. Late Perpendicular are the choir-stalls and the fine stone screen; in the nave, the greater part of the arcades must be early-sixteenth-century, though a vault was

never completed here in stone, while enough relics survive of the late-twelfth-century church to keep you interested throughout a long sermon. Under the crossing, St Wilfrid's crypt now incongruously houses Ripon's mediocre church treasures. But go down there all the same. If this originally relic-holding crypt truly belonged to the saint's own church, it is a near-unique survival of the Anglo-Saxon Conversion, recalling a seventh-century bishop who, for all his zest for controversy, was more in touch with the realities of the Conversion than almost anybody known to us from that day. Other details worth remarking include the Perpendicular marble font, with concave side panels, towards the west end of the south aisle, the nice early-fourteenth-century glass roundels in the window immediately south of this font, the luscious Decorated sedilia in the spectacular chancel of *c.* 1300, and the great east window (surely among the most gorgeous examples of its kind) also attributable to this date. Go back now to the crossing and look west down the nave to get the full effect of the Early English lancets in their grand double tier, even nobler inside than out. For a cathedral, Ripon's nave is unusually short. However, its breadth and the spaciousness of the crossing restore dignity and grandeur to the building. Were one able to see through, beyond the screen, into the great chancel to the east, this would indeed be a notable interior.

Sheriff Hutton Modern housing estates have robbed Sheriff Hutton of much of its charm. Nevertheless, this is a village full of interest, with a great late-fourteenth-century castle at the west end of its street, a large parish church at the other end to the east, and a grassed-over market-place in between them. The castle, unfortunately, is private property and is much overgrown these days. However, a public footpath runs past its north face, and it is possible from here to get a good impression of what was once a large rectangular building, with squared-off towers at the angles (not unlike Bolton, on which it may very well have been modelled), and with a gate-house on the east side (now hidden by farm buildings) opening into a great outer court on the site of the present-day farm. Sheriff Hutton was built by the Nevilles of Raby: by John Lord Neville (d. 1388) and by his son Ralph (d. 1425), the first Neville earl of Westmorland. Like Raby, the original family home, it was built on the grandest scale, celebrating the rise of a Marcher clan that was coming to rival the Percies. For such Marcher lords, an important require-ment in their castles was plentiful accom-modation for retainers, many of whom were scarcely less noble than themselves. Accordingly, private suites with fireplaces and garderobes of their own were provided in the towers and can still be identified in the ruins. The hall was probably on the south side of the courtyard, adjoining the great south-west tower which remains the best preserved in the castle; other domestic ranges backed on the curtain walls to the north and west but have now almost entirely disappeared.

At Sheriff Hutton, the original castle lay south of the parish church, with a deer-park (enclosed in the 1330s) to the south again. The former has left considerable earth works, confusing but still traceable on the ground. As for the church itself, it con-tains twelfth-century work, including the base of the west tower, but was much enlarged when Sheriff Hutton rose with the Nevilles in the later Middle Ages, acquiring its aisles (north and south of the nave) in the fourteenth century and its chancel chapels and vestry in the fifteenth. The north chapel, built as the chantry of Thomas Wytham (d. 1481), whose memorial brass survives there to record it, also houses two good monuments, the earlier being a knight effigy thought to be Sir Edmund Thweng (d. 1344) and the later an elaborate alabaster monument to Edward Prince of Wales (d. 1484), son of Richard III and of his Neville wife, Queen Anne. Worth noticing too are the good late-medieval roofs of the chancel and aisles; also the fourteenth-century glass surviving in the heads of the north aisle windows.

The handsome box pews, such a feature of the church today and particularly interest-ing in the south chapel, date for the most part to 1838.

Thirsk Take the road out towards North-allerton from Thirsk's busy market-place and you will get the best view of the borough's parish church, round which Kirkgate loops at its northern end. Nicely framed by the Georgian red-brick of Kirk-gate, it is a lavish exterior, rich in pinnacles and in pierced battlements, and especially handsome in its clerestory. The inspiration for such a massive fifteenth-century rebuilding, not all that common in York-shire, probably came initially from Robert Thirsk's bequest, recorded in his will of October 1419 and directed towards the foundation of a chantry of St Anne, endowed sufficiently to maintain three priests. Robert's brass, recording his founder's role, remains at the east end of the south aisle, his burial-place and the site of his chantry. In this south aisle, too, the east window assembles what is left of Thirsk's fifteenth-century glass, and the delicate screens here and at the east end of the north aisle are Perpendicular, as is at least part of the much-restored font cover, the font itself being Victorian. In general, the restorers have been too busy here, and the church is not as attractive inside as out. However, the fine timber roof of the nave is genuinely late-fifteenth-century, which is the date of the clerestory. And one excel-lent product of the restorations was a roof almost as handsome for the much lower chancel, although the contemporary replacement of the chancel arch was singularly ill judged, being exactly where restoration hurts most. Victorian church furnishings and ugly tiled floors complete the alienation of the medievalist. But spare a moment for the ingeniously telescoping brass altar rail, a nice example of nineteenth-century inventiveness in the spirit of Prince Albert's Great Exhibition.

West Tanfield Church and castle gate-house, sited right next to each other at West

Tanfield, make an unusual pair, easily seen and most impressive from the road. Unfortunately, the church was drastically restored (almost rebuilt) in the 1860s. Nevertheless, it retains features of interest and merits a visit, especially for its late-fourteenth-century Marmion tomb and for an odd little construction (perhaps a chantry chapel) in the north-west angle of the chancel, which it surveys through a pattern of diminutive windows, like the box of an anchorite or recluse. On a plain tomb-chest, the two alabaster figures probably represent Sir John Marmion, killed fighting under John of Gaunt in Spain in 1387, and the Lady Elizabeth, his wife. Over them both, a crenellated iron hearse, retaining the original prickets for its candles, is a most exceptional survival. Other Marmion monuments line the north wall of the aisle, but are badly damaged and are not in their original positions. In the same aisle, one window preserves some interesting fifteenth-century glass, including a Crucifixion and four other figures.

Immediately to the south-west, the so-called Marmion Tower is a handsome fifteenth-century gatehouse, with two comfortable apartments on the first and second floors, and with a guard-chamber next to the gate-passage. Note the nice oriel window lighting the hall at first-floor level, and the garderobe projecting from the chamber above. Together, they make up a typically late-medieval private suite, no doubt repeated several times in the buildings of the now demolished castle beyond. Most of the windows in the gatehouse are sixteenth-century replacements, but the substitutions have been made with skill and improve rather than detract from the building.

HOTELS AND ITINERARIES

Yorkshire is a welcoming county. You will find yourself more warmly greeted at the hotels on this tour than anywhere else in England. Happily, too, there is a wide choice. One unusual opportunity is to stay immediately next to the ruins of a Cistercian abbey. **Jervaulx Hall** is a country house hotel of great charm. It looks out on the abbey over gardens and parkland; just the place for the most tranquil of weekends. Take your tea on the lawns of Jervaulx, or cross the county to live as quietly at the **Lastingham Grange Hotel**, ideally set in a hollow of the moors midway between Helmsley and Pickering. Neither is a building of great antiquity, but the location is ancient and the rooms are comfortable. Some find this combination the best.

For those who prefer the busier setting of a country town, North Yorkshire again has much to offer. Richmond, certainly, is a town to linger in, with the **King's Head Hotel** right on the market-place where you can best take advantage of your stay. This is a businessman's hotel and the decor reflects it: one night would probably be sufficient, as it would be also at the **Golden Fleece** at Thirsk — a nice Georgian building like Richmond's King's Head but caught up in the hurly-burly of commerce. To get away from all this, there is no better place than Helmsley, on the southernmost edge of the North York Moors and a well-known centre of tourism. Of course, tourists create problems of their own, but here at least

80 The southern show front of Fountains Hall, a Northern Renaissance mansion of the early seventeenth century, re-using stone from the adjoining abbey ruins

they have caused the Trusthouse Forte chain to put considerable investment into rebuilding the **Black Swan**, and the job has been very well done. Both the Black Swan and the more modest **Crown Hotel**, immediately next door, claim to be sixteenth-century in origin, and both make a feature of their oak beams. For comfort in the international class, for space, and for the pleasures of a long-drawn-out meal, go to the Black Swan. For value for money and for the genuine feel of Yorkshire, book in rather at the Crown; the rooms are excellent, but good though the food is, you will have to dine early with everybody else, and then how will you occupy the long evening?

*   *   *

The Great North Road, as it has done for so long, still marks the division between one side of North Yorkshire and the other; for us, it will serve as a boundary. To the west of it, a busy day might begin in the south with **Fountains** and **Ripon**; a short pause will be all you should require at **West Tanfield**, at **Masham**, or at **Bedale**, but you will need longer for **Jervaulx** just getting to the site, which is something of a trudge across the park, and **Middleham** will again cost you some time. Do not miss **Bolton Castle**, whatever else you may have to sacrifice. It will take you out among the beauties of remoter Wensleydale, and will give you moreover a breathtaking drive across the top of the moors to **Grinton**, on the Swale, before heading east again for **Richmond** and then **Easby**.

East of the A1, **Thirsk** is still in the flat Vale of York and need not detain you for long. Go north to **Mount Grace** and then perhaps, if you have time to spare, take the longer route to **Helmsley** by way of Stokesley (a pretty Georgian town) and the Cleveland Hills (B1257); it will bring you there by way of **Rievaulx** and will tell you more of the isolationist ambitions of the first Yorkshire Cistercians than could any approach from the south. If you have returned to Thirsk, go to **Coxwold** first and then to **Byland**, for this way you will see Byland at its best. From there, it is a short trip to Helmsley and to the start of a broad sweep to the east that will take in **Lastingham** and **Pickering**, **Malton**, **Kirkham**, and **Sheriff Hutton**, none of which ought really to be missed.

If you do not know Fountains already, of course you must go there without fail. Byland and Rievaulx are similarly high priority, but there is something rather special about both Easby and Mount Grace, not least that they are comparatively little known. Of the castles you must see, Richmond, Helmsley, Pickering, and Bolton are the first priority, with Middleham and the inaccessible Sheriff Hutton in the second rank. Try not to miss the crypts at Ripon and at Lastingham, the iron hearse over the Marmion tomb-chest at West Tanfield, or the wall-paintings in the parish churches at Easby and at Pickering. Kirkham is important but not as beautiful as it surely ought to be; for this, go rather to Jervaulx and set aside your alarm at the state of its ruins for at least long enough to appreciate the romantic attractions of neglect. Save Jervaulx for that precious flask of tea!

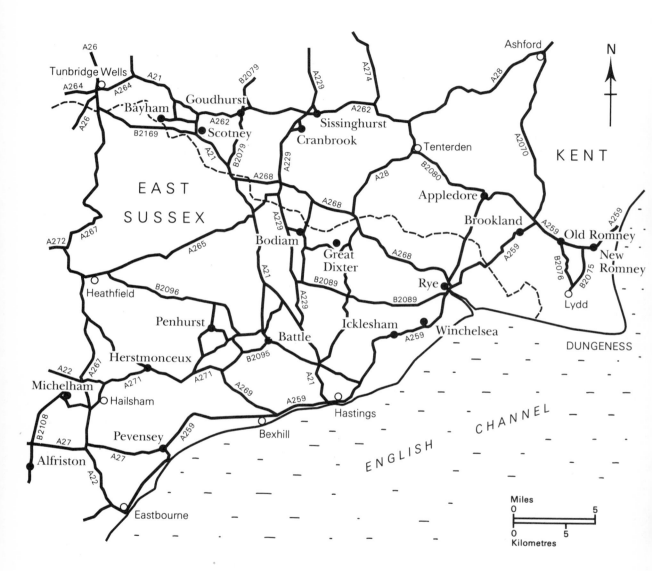

Chapter 8

East Sussex and the Weald of Kent

Clapboard and fine brickwork, white paint and roses – such are coastal Kent and Sussex as we know them today. Yet these shores have been battle-grounds for centuries. Take **Pevensey**: it was here within the circuit of the Roman walls that Duke William set up his original base camp after an unopposed landing; shortly afterwards, the Conqueror's half-brother, Robert Count of Mortain, built the first Norman castle here in the south-east corner of the enclosure; further major works followed John's loss of Normandy, and the fortress had been thoroughly modernized by the mid-thirteenth century to meet the new threat from across the Channel, keeping it secure against all subsequent French raids. Most recently, Pevensey was re-fortified in the Second World War. We do not know when its turn will come again.

81 Mid-thirteenth-century interval towers behind the inner moat at Pevensey Castle

It was just inland from Pevensey and a few miles north of Hastings that Duke William's army met King Harold and his thegns. We know the site and the circumstances especially well, for the Conqueror had vowed, if victorious, to establish an abbey, dedicated to St Martin, that warrior saint, and soon known familiarly as **Battle**. It was the Conqueror's express wish that the monks' high altar should stand on the exact spot where Harold fell: a waterless eminence amongst sandy scrubland, with an awkwardly steep descent towards the south. Wine, William promised (and did not keep his word), would flow as freely at Battle as might water in a better-sited monastery. Today, after generations of settlement and cultivation, it is not easy to appreciate the scale of the problems with which the Benedictines imported from Marmoutier had to wrestle. But look at Battle's only substantial surviving building, the great dormitory south-east of the cloister. As reconstructed early in the thirteenth century, it had to run at its south end over an expensive double-height undercroft, compensating for the slope which, in 1066, had protected Harold's position.

With associations like these, Battle requires to be visited. However, its most spectacular memorial, the magnificent abbey gatehouse, has nothing to do with the Conqueror's decades, being the product of a much later struggle. John's expulsion from northern France in 1203-4 had raised the spectre of another invasion to which the south coast, especially, was vulnerable. Pevensey's re-fortification followed the landing of Prince Louis in 1216. At **Rye**, the king's Ypres Tower, facing the sea, is another mid-thirteenth-century exercise in coastal defence. Then in 1338, just after the beginning of that prolonged struggle with France which has since come to be known as the Hundred Years War, French warships arrived (as they had long been expected to do) in the first of many successful raids on the coast. Battle's gatehouse, itself the focal element in a more general fortification of the abbey site, belongs to these years. It had numerous later imitators in the region.

Crucial to the defence of England's exposed southern shores was the confederation of boroughs known as the Cinque Ports. In the absence of a formally organized and permanently effective royal navy, the Cinque Ports had provided a fleet throughout the thirteenth century that could be used to patrol the length of the coast and that was ready to meet most emergencies. In return for such services, the Cinque Ports accumulated privileges. Their 'barons' (as the burgesses and sea-captains liked to be known) grew increasingly restless; they turned to piracy and eventually lost the confidence of the king. Nevertheless, the Cinque Ports were still very strong in the late thirteenth century when **Winchelsea**, one of their number, was re-sited. East Sussex's flat and low-lying estuarine plain had long been vulnerable to more than overseas invaders. There had been good times in the past, when the expansion of the Cinque Ports had coincided with what we now recognize as a prolonged climatic optimum. But the marked deterioration of the weather from the mid-thirteenth century had had an immediate effect on Old Winchelsea. Already in the 1240s, considerable sums were being spent on port works and on defence against the inroads of the sea. Then in 1250 and again in 1252, great storms swept away many houses and churches, beginning a long process of deterioration. It was not until 1288, in another great storm, that the old town was finally lost. However, preparations to move the community, initiated by the king himself, had begun a full decade earlier. Edward I was no stranger to the building of new towns. He had learnt the value of such foundations in the defence of English-held Gascony, and was currently applying those very lessons in North Wales. Each of these towns was laid out, where the site allowed it, in a geometrically perfect grid, never filled at Winchelsea but traceable still on the ground. Defences were constructed, of which Winchelsea's Strand Gate is one of the better survivals, and parish churches, of course, were supplied. Little remains above ground of Edward's borough except its gates and a fragment of the principal church. But if you would like some idea of the scale of the king's enterprise, all you have to do is to enter this church, appreciating that what you are seeing is no more than the original chancel, east of the crossing. Rarely in England has the Decorated style taken off to more dramatic effect. Look at the quality of the piscina and sedilia sets (two of them, no less!) and the exceptional magnificence of the canopied tombs, all of them dating to the early fourteenth century. No expense, it is obvious, was being spared.

In the event, Winchelsea's resurrection from the sea was miscalculated. The significance of the Cinque Ports was already on the wane. The king was beginning to build and maintain his ships elsewhere, in better protected anchorages. The Gascon wine trade, badly affected by French piracy and by the growing need for expensive convoy systems (driving up the cost of transportation), had entered a pronounced decline. Winchelsea itself, despite its lofty situation and new defences, was twice sacked (in 1360 and 1380), and its burgesses put to the sword. Worse even than these raids, over the region as a whole, was the constant threat of more. No area in England (which generally escaped the worst consequences of a struggle always more harmful to France) reflects more obviously the arbitrary brutalities of the war. **Appledore**'s curious church interior – nave and north aisle incorporated under one roof – is the result of a raid in 1380, when the French burnt both parish church and village. Clerical immunities were as nothing. The defender of Winchelsea in 1377, successfully beating off the raiders, who then fell on Hastings instead, was Hamo de Offyngton, abbot of Battle. Neither he nor his associate, Sir Edward Dalyngrigge, were as lucky three years later. It was in 1380, when Appledore was burnt, that Abbot Hamo failed to rescue Winchelsea and

82 The early-fifteenth-century gatehouse tower, with two suites of lodgings over the gate passage, of the moated priory site at Michelham, thus defended against possible French invaders on the South Coast

that Sir Edward was seriously wounded fighting the French. Small wonder, then, that every man who could reasonably afford it in the region turned his mind to the problems of defence.

England is not known for its fortified monastic sites, much more common on the war-torn Continent. Yet here in Sussex, at Battle, and again at **Michelham**, we have what are certainly two of our best examples, the fortification of Michelham coinciding precisely with the worst of the threat to property in the region, at the turn of the fourteenth and fifteenth centuries. Prior Leem's gatehouse at Michelham and his re-dug moats are easily dismissed as militarily of very little value. Today they are merely picturesque. However, it is deterrents that are needed in a warfare of raids, and it would have been these that the prior had in mind. Very similar concerns obviously moved Roger Ashburnham, a local Conservator of the

Peace with Abbot Hamo of Battle and Sir Edward Dalyngrigge of Bodiam, to fortify his manor-house at **Scotney**. This was no conventional fortress. Perhaps never completed, it was overlooked and commanded from the steep rise immediately to the north. But its moats were wide and its approaches were complex. Towards the south, where the moat was broadest, Scotney's machicolations bristled at the road along which the French might have been expected to advance. They never came that way, and Roger and his family slept secure.

Part of the reason for this security was the greater state of readiness into which the south coast as a whole had been brought. Local commanders, among whom Sir Edward Dalyngrigge was prominent, were professional soldiers schooled in the wars in France. They had come home from those wars with a good knowledge of the latest defensive techniques and with a fair understanding of the psychology of the raider, being a role they had experienced themselves. **Bodiam Castle** encapsulates these lessons, for Sir Edward built it in the late 1380s (a decade after Scotney) at the very end of his military career. Once again Bodiam is as much manor-house as castle. However, more than Scotney, its defences are serious and, in its gatehouses especially, Bodiam shows the hand of the wily old soldier. Right-angled causeways and multiple drawbridges, machicolations and barbicans, triple portcullises and murder-holes (*meurtrières*) in the vaulting of the gate-passage – much of this had been learnt or perfected in the French wars, to be re-applied when Sir Edward and his companions-at-arms came back home. Bodiam has gun ports also in the gatehouse walls. But guns in the 1380s were more terrifying than effective, and the weapon that in the end would out-mode the castle still favoured the defender above his opponent. At Bodiam, provision for guns is only one more instance of the up-to-date quality of the fortress that Dalyngrigge had commissioned.

Bodiam was modern in another way also. One of the qualities of lordship most admired by contemporaries was the maintenance of a generous household. Thus Bodiam – like Bolton or Sheriff Hutton in the North, or like the earlier Goodrich on the frontiers of Wales – had to be equipped with numerous separate suites of individual lodgings, each with a garderobe and a fireplace of its own, in addition to the normal public rooms. Such private lodgings, being the architectural manifestation of 'livery and maintenance' and of the private armies which became such an abuse in late-medieval England, were an inseparable element of domestic planning on the grander scale. In Bodiam, a one-period building, they are contrived with exemplary ingenuity. But they occur also, of course, on the two upper storeys of Prior Leem's contemporary gatehouse at **Michelham**, and would certainly have been a feature of the accommodation at Sir Roger Fiennes's **Herstmonceux** before the many demolitions and remodellings it later suffered. Herstmonceux these days is a hollow crown. There is little inside it worth inspection. But its exterior walls still carry the heraldry of Fiennes himself, builder of the fortress in the 1440s, and its scale and extravagance are appropriate reminders of the fortunes that were yet to be won in the wars in France or at home in the service of the Crown. A clear manifestation of this extravagance was the choice of brick as a building material at Herstmonceux, being in the latest and highest of fashions. Skilled bricklayers at this period were still having to be imported, at considerable expense, from Flanders, where the technique was much older. Here at Herstmonceux they were employed not merely on the castle itself but also on the contemporary addition of a family chapel to the parish church, a short way off to the south-west. Now known as the Dacre Chapel after the noble family into which Sir Roger's son and heir married, it houses the magnificently pompous Dacre monument, pieced together economically from earlier elements but nevertheless an expression of dynastic pride which, in its gaudy but authentic coat-of-many-colours, is a fine expression of the last voice of high chivalry. Of the two Dacre lords represented in pious effigy on the tomb-chest, one was the associate of thieves and miscreants, the other was hanged publicly for murder. Yet there they lie in full plate armour under a canopy rich in family heraldry. The new Tudor aristocracy may have had its faults, but the old was surely ripe for a change.

Alfriston The charms of Alfriston have become too well known; you may find yourself sharing them with half-a-dozen coach-loads of pensioners. Avoid mealtimes, however, and you may be lucky. There is certainly plenty to see, starting with two fifteenth-century timber-framed houses (the Star Inn and the George Inn) facing each other across the delightful main street. Tucked away to the east, behind the broad village green and not easily seen from the street, Alfriston's parish church is a substantial cruciform building datable to the mid-fourteenth-century. Over-restoration has largely ruined its interior. Nevertheless, the fine Easter Sepulchre on the north wall of the chancel is worth inspection, being comparatively rarely found, and there is an interesting piscina and sedilia set, all under canopies, on the south wall facing the sepulchre. Notice too the distinctive concave-sided piers, capitals, and bases of the crossing at Alfriston, anticipating by several decades the development of this design in great Cotswold churches like Northleach and Chipping Campden. But do not linger here. Alfriston's star attraction is not the church but the vicarage, or clergy house, immediately to the south, a timber-framed cottage of the Wealden hall-house type, similarly attributable to the mid- or late fourteenth century. In the care since the 1890s of the National Trust, Alfriston Clergy House has been well looked after and carefully restored. But it was always a building of some quality, as can still be seen in the decorative finish of its doors, in the moulded and crenellated beams at either end of the hall, in the prominent jettying and little oriels. Confirming the purpose of the building, the east bay (where the servants lived) was inaccessible internally from the priests' quarters in the hall and its adjoining store-room and solar. After the Reformation, when priests might marry if they wished, this internal division was done away with and the whole house thrown open to the vicar's family. Poor fellow! To judge from the experience of many

Elizabethan pastors, crushed by the burden of their numerous progeny, he may have wished it had never been so.

Appledore A troubled history adds interest to a church which (in its pleasant, tranquil, present-day setting) is already very appealing. In 1380 French raiders, coming up the still-navigable Rother in their ships, burnt both the church and the village at Appledore. And while the village, of course, shows nothing of this now, the church still bears the scars of their visit. An Early English west tower, with attractive quatrefoil belfry openings, is the principal survival from the pre-raid church. Inside, the odd lopsided look of the nave, with only one broad aisle on the south, is itself most probably a consequence of the raid, after which the former north aisle would seem to have been abandoned, to be incorporated with the nave under one roof. Amateurish reconstruction did not stop there, for the chancel arch (most unusually) is of timber and the south arcade is a primitive job, fairly obviously put together in a hurry. Overall, the effect of these alterations is curious rather than unpleasing, and there are several other features of interest. North of the chancel, the present vestry

83 The fourteenth-century Clergy House at Alfriston: a comfortable timber-framed building in the local Wealden hall-house tradition

is a thirteenth-century chapel, very complete, with a little sanctuary all of its own. Across the church, the parclose screens are late-fourteenth-century; they are intact apart from their Victorian cresting and are a little bit earlier than the central rood screen. The chancel roof is a Victorian rebuild, but the crown-post roof of the nave is original, being best seen from the east through the contemporary woodwork of the chancel arch – an effective and unusual composition. A sympathetic restoration in the mid-1920s resulted in the laying of the present very attractive tiled floor, incorporating what survived of the medieval tiles, some of which have been re-set in the south chapel. In the floor of this chapel, too, there is a medieval stone altar-slab; against the south wall, the handsome tomb-chest and canopy are late-fourteenth-century and may be the monument of William Horne, whose nearby manor-house was attacked in the Peasants' Revolt of 1381 and who then served as one of the king's commissioners, restoring order after the troubles.

Battle Visit Battle – everybody must – but you may not be too excited by what you find there. The interest of the site is, of course, its association with the Conqueror's defeat of Harold on this spot, commemorated thereafter by the foundation of an abbey: its high altar placed where Harold is reputed to have fallen. Inevitably, a town grew up at the abbey gate, and it is this (with its triangular market-place just opposite the gatehouse) that you will see first. Linger at the gatehouse especially. Built by Abbot Alan of Ketling after obtaining a licence to crenellate (fortify) the abbey site in 1338, it is one of the earliest and most handsome of the great fortified gatehouses subsequently built by many monasteries. Within the enclosure, only the west claustral range remains in occupation. Formerly an elaborate abbot's lodging, extended in at least three separate campaigns from the mid-thirteenth century, it was preserved and re-modelled after the Dissolution by Sir Anthony

Browne, master of the king's horse, to whom the site was granted in 1539. Rebuilt again in the mid-nineteenth century, it has long been in use as a girls' school, old-fashioned and distinctly unwelcoming. Skirting the school buildings, you will find yourself overlooking the battle site, with the abbey's guesthouse range immediately behind you. Notice the characteristically tall and slender Tudor turrets still standing to their full height at the west end of this range, being all that remains of the lodgings Sir Anthony began here for the Princess Elizabeth, briefly entrusted to him as his ward. If you follow the path as directed, the next thing you will come to is the south gable end of the monks' great dormitory, one of the many improvements and enlargements to the house which began in the early thirteenth century. Although the dormitory behind it has now gone, the fine vaulted chambers of its undercroft remain intact; more even than the gatehouse, they can tell us something of the scale and importance of the Conqueror's foundation. Beyond these again to the north, the apsidal-ended chapter-house stood on the east of the former cloister, now a private lawn with parts of the otherwise vanished cloister arcade preserved in the school buildings to the west. Of the church to the north, whereas the layout is reasonably clear in the modern gardens, only the east end of the fourteenth-century crypt is exposed. It records an ambitious enlargement of the abbey church during the first half of that century, with a greatly extended choir and presbytery, dwarfing the original nave. After this, the abbey came on harder times and little work was done on its fabric, save further additions to the abbot's lodgings – a characteristic improvement of the last period.

***Bayham** The picturesque quality of Bayham's ruins has been appreciated since at least the mid-eighteenth century, when a 'Gothick' villa (look at it from the north to see its earliest façade) was built on a rise to the west. Since then, the site has been landscaped by Humphry Repton in 1799–

84 A vaulted undercroft, usually identified as the Novices' Chamber, in the east (or dormitory) range at Battle Abbey

1800, remaining for many years the private ruin of the Camden family until its transfer to public guardianship in the 1960s. All of this has given Bayham a slightly artificial air. It is almost too romantic, as a great beech grows out of the eastern apse of the presbytery and as the slopes to the west get mixed up with the garden terraces of the villa. Even the distant gatehouse, off to the north-west, has been incorporated in Repton's grand design. But get into the spirit of it. Bring your picnic here, to enjoy it in the quiet surroundings of one of the more important of England's Premonstratensian houses, the proud possessor of the miraculous bed of St Richard, bishop of Chichester (d. 1253), and of the rare privilege of a nominal foundation direct from Prémontré. The canons of Bayham were not especially wealthy — Premonstratensians seldom were — and their earliest buildings were not, in consequence, very remarkable. However, what makes a visit to Bayham particularly worthwhile is the work carried out here in the 1260s and 1270s during an ambitious extension of the canons' church. Compare the scale of the earlier nave and adjoining cloister, laid out shortly after the canons' transfer here from a less favourable site at Otham in c. 1208, with the rebuilt choir and presbytery of the second period, dwarfing every other building in the complex. And consider also, from what remains of the north transept especially, the high quality and great expense of the new stonework. Bayham's masonry, in this quarter of the abbey, bears comparison with the king's works, going on at this time, at Westminster. Obviously, a costly programme of this kind would strain the resources of the house, and this may be one of the reasons why the canons engaged in a lengthy legal duel with the Augustinians of Michelham over the rights both claimed to the patronage of Hailsham Church. In the end, these two well-off houses fell upon hard times, suffering problems in particular of recruitment. Thomas Cromwell kept his sights on Michelham Priory, which he secured for himself in the first round of suppressions in 1536. Bayham had collapsed even earlier, being the victim of a disreputable deal which transferred its assets to Cardinal Wolsey in 1525 as endowment for his colleges at Oxford and at Ipswich. It says something for Bayham's continuing reputation at this period that the cardinal's suppression met much local resistance, requiring to be imposed there by force.

***Bodiam   Prepare yourself for a trudge from car-park to castle, but you will agree that the separation is essential. Bodiam is everybody's dream of a fortress. Bring a child here, of any age up to the fickle mid-teens, and he will remember Bodiam for the rest of his life. Adults invariably are enchanted by it. Consider carefully, though, what you are looking at. Bodiam is a castle of the Hundred Years War. Although built by an old soldier under licence from the Crown, its purpose was not wholly defensive. Like other castles of that period, including Roger Ashburnham's Scotney, Bodiam was designed to celebrate a life of achievement. It was the plaything of Sir Edward Dalyngrigge's declining years; he put everything he had learnt into its construction. Buy Catherine Morton's excellent guide. You will need a plan anyway to make the most of your tour, and the text will make good reading with your picnic. Study the arrangement of Bodiam's approaches. If raiders from France (against whom the castle was built in the late 1380s) had wished to enter Bodiam, they would have had to cross three drawbridges and penetrate a barbican before even reaching the main castle entrance. Over this, machicolations defended the first of three gates; there were three portcullises and a vaulted entrance passage, with 'murder holes' pierced in the roof. Sir Edward's precautions may seem over-lavish. Yet they are very much in tune with the military thinking of his generation, which continued to place the main defensive emphasis of a castle on its gatehouse. Once inside, the picture becomes very different. Throughout

85 Sir Edward Dalyngrigge's castle at Bodiam, built by an old soldier in the 1380s and making use of his experience in the French wars

Bodiam, as you will find when you come to explore it, there are comfortable suites of private apartments: the grandest in the east range, where the old knight lived, but many others filling the towers at the angles, each with its fireplace and garderobe. Take yourself in particular to the south-east tower; here there is a vaulted undercroft just below courtyard level, with lodgings stacked on three floors above it, each of them fully independent. To preserve appropriate state, Sir Edward felt obliged to maintain a large household, to keep a good table in the two castle halls, and to surround himself with gentlemen of rank. Over Bodiam's entrances, prominent heraldry announces Dalyngrigge's own loyalty to Sir Robert Knollys, his former war captain in France, and records (over the north gate) the family connections: Dalyngrigge flanked by Wardeux and Radynden. Of course Bodiam had its role in deterring the French. After the recent raids on Rye and Winchelsea, it was recognized by the king as an element in the defence of the south coast. But it was also an old warrior's reward.

***Brookland   Do not miss this marvellous church. It is a muddle of dates and of styles, nor is there much in its setting to admire. But Brookland's exterior is already highly promising, its interior one of the most charming in England. Look first at the strange free-standing belfry; it is as early as the thirteenth century in its original timberwork, although of course it has been much tampered with since. Then admire the north porch, rebuilt too at various times but with its fourteenth-century arch (note the characteristic quatrefoils in the spandrels) still intact. Inside, the nave arcades have an intriguing outward lean, but especially striking is the absence of any division between chancel and nave, normally marked by the intrusion of a chancel arch. Work on the present building, no doubt replacing an earlier church on the same site, clearly began at the east end. Here the chancel is of good-quality mid-thirteenth-century work, with the typical roll moulding of the period continuing (in the absence of a chancel arch to break its line) over the nave arcades. Sadly, the original triple lancets of the east window have been replaced, but the piscina and double sedilia on the south wall are authentic, the whole ensemble being a tribute to the generosity

86 The lead font at Brookland Church, with Labours of the Months on the lower tier and Signs of the Zodiac above them; French work of the late twelfth century

period that most of the (very charming) church furnishings belong, including the good double-decker pulpit and box pews. Look especially carefully, before you leave, at the font. It is of lead and carries representations (in the lower tier) of the Labours of the Months — hawking, threshing, haymaking, harvesting, treading grapes etc. — with the Signs of the Zodiac above. It dates to the end of the twelfth century, and probably originated in France, for there is little at all like it in England.

**Cranbrook In this pretty Georgian town, a great Perpendicular 'cloth' church comes as a considerable surprise. Like many of its kind in the West Country and in East Anglia, Cranbrook Church was completely remodelled in the Late Middle Ages. A good brass preserved here is to the clothier Thomas Sheaffe (d. 1520), with his merchant's mark and with a chrysom child (died in infancy) shown next to him. It was by men like Sheaffe that the church was rebuilt, and they made a remarkable job of it. As you go in, notice the unusual outer door to the south porch, said to have been put there in 1569. However, it is the noble and very light interior that you will most likely remember, set off most beautifully by a lovely stone floor and handled unusually sensitively by Victorian restorers, to whom the handsome nave roof is, of course, attributable. From an earlier roof, perhaps as early as the fourteenth century, four carved oak bosses (three of them with 'Green Man' themes) have survived and are now fixed against the wall across the tower arch. They are accompanied by a particularly splendid royal arms, presented in 1756. In the north aisle, the fifth window from the west preserves good sixteenth-century glass, pre-Reformation and very complete, but obviously re-set in this postion. Elsewhere, it is the eighteenth-century monuments that catch the eye, especially the Roberts family tree on the south aisle wall, enough to turn anybody against the gentry. Who now cares a whit for the claim that Sir Walter Roberts, that egregious

of the monks of St Augustine's (Canterbury), holders of the advowson and then appropriators (in 1349) of Brookland. There is good early-fourteenth-century glass in the head of the east window of the north aisle. In the south aisle, again at the east end, a fragmentary but still impressive wall-painting depicts the murder of Thomas Becket at Canterbury, probably dating to the late thirteenth century (a high point in Becket's cult) although re-painted in the Late Middle Ages. Nice crown-post roofs survive in the nave and south aisle, but the aisle windows are eighteenth-century replacements, and it is to this

87 High-quality wood and gesso effigies, in the pre-Reformation style, of Sir Alexander Culpeper (d. 1537) and his wife, at Goudhurst Church

'Baronet of Glastenbury in this Parish', was 'Descended of an Ancient Family Settled there, and in the Neighbourhood for Many Centuries'? It serves him right that he should have become the occasion for our sniggers.

*Goudhurst On the road (A262) between Sissinghurst and Scotney, Goudhurst village makes a pretty composition as it sinks unexpectedly down its hill. But its over-restored church would scarcely be worth the halt were it not for two features of considerable interest. The first of these you can see from the road. It is the west façade of the tower, hesitant Gothic and Renaissance classicism combined, typical of the later 1630s. Evidently, old habits died hard, and when reconstruction began after the lightning-strike and fire of 1637, no countryman was prepared for the Italianate styles winning a more thorough recognition in London. Inside the church, a similar con-

servatism is evident in the rare wood and gesso effigies of the iron-master Sir Alexander Culpeper (d. 1537) and his wife. They are placed on a tomb-chest ornamented with heraldry, and their style (despite the date) is still unequivocally medieval. But notice the clear attempt here at accurate portraiture, and look above them too at the little relief on the wall, again dated 1537 and this time distinctly Italianate.

*Great Dixter There is not all that much, it has to be said, for the blinkered medievalist at Great Dixter. Although fifteenth-century in origin, the house in its present form is largely Lutyens-built, commissioned by Nathaniel Lloyd (the architectural historian). And it is for the garden – surely one of the most sensitively planted in England – that most of us will come here. But Lutyens and Lloyd made a formidable team. The busy timber-work of the main front is a Lutyens conceit for the most part.

88 A fashionable brick castle of the 1440s, built for Sir Roger Fiennes, another returned warrior of the Hundred Years War, establishing his dynasty at Herstmonceux

But the grand two-storey porch is essentially authentic, as is the great hall behind it, although made more splendid by interpolated bay windows. Perversely, the mixture has been complicated still further by the re-erection of a Wealden hall-house (imported timber by timber from Benenden, in Kent) against the back of the service range of the hall. Treat every detail at Great Dixter with the utmost scepticism, but allow it the tribute of your cautious delight, for this is Lutyens very much at his best. Three stars for value, one for authenticity. Take your pick.

***Herstmonceux** Sir Roger Fiennes's magnificent brick castle at Herstmonceux, put up in the 1440s while other fortresses of its kind were rising at Caister (Sir John Fastolf), Tattershall (Ralph Lord Cromwell), and Rye (Sir Andrew Ogard), is today no more than a shell. While authentic enough on the outside, its interior was gutted in the 1770s, to be rebuilt once again on quite a different plan in the earlier decades of this century. In effect, our failure to gain admission beyond the castle gates is no great loss; almost everything we would like to see is external. Note in particular those outstanding characteristics of the French-influenced castles of the Hundred Years War: the wide water-filled moat, enlarged to a lake on the east; the lofty turreted gatehouses, machicolated proudly at the top; the heraldic panel, carrying Fiennes's arms, over the main gate on the south; the ornamental arrow-loops on the gatehouse towers, with circular gun-ports (largely ineffective but very up-to-date) at their base. Sir Roger and the other notable castle-builders of his time had all fought with the king's armies in France, many of them in more than one campaign. When they built their fortress-palaces towards the end of their lives, they were perfectly aware of the latest military thinking and did what they could to take account of it. A fortress like Herstmonceux made a powerful statement about the dignity of its builder, and of course it demonstrated the wealth Fiennes had brought home from campaigning in France and from offices of profit (he was Treasurer of the Household) under the Crown. But its defensive purpose was serious as well. Sir

Roger's younger brother, James, first lord Saye and Sele, was murdered in 1450 by Jack Cade's rebels. For the landowning classes, these were not reassuring times.

Over the road, Herstmonceux Church is similarly well worth a visit. Nasty Victorian dormer windows have given a seaside effect to the aisles. But the arcades are Early English, particularly good on the south, and the monuments especially are important. Of these, a fine military brass in the chancel floor is to Sir Roger's father, Sir William Fiennes (d. 1402); its inscription promises (on what authority God knows!) 120 days' pardon to all passers-by who should say a Pater Noster and an Ave for his soul. Sir Roger's son married a Dacre heiress, and the Dacre Chapel (a brick chantry chapel north of the chancel) recalls the union of the families. Between this and the high altar, piercing the wall, there is a splendid canopied tomb to Thomas Lord Dacre (d. 1533) and his son. The two excellent Caen stone effigies are thought to be bargain purchases from Battle Abbey (suppressed in 1538), and the tomb-chest may also be earlier. But the monument as a whole, with its canopied niches (now robbed of their saints) and bold heraldic display, is an outstanding example of Late Gothic pageantry, barely antedating the iconoclasm of the reformers. In Thomas's will, there had been provision for a chantry. An honest priest, 'being an englisheman borne', was to sing masses for Dacre's soul for seven years. It was to be among the last of such pious memorial foundations, judged superstitious and ineffectual by the Protestants.

*Icklesham Confirmed church-spotters will want to stop here; with reason, for there are several points of interest to explore. However, a mid-nineteenth-century restoration has done much harm, both inside and out. You will need a strong stomach or a blind eye to emerge with your affection for the building still intact. Notice the good Late Norman three-bay arcade, with the Norman south aisle windows surviving (most unusually) and with a nice

oculus window of the period over the arch between this aisle and the south chapel. The base of the north tower is Late Norman too, but the exceptionally large chancel (tilted to the north) is of a later date, giving the church the spacious feel which is now one of its principal attractions. Good Early English blind arcades have been preserved in the north and south chapels, the former with original lancets over, the latter possibly re-set. Externally, the three east windows, with their splendidly ornamental tracery, will have been the most powerful inducement to stop here. But the central (chancel) window dates to the restoration of 1847-52, as do the dauntingly heavy roofs throughout and the greater part of the present church furniture. Above all, turn that blind eye to the corbels of the nave roof, each a *tour de force* of Victorian naturalistic stone-carving but savagely out of character with the Norman arcade just below: they can give you a nasty queasy feel.

***Michelham There comes a point when a medieval building can be exploited too far, and Michelham, one feels, has gone beyond it. Nevertheless, this is an enchanting spot, and if the house is too full these days of the bric-à-brac collections of the Sussex Archaeological Society, there is much left for the medievalist outside it. In particular, Michelham's importance is to be found in the moat that still circles the priory and in the gatehouse, once fronted by a drawbridge, that protects it. Most probably, the moat on the western (or gatehouse) side of the present island has been there since the priory's foundation (relatively late for an Augustinian house) in 1229. However, the completion of the circuit and the building of the gatehouse are usually attributed to John Leem, prior of Michelham for some forty years in the late fourteenth and early fifteenth centuries, which makes them contemporary with many local defensive works, primarily constructed against the French. Take your time over the gatehouse. It is the least restored of the priory buildings and is much the most interesting survival. On the ground floor are the porters' rooms, with an original spiral stair rising through two floors above, each with its garderobe on the landing and with a generous well-lit and well-heated private lodging. Such lodgings, of course, were routine accommodation at contemporary castles: you will find them, for example, all over Bodiam, on the Kentish border, or in castles of the North like Richard le Scrope's Bolton or the great Neville fortress at Sheriff Hutton. Here at Michelham they probably served as private suites for lay officials of the priory or for important long-term guests – the corrodians of which we hear much in Michelham's later history, some of whom were sent here by the king. Look back at the gatehouse from the priory side and you will see the neat arrangement of its garderobes, draining directly into the moat below. Then go on to what is left of the priory buildings and remember that you are approaching them from the western side: demolished church on the left, cloister (now the entrance court) at the centre, prior's lodgings at the surviving southern end of the west claustral range, refectory in the south range on the right. You will have trouble – we all do – in unpicking these buildings. They preserve a splendid vaulted chamber (the former parlour) on the ground floor where you enter, with the prior's very grand guest chamber immediately above it; on one side of the staircase, oddly, the thirteenth-century west window of the canons' refectory has survived. But think of this rather as one of our better examples of a very common Tudor practice after the Dissolution: church and east claustral buildings being almost instantly demolished, while the south and west ranges were preserved as a farmhouse, later developed (in the 1590s) into a small mansion. Michelham's situation in rich farming country was, of course, the main reason for its survival. Yet the charms of its water-bound site were important too, nor was antiquity (best seen in the gatehouse) a matter of small value to the Elizabethans. Even before Michelham's

suppression in 1536, Thomas Cromwell (a connoisseur in such matters) had marked the priory out for his own. It was the first of his many acquisitions as the religious houses fell, the most important of which was to be neighbouring Lewes. When Herbert Pelham built here just before the end of the same century, the melancholy of the ruins had had time to dissipate, while the beauty of Michelham remained.

***New Romney** Two churches have been sewn together at New Romney in a most unusual fashion. To appreciate it fully, go first into the churchyard to the south of the building, and you will see how an ambitious early-fourteenth-century restyling, starting from the east-end, has embraced the greater part of an already grand Late Norman church. Take the opportunity to stand back far enough to get a good look at the exceptionally handsome west tower. Then go inside and what you will find is a good-quality Norman nave – clerestory and original aisles still partly in place – tightly wrapped for half its length in Decorated outer clothing, and then expanded into a spacious triple-pronged east end. Notice the great early-fourteenth-century windows on the east, with their characteristic reticulated tracery: as nice a set as any in England. They flood the church with light, increasing the contrast between the notably generous feel of the Decorated east end and the cramped effect of the Norman arcades, which, were they to be seen in any other setting, would no doubt have appeared to us very handsome. New Romney, on the brink of comprehensive restoration in the 1880s, was rescued by William Morris and his friends. And one of the things we have to thank them for is the survival of a charming irregular floor of stone, brick and tile, nicely setting off this interesting interior. In the town itself there is less to admire. But Priory House (back down Church Approach and across the High Street into Ashford Road) may incorporate the remains of the former hospital of St John Baptist, suppressed in

1495, though its medieval fragments look suspiciously re-set.

**Old Romney The separation of Old and New Romney dates back a great many years, being recorded as early as the twelfth century. Now New Romney flourishes while the older borough has totally decayed. Old Romney Church, a melancholy relic, sits alone among its fields; it would take a heart of flint not to stop there. Furthermore, your sentiment will be pleasantly rewarded. Because of its situation and lack of wealthy parishioners, Old Romney escaped the restoration that ruined many grander churches in Victorian times. Such repairs and alterations as it has experienced in our own era have been done with the greatest sensitivity. While not as interesting as Brookland, just along the way, Old Romney rivals its neighbour in charm, for here also the eighteenth-century church furnishings (though modified and re-painted in a new pink-and-black livery since that time) have been left largely intact. Features of the church are the late-medieval roofing throughout, the nice tiled floor (except in the chancel), the wall-texts, the good Decorated windows at the east end of the south chapel and west end of the nave, and an unusual font of *c.* 1300 with plain Purbeck bowl and dumpy little corner shafts – an odd stitching together of different elements which must cover a wide range of dates. Of similarly mixed date is the strangely narrow chancel arch (more a door, and closed off now by delightful eighteenth-century gates in the 'Chinese' taste), with generous squints on either side. In its present form, it can hardly be earlier than the Georgian refurbishing which once surrounded it with panels; its appearance these days is peculiar.

*Penhurst Much of your satisfaction in this rustic little church will come from its approaches and its setting. Take the A269 out of Battle towards the west; then, as you join the B2204, there is a phone box on the right and a narrow road without a signpost runs off to the north; follow that and you will get to Penhurst, although the signs (when they come) are for Ashburnham. The reward is a simple but charming country church, with a handsome seventeenth-century farmhouse immediately to the south. Good features include nice original roofs – kingpost in the nave, wagon in the chancel – with a simple early screen and Jacobean paired pulpit and reader's desk. Fragments of late-medieval glass have been preserved in the east window, in the north windows of the nave, and in the chancel, on the south. To the north of the chancel, entered through a broad round-headed arch, the chapel dates to the seventeenth century and was probably built as a family pew. Under the tower and behind the present bookstand, the incised slab, with its geometric patterns, may be the setting-out stone of a late-medieval mason, giving him the pattern for window tracery. Outside, the west window is unexpectedly grand on a tower of this scale; round to the south, the timberwork of the porch, although badly worn, is authentically late-medieval.

**Pevensey The castle at Pevensey has a church at each gate: St Nicolas (Pevensey) to the east, St Mary (Westham) to the west. Each of these buildings will be worth a visit, though it is at the castle, of course, that we begin. Most obvious here are the fourth-century Roman walls, patched but little altered by the Normans. They defend a great oval enclosure, re-used by Duke William in 1066 as the first collecting-point in his invasion of England. A Norman ditch at the west gate, now re-filled and not traceable on the surface, is probably all that survives from that episode, the next stage of post-Conquest fortification being the cutting off, before the end of the century, of the south-east angle of the Roman fort and the building there (behind ditch and palisade defences) of a substantial stone tower-keep of which only the base now remains. The east wall of this keep has collapsed, leaving an irregular mass of masonry supplied with curious apsidal buttress-like projections to west and north, the western probably dating to the late twelfth century, when they may have had something to do with a re-sited first-floor entrance on this quarter. Early in the thirteenth century, a rebuilding of the timber defences in stone began with a substantial twin-towered gatehouse on the west of the Norman inner bailey, the circuit being completed in the mid-century by a curtain wall with interval towers, two on the north and one on the south, each of them commanding its own postern. Pevensey was thus brought dramatically up to date, anticipating by some decades the sophistication of the Edwardian castles of North Wales, where the emphasis would rest on the mobility of the defenders, needing to get out quickly themselves for sorties and counter-attacks at least as much as to prevent the enemy getting in.

Pevensey's interest falls off at this period, and you are likely to find its Second World War re-fortification (carefully preserved in the present buildings) both distracting and something of a bore. Go instead to Westham Church, the earlier of the castle's neighbours, where you can see some nice Early Norman round-headed windows high on the south wall, with a fourteenth-century arcade to the north, a pleasant Perpendicular rood screen (best seen from the east) closing off the chancel, and some good fifteenth-century glass (thirteen complete figures) in the head of the grand east window. Outside the church and nicely placed by its gate are two fifteenth-century timber-framed houses: the Oak House with prominent jettying towards the road, the Old Dial House preserving what looks like an original first-floor oriel.

Westham's exterior is the best feature of the church; back in Pevensey, it is the interior of St Nicholas that scores. Good Early English arcades to north and south make a nice frame for the handsome (but considerably later) king-post roof. In the chancel, also Early English, there are the usual triple lancets at the east end, with a splendid internally shafted double lancet on the south wall, virtually in mint condi-

tion. The younger George Gilbert Scott carried out some rebuilding and restoration here in the 1870s, which is one reason why St Nicholas is less appealing outside than in. Yet this remains a pleasant and a rewarding building, especially refreshing after the barrenness of the castle next door.

***Rye**   Many remember Rye as a town of flower-gardens, and you should come here, if you can, in the summer months when every street is ablaze with roses and geraniums and each house looks more covetable than the last. Of course, it is a town with a long history too. Everywhere there are fragments of the medieval borough. On Conduit Hill, the chapel of the Austin Friars, although much knocked about, and re-roofed comparatively recently, is still recognizably a building of the late fourteenth century; in Church Square, facing the south porch of the parish church, a medieval stone gable (with hall behind) is associated with the Friars of the Sack, while there is a particularly attractive timber-framed house (St Anthony of Padua) at the choice position on the corner of Watch Bell Street, prominently jettied and dating to the fifteenth century. The Mermaid Inn (an excellent place to stay) is itself a good building of the fifteenth and sixteenth centuries, situated in one of Rye's prettiest streets. But remember that what you see on the surface is only a small part of the treasures that lie hidden beneath. Like Winchelsea, Rye was equipped with vaulted stone wine-cellars under timber-framed houses frequently given a new façade in the eighteenth century. Walk its narrow and sometimes precipitous streets, and you will quickly come to what remains of Rye's defences: the impressive fourteenth-century Land Gate through which you will have driven to reach the town centre, and the more interesting Ypres Tower at the south-east angle of Church Square – mid-thirteenth-century and (with symmetrical towers at the angles) very up to date, being one of the earliest examples of systematic coastal defence, commissioned and financed by the king. Look out from the gardens just south of this tower, and you will see what Henry III and his advisers were afraid of. Rye was to be sacked by the French on at least two occasions, in 1339 and 1377, and would be threatened many times more. The danger, in each case, was of sea-borne attack, to which Rye, like its neighbours, was most vulnerable.

Partly as a consequence, one must suppose, of these raids, Rye Church is something of a mess. It is an imposing building, particularly impressive at its spacious east end, where great chapels flank the chancel on each side. Here there is some nice Early English work, most notably in the south chapel lancets. But the crossing has fragments only of its original Norman blank arcading; in the nave, the arcades are rather heavy Transitional work of *c.* 1200, nor have they been helped by a sad Victorian clerestory or by the woodwork, again of that period. Burgess pride in this church is reflected in its scale, but in little else.

***Scotney

The grounds of Scotney New Castle (built in 1837-41) are in the great Romantic tradition of English landscape gardening, descending one hill and climbing another, with their focus on the Old Castle at the bottom. Go first after you enter to the Bastion towards the top of the slope, from which a carefully contrived view is obtained of the picturesque moated castle below. Only one tower of the old fortress survives reasonably intact. Its pretty roof and central lantern, supplied in the seventeenth-century rebuilding of Scotney, give it a thoroughly domestic look. But the very French machicolations under this cap are military enough, and what survives of Roger Ashburnham's castle, both here and elsewhere between its moats, is certainly sufficient to establish a more serious defensive purpose. When you get down to the river (diverted to make the moats which are Scotney's principal defence), you will see that Roger's castle is on an island of its own, approached over stone causeways which, as at Bodiam, would have been broken in two or more

89 Mermaid Street in Rye, with the fifteenth-century Mermaid Inn on the right

places by drawbridges. A central gatehouse gave admission to an irregularly shaped inner court, protected at each angle by the sturdy drum towers, of which one remains and of which the emplacements of three others are still visible. In the late 1370s, when the castle was laid out, domestic buildings would have run across the centre of the island, with the hall door opposite the gatehouse. But only fragments of these remain at Scotney today, much complicated by work of the 1580s and by a further considerable rebuilding programme undertaken about fifty years later. All these together make an assemblage of great charm, outstandingly photogenic from almost any angle but loveliest of all from across the moat. Linger here in these gardens for as long as you can. They are historically important for more than one reason, preserving a record at one level of the local response to invasion threats at a particularly low ebb of the Hundred Years War, at another of the sophisticated aestheticism of Late Georgian high society in its final generation, before the vulgarities of industrialization dragged it down.

***Sissinghurst   Our excuse as medievalists for visiting Sissinghurst is that we are here reaching the end of the line. This beautiful house in its still more lovely garden is of mixed date: there are even the ditches (water-filled on two sides) of the medieval manor-house to the east. But the earliest standing work here is of the late fifteenth century, while the tower – Sissinghurst's most prominent feature – is certainly no earlier than the 1560s, for all the pomp of chivalry it recalls. Buy Nigel Nicolson's excellent short history of the house he himself made over to the National Trust; then take yourself to read it in a quiet corner of the garden his mother created. What is immediately obvious is that Sissinghurst's tower is no more than the inner gatehouse of a much grander mansion (now demolished in all but its southern angle) that lay across a courtyard to the east. In one of the upper tower rooms, there is a useful display which makes these relationships at once clear. But you must climb the tower anyway, for it is from its parapets that you will get your best view of the enchanting gardens below, as well as appreciating the more distant prospect away to the North Downs, certainly enjoyed by its Elizabethan builders, whose appetite for such viewpoints was insatiable. Sissinghurst, it has now been concluded, was rebuilt almost entirely by Sir Richard Baker (d. 1594), who had inherited the estate in the late 1550s from his more famous father, Sir John. The entrance range, with another handsome gatehouse, is earlier, the main bulk of it dating to the late fifteenth century, while the gatehouse (of the 1530s) is Sir John's. But note the assured Renaissance detailing – the Tuscan pilasters and Italianate entablatures – of the inner gatehouse and tower. All this was repeated (as we know from eighteenth-century illustrations) in the lost mansion behind: a splendid cocktail of motifs from the Elizabethan Renaissance, as wilful as any in the land. Sissinghurst is called a 'castle', but of course it is nothing of the kind. The tower is a place for flags, a platform for promenaders taking the air, a talking-point, and a folly or conceit. It belongs to the late-medieval tradition of the tower-house, which was often combined with the gatehouse as here, but was itself never designed as a fortification. Compare Sissinghurst with Scotney, with Herstmonceux, or with Bodiam. There are points of resemblance, one would have to admit; but the purpose is no longer the same.

***Winchelsea   Repeated storms and coastal inundations forced the re-settlement of Winchelsea on its present site, to which the burgesses of Old Winchelsea removed in the 1280s. At that time, it was Edward I's intention to build up his new town as a port for the Gascon wine trade, then reaching its peak, and as a centre for the defence of this especially vulnerable stretch of the south coast. Consequently, the town was laid out with great optimism and on a scale soon to prove much too generous. Today, many of the original house-plots, although traceable still on the grid of Edward's late-thirteenth-century town-plan, remain undeveloped. Winchelsea has the look of a failed garden city of the 1920s, but it was failing already in the 1330s, before ever the French came to sack the town and within a generation or so of its re-founding. Settlement had concentrated from the first in the north-east corner of the grid, and it is here that many stone vaults of the town's earliest period survive under neat eighteenth-century houses. They were built, almost certainly, as wine vaults, though they have served a variety of purposes since that time and are many of them still in use. Almost at the centre, an entire block is given over to the parish church, dedicated to that very English saint, Thomas Becket of Canterbury, and one of two churches (the other was St Giles) re-founded on the site of the new town. As you will see immediately, the church is incomplete, nor is it at all clear that it was ever finished. Very probably, work would have slowed down with the increasingly obvious decline in Winchelsea's fortunes, with the withdrawal of royal patronage, and with the mounting risk (confirmed in the raids of 1360 and 1380) of sea-borne attack by the French. Yet what had been achieved before that time was already very impressive. What we enter today through an absurd little Late Perpendicular porch in the blocked eastern arch of the crossing, is the former chancel, with raised sanctuary at the east end and with spacious chapels (now serving as aisles) to north and south. All this, as are the ruins of the transepts to the west, is early-fourteenth-century in the richest imaginable Decorated taste and of the proportions, had it been completed, of a cathedral. Much of the stonework, including the lavish window traceries, has been renewed, and the interior has a somewhat too perfect look. But the reconstructions have been carried out with sympathy, and Winchelsea remains one of our better examples of the Decorated tradition near its climax. Notice especially the elaborate piscina and sedilia sets both in the chancel and (a little later) in the south chapel. But particularly interesting at Winchelsea are the five canopied tombs, all of this period, in the north and south walls of the church. Observe especially the high realism of the clothing of the effigies on the south, their belts spilling over the tomb-chests. This is the style that would culminate soon after in the Grandison monument at Much Marcle.

HOTELS AND ITINERARIES

Nobody could fault the **Mermaid Inn** for oak beams or for period atmosphere. Ideally placed on one of Rye's most ancient streets and tucked away from the noise of all the traffic, the Mermaid makes an obvious choice for this tour, compared with which everything else is bound to look a little second-best. However, the Mermaid is small and not too easy to find on first arrival. A reasonable alternative, impossible to miss as you drive through Rye's centre, is the **George Hotel**, on the High Street. Although hiding behind an eighteenth-century façade, this is a building almost as old as the Mermaid. You will not be disappointed by it as a base for your visit, even while the Mermaid still rouses prickles of envy. A third possibility is the **Hope Anchor Hotel**, at the far end of Watchbell Street: not an old building, but comfortable and magnificently situated. Go to the Hope Anchor Hotel if what you dream of one day is a restful retirement to this very perfect little town of Henry James, of E. F. Benson, and the Worshipful Lucia. No quarter of Rye feeds fantasies as busily as does the junction of Watchbell Street and Church Square. Here the flowers of Rye suggest a tranquillity which even the trampling of foreign teenagers cannot shatter.

Strangely, this opulent region – so much the home of the leisured middle classes – is also uniquely rich in bed-and-breakfast signs, placed improbably in the windows of the sort of period houses which, everywhere else

90 The outer porch door at Cranbrook Church: an unusual feature of
this fine building

in England, are most definitely off limits to the visitor. You could do worse
than take a chance this time, finding your lodgings as you travel. But if
unwilling to risk this, there is the **Star Inn** at Alfriston, a fifteenth-century
building which claims to be even earlier, being much bigger than it looks
from the street. Opposite the Star, the **George Inn** is of a similar date,
seems well kept, and is noticeably cheaper than the Trusthouse Forte alternative. You would be happy in either, and Alfriston certainly, although

awkwardly placed on the extreme western limits of this tour, is not a village you should allow yourself to miss.

* * *

For the gardener and really for everybody else, this area favours summer touring. It would take some doing, but three of England's best gardens – at **Sissinghurst**, at **Scotney**, and at **Great Dixter** – could be visited in one weekend day if you started with Sissinghurst in the morning. **Bayham** and **Bodiam**, both in this northern sector of the tour, have long visiting hours, and could either be taken in first thing in the morning or left till the evening shadows have lengthened. Include **Cranbrook** if you can (it is very close to Sissinghurst), but the best of **Goudhurst** may be seen from the road, and you will not want to delay here if time is pressing.

Along the line of the coast, your itinerary will be determined by where you stay. From **Alfriston**, the castle and churches at **Pevensey** might begin the morning, with **Michelham** by lunch-time and **Herstmonceux** to start the afternoon. **Battle**, **Winchelsea**, and **Rye** must certainly be visited, but the group of churches to the east of Rye is probably for those who have started at that end and whose base for the night has been at the Mermaid, or at the George or Hope Anchor hotels. **Brookland** is very much worth seeing if you can get there: it is a church of great individual character and charm. But attractive also are **Appledore** and the two **Romneys**, and should you have the time, there are those other neighbouring marshland churches (not included here for fear of over-burdening the itinerary) like Ivychurch and St Mary in the Marsh.

What you will not wish to miss is the castle at Bodiam, the priory gate-house at Michelham, or the parish church at Winchelsea; after which, Bayham and Brookland, Herstmonceux, Rye, Scotney, and Sissinghurst are similarly high priority. Pevensey and Battle both have their disappointments. Nevertheless, they should be seen for their historical significance, the charm coming rather in other monuments of the second rank, including the Romneys and Appledore, Alfriston and the 'cloth church' at Cranbrook. To Great Dixter I gave just a single star, but that is because I am not much of a gardener; others, I know well, would rank it higher.

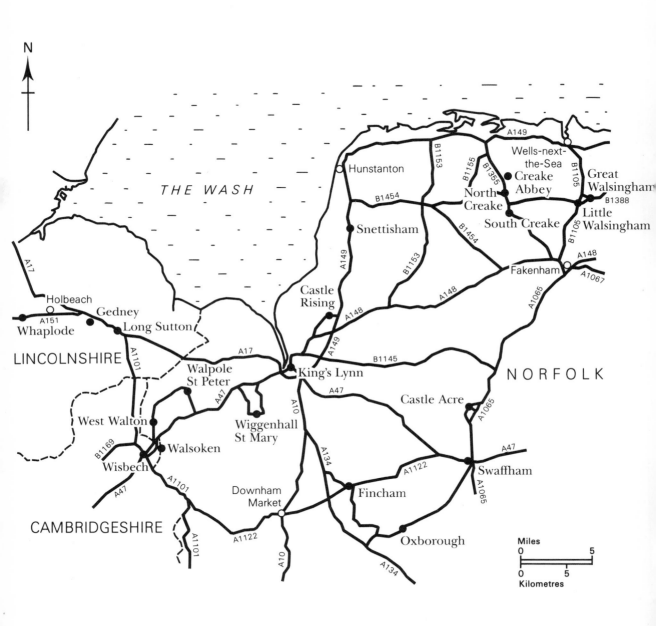

Chapter 9

North-West Norfolk and the Fens

Economic growth and at least a doubling of population were common to the whole of England between the Conquest and the onset of plague in the mid-fourteenth century. However, there was one area in particular – the silt fens round the Wash – that experienced spectacular expansion. In the Middle Ages, it was the parish churches that gave notice of prosperity. Here in the Fens, they seem to shout their riches to the heavens.

Compare the little post-Conquest church, preserved under the ramparts of **Castle Rising**, with its ambitious replacement in the re-sited village, not much more than a couple of generations later. Castle Rising's old church was small, cramped, and very dark; it had a diminutive 'choir' and tiny eastern apse, without room to turn a priest or swing a thurible. In contrast, the new church was exceptionally imposing, conceived on an entirely different scale. An ornate west front was the prelude to an interior which could have swallowed several buildings of the size of its predecessor, whether stacked or laid end-to-end. Moreover, particular investment had been put into the grand central tower, with its cathedral-like mural passage opening into the nave, and with its expensive zigzag-decorated rib-vault. This was not in any sense an economical building. Its purpose was to publish the wealth of its builders, as much as to do honour to God.

On its own, Castle Rising could perhaps be explained as another demonstration of the building zeal of William d'Aubigny, first earl of Sussex and originator of the great fortress on the hill. In electing to do away with the existing parish church, he must have felt some responsibility for its successor. Yet within decades, churches on a comparable or even greater scale were being built everywhere in the region, reflecting local enterprise in taming the marshes and the increasing inadequacy of existing buildings. **Long Sutton** was one of those parishes, just south of the Wash, in which growth in the twelfth century was especially vigorous. Certainly, before 1180 the community had outgrown its inherited timber church and was ready for a reconstruction in stone. It is from this period that a charter survives to record the gift of a new plot, away from the last, on which the parish church should be built. It was the donor's wish, he added, that 'the earlier wooden church of the same vill, in place of which the new church will be built, shall be taken away and the bodies buried in it shall be taken to the new church.' There, presumably, they must rest to this day, in the shadow of the fine church which has itself been preserved by a later casing of aisles and clerestory, the product of still further expansion.

One of Long Sutton's better features is the Late Norman clerestory, decorated externally with a handsome blind arcade now protected by the roofs of the aisles. It is a device repeated at **Whaplode**, to the west, and here the progressive extension of the church is of particular interest and importance. What you will see at Whaplode is a seven-bay nave arcade of which the first four bays are in the monumental tradition of the earlier twelfth century, the last three (much lighter and more sophisticated in character) being of the 1180s or a little later. Internally, the enlargement of the building – presumably to cope with a local population increase – is well marked by the change in floor levels; and while externally the break is harder to recognize, the blind arcading of the clerestory stage shows characteristically greater elaboration towards the west. A growing confidence and improving technique were both apparent in this so-called Transitional phase at the turn of the twelfth and thirteenth centuries. Very quickly, they would flower into Early English, this being the style of Whaplode's magnificent four-stage tower, three stages (below the belfry) expensively finished with blind arcading.

Whaplode's tower was extravagant enough, but take a look now at the even grander **West Walton**, on its barren fen between Wisbech and the Walpoles. West Walton's beautiful free-standing tower is an architectural *tour de force*, dating like the rest of this marvellous church to the 1240s and very much the finest of a distinguished group which includes such other fine towers as Long Sutton's. Happily, West Walton's tower is to be restored and maintained by the State. But a tiny congregation is now otherwise responsible for the fabric of a mighty church, totally out of proportion to its present communicants' resources. More secure is its neighbour, **Walpole St Peter**, 'Queen of the Marshlands' and 'Cathedral of the Fens', a building in the Late Decorated and Early Perpendicular styles which is unquestionably among the finest in England. Yet Walpole's story of collapse and rebuilding, following the flood of 1337, should remind us that there was a price to be paid for living in the Fens, where the fury of the sea might snatch away the wealth that the silt-laden rivers had deposited there and that man had only lately learnt how to exploit.

It is a striking fact, very important to our understanding of this region, that whereas in the Domesday statistics of 1086 the silt fens appear to have been poorer than the uplands on each side, the balance of riches had shifted

91 The detached bell-tower at West Walton Church: Early English work of
the highest quality in this barren Fenland parish

dramatically by the time that the next convincing figures were compiled
for the taxation returns (the lay subsidies) of 1334. In the 1330s, just before
the Black Death, the Fens were many times richer and more populous than
their neighbours. At Fleet, next to **Gedney**, the increase in tenants had
been sixty-two-fold since Domesday, and while this was certainly exceptional, it informs us (even more than do the buildings themselves) of the
pressures that made the church at Gedney so spacious. Indeed, the unusually broad aisles at Gedney, datable like the bulk of the body of this church
to the early fourteenth century, are just what one would expect of a building where what had come to be necessary was more space for a swollen
congregation. Fleet Church was rebuilt at exactly this time and obviously
for identical reasons.

It was the prosperity of this rich hinterland that most materially assisted the growth of the bishop of Norwich's new town at **Lynn** (later King's Lynn), one of the most immediately successful urban plantations of twelfth-century England. Lynn peaked earlier than many other ports, being relatively at its wealthiest in the thirteenth century. But it remained rich and energetic throughout the Middle Ages, many of its finer architectural survivals (in particular the great 'chapel' of St Nicholas) belonging to those decades in the late fourteenth and early fifteenth centuries when its trade was supposedly in recession. Among the attractions of Lynn, especially alluring in the thirteenth century when England was still largely feudalized, was the light lordship which it shared with the more fortunate settlements on the reclaimed marshlands of the locality. To this cauldron of commercial activity, as yet inadequately colonized by the Church, the friars were attracted like bluebottles. One day, it would be recorded in the proverbial wisdom of late-medieval England that 'a fly and a friar will fall in every dish'. In the thirteenth century, however, men still welcomed the friars, for they brought a vigorous religion direct to the market-place, where the word of God was as yet no louder than a whisper. Franciscans and Dominicans, Carmelites, Austin Friars, and Friars of the Sack – all had settled in Lynn by the late thirteenth century. Only the tower of the Grey-friars (Franciscans) remains to commemorate an episode of high importance in the faith. But we can use our knowledge of the friars' settlement in another way too, for it tells us much about the prosperity of the community that welcomed them and of the freedoms which Lynn's burgesses enjoyed.

It was a full century later, and in very different circumstances, that the Franciscans were invited to **Little Walsingham**. They came as the protégés of Elizabeth de Clare, a wealthy heiress whose interest in religion and learning included a devotion to St Francis (to Franciscan minoresses as well as to the friars) and the foundation of Clare College (Cambridge). Predictably, the Augustinian canons who were already at Walsingham, and who were drawing large profits from the custody of its shrine, objected to what they rightly saw as a significant threat to their revenues. To the usual arguments so often advanced against the friars' settlement in the past – the loss of tithes and other revenues, the 'enticements, blandishments and deceptions' by which the friars unfairly attracted to themselves the charity of gullible parishioners – they added more reasonably that there were Carmelites already at Burnham and at Blakeney (both within a few miles to the north) and that the Franciscans could be expected to take advantage of the locking of the priory gates against thieves every night (very necessary in such violent times and with such valuable relics to protect) to ensnare late arrivals and their offerings. To all these separate arguments, totalling seven main reasons and several sub-clauses, the Lady Elizabeth turned a deaf ear. By 1348 there were Franciscans established in Little Walsingham, occupying a choice site right next to the main pilgrim route, between the

Slipper Chapel (where pilgrims customarily removed their footwear) and the gates of the priory itself. As the canons had foreseen, an important building at the friary, the gables of which still rise above the rest, was to be the guest-house next to the great cloister.

In favouring her Franciscans above the Austin canons of Walsingham, Elizabeth de Clare was backing excellence as she saw it, but in a thoroughly traditional way. More innovatory was her endowment of a Cambridge college, originally University Hall, which she supported so liberally that it came to adopt her name. These were early days yet in the transformation of religion. However, in 1348 (the very year that the Franciscans settled in Walsingham) the Black Death visited England in full fury. After this and in the wake of successive visitations of the plague, a line would be drawn across the faith and nothing thereafter would be the same. Walsingham Priory, protected by its cult, suffered less than most. But **Creake Abbey**, its nearest Austin neighbour, was not as fortunate. Creake had never been a rich house, even by the standards of its undemanding order. At its best, Creake had had difficulty in balancing its books, the canons remaining dependent on the generosity of their benefactors and on the occasional fresh appropriation of a parish church. Then, as enthusiasm cooled and as the springs of benevolence ran dry, the abbey descended

92 Blocked Early English lancets in the presbytery at Creake Abbey, one of the smaller Augustinian houses

into poverty. In these latter days, donors had come to favour the reclusive orders – the Carthusians especially, and the Bridgettines; they put their money more readily into chantry foundations, and gave regularly (but sparingly) to the friars. Creake might well have survived, as others did, on the modest returns of its endowment. But a great fire in the 1480s, followed closely by the fatal epidemic of the early 1500s, proved too much for it. Creake's church, after the fire, was patched but was never rebuilt. Picked off one by one in the plague, the community expired on 12 December 1506 with the last breath of Giles Shevington, the abbot.

What then happened to Creake, as it escheated to the Crown, was very much in harmony with the times. There was to be no attempt, then or later, to re-establish a community of Augustinians at the abbey. Instead, Creake's properties were assigned to the support of a favourite project of the king's mother, Margaret Beaufort, that great and pious lady of whom, so Fisher said, all England 'had cause of weeping' on her death. Creake's lands went to Christ's College (Cambridge), but Margaret Beaufort's advanced religious views had already led to the endowment of a divinity professorship at Cambridge of which Erasmus (savage critic of Walsingham and of all its ways) would very soon afterwards be an ornament. Margaret Beaufort – and the much earlier Elizabeth de Clare too in her fashion – had sowed the wind; others reaped the whirlwind. Folly or wisdom; wickedness or solid achievement? You choose.

***Castle Acre**   Priory, parish church, and castle together – this is one of the most important and least spoilt medieval groups in England. You must allow it plenty of time. And if there is any time to spare, of course, there is South Acre to visit and West Acre too – the first with a pretty church (good hammer-beam roof and fine late-fourteenth-century military brass), the second with the remains of West Acre Priory (one of the most substantial Augustinian communities, of which the fourteenth-century gatehouse and other fragments still survive). But first go to the castle site at Castle Acre.

This great late-eleventh- and twelfth-century fortress was the Norfolk estate-centre and then castle of the wealthy Warenne earls of Surrey. Major excavations have recently established a sequence here from unfortified palace/hall to ambitious ringwork-and-bailey castle, all occurring within a handful of decades from the 1070s into the mid-twelfth century. The substantial curtain wall which still surrounds the upper ward must belong to the late eleventh century; within it are the remains of William de Warenne's first hall, later modified and reinforced to make a tower keep; from it to the south, a defended bridge gave access to a substantial inner bailey, similarly walled, just below. Another gate (now the approach from the west) opened from this lower bailey into a still larger enclosure, formerly the defences of a small market town. During the days of the castle's prominence, the borough would have supported an active trading community, and it was for this that a substantial parish church was built, just beyond the western limits of the outer bailey.

Externally, Castle Acre Church is typically Perpendicular, with a great west tower and with a handsome north aisle embracing half the chancel and finished off with a neat two-storeyed vestry capped with delightful stone animals. Inside, as is so often the case with churches of this date, the total effect is somewhat bare and austere. Yet this, of course, is not how it looked in the later Middle Ages, as the survival of some important painted church furnishings makes clear. Study, in particular, the magnificent fifteenth-century telescoping font cover; it has traces of former painting (probably once very gaudy) on the canopy. But hardly less impressive is the splendid little contemporary pulpit, conventionally painted on its four side-panels with the Latin Doctors – St Augustine, St Gregory, St Jerome, and St Ambrose – and of high-quality work for this location. Of similar quality, and dating (like the pulpit) to the early fifteenth century, are the twelve saints' figures on the surviving dado of the rood screen, the sixth from the left being Castle Acre's patron, St James. Other painted panels, probably taken from the mutilated parclose screens in the aisles, have been used as fronts for the stalls (complete with their carved misericords) which face east into the chancel. Several good fragments of late-medieval glass, including a fourteenth-century St George, have been re-set in the east window of the south aisle, another interesting feature of Castle Acre being the way its fifteenth-century builders have made use of the thirteenth-century piers from the earlier building to support their Perpendicular arcade. Recent modernizations in this much cherished church have left its early fittings, including some charming low benches with poppy-heads, looking distinctly out of place. Yet even this is a stage better than inspecting them in a museum, and one leaves the building much in debt to its custodians.

Down the hill to the south-west of the church are the priory ruins: the third and the prettiest element at Castle Acre. The first thing you will see is an early-sixteenth-century gatehouse, with characteristic display of heraldry, the arms of the priory's founders (the Warenne earls) quartered by those of their successors (the fitz Alans). Then, framed by the great car-

93 The pulpit in the parish church at Castle Acre: fifteenth-century work of good quality painted with representations of the four Latin Doctors

riage arch and at some distance down the slope, is a thoroughly domestic-looking building, being the late-medieval prior's lodging of this wealthy Cluniac house, combined with guests' quarters in a greatly enlarged west claustral range. Like many such ranges all over the country, the prior's lodgings at Castle Acre were the only part of the priory buildings to survive the Dissolution. They had just before been converted into a spacious manor-house, appropriate to the prior's rank and his high local standing, and were too comfortable and convenient to be demolished. The

94 The twelfth-century west front of the church at Castle Acre, with the late-medieval prior's lodgings on the right

prior's personal quarters, his solar and his chapel, were on the first floor of this range at its northern end, the solar (or study) being an especially handsome apartment, with lovely oriel windows to the north and the west. Notice the fine fireplaces, backing onto each other, in both chambers. They belong to the final programme of improvements to these lodgings, which included the building of the great bay window overlooking the west end of the priory church, and date to the late fifteenth or early sixteenth centuries. No doubt because of the survival of the lodgings, the immediately adjoining west façade of the church was preserved reasonably intact. Here a large Perpendicular window has been thrust through the front, but quite enough survives of the mid-twelfth-century blind arcading to demonstrate the character and richness of the other priory buildings, almost all of which have suffered such extensive stone-robbing as to be left like a skeleton of coral. Other touches of magnificence include the lofty chapter-house, going up through two floors and formerly ornamented with blind arcading like the church; also the extraordinary elaboration of the great reredorter over the main drain at the southern end of the monks' dormitory, to which it was joined by a bridge. To the reduced community of the later Middle Ages, this lavish provision of lavatory seats (many of the brackets of which still survive) must have seemed to argue for an earlier incontinence and – in the winter especially – appeared excessive.

***Castle Rising** What used to be thought, until very recently, to be an earthwork and stone castle of two distinct periods, has now been reinterpreted in a very different way, which of course adds to its interest. Buy Allen Brown's excellent guide to Castle Rising; it makes characteristically good reading, but is a lengthy work and will probably have to be put aside for later study. Professor Brown's belief is that both the stone keep and its surrounding earth-works date to the late 1130s, following the marriage of William d'Aubigny (or 'de Albini') to Alice the Queen, widow of Henry I (d. 1135). Much later in the same century, the earthworks (hitherto thought to have pre-dated the keep) were enlarged and the ditches re-cut to something approaching their present form, hiding the two-storey keep in the inner ward but still following the line of Earl William's original enclosures. What we have here, then, is a palatial hall keep of a rather old-fashioned form – its parallels are with Norwich, Colchester, and the White Tower – surrounded by a defensive bank and ditch, with stone again used for a gatehouse on the east further protected by an enclosed outer ward on this quarter; yet another (much smaller) ditched enclosure guards the castle's approaches from the west. Notice how unsophisticated these arrangements still are. As at Castle Acre, much reliance is placed on the steep banks of the inner ring-work; the gateway passage, with banks on either side, comprises the ground floor of a simple tower, the present barbican being a later addition; the keep itself is a solid rectangle, with very little development of the mural passage already seen at Norwich and with a straight stair approach to the forebuilding, in which an open galleried vestibule gave access immediately to the earl's hall. Certainly, there are three heavy doors on this stair. But William d'Aubigny's keep should be seen first for what it was: a residence for the earl and his lady. Beyond the handsome vestibule, at first-floor level, a hall and chamber were equipped with their own kitchen (west of the hall) and chapel (east of the chamber); for each main apartment there were two private garderobes; below them, there were basement stores; above, just one further chamber (perhaps for the priest) immediately over the chapel. Early in the fourteenth century, repairs and modifications led to a heightening of the keep and to the addition of another chamber over the vestibule in the forebuilding, then given its present pointed roof. However, the building in most respects is as William d'Aubigny first intended it, giving us precious evidence (especially complete in the chapel and kitchen arrangements) of the accommodation expected by a great lord of the period, while domestic quarters were still comparatively austere. Other quarters, for retainers and guests, would have been built within the banks of the inner and outer wards, although nothing of these is now visible. They may be expected to have taken the form of another hall, great kitchen, and independent lodgings, much added to and extended over the years and probably at their most complete in the middle decades of the fourteenth century when Isabella, the Queen Mother, was in residence.

Today, confusingly, the only stone foundations exposed within the inner ward are those of an earlier parish church, known to have pre-dated the entire complex. A building of the late eleventh century, it provides interesting evidence of the plan of a subsequently little-disturbed church of the immediately post-Conquest decades, having a diminutive and dimly lit apsidal chancel at the east end, a central presbytery or choir (again very small), and a larger nave to the west, supplied with opposing entrances near the end wall and with – a rare survival – wall-bench seating. Compare this very humble little structure with the much grander parish church which soon replaced it. Castle Rising Church, hideously over-restored externally, lies away to the north where it must have had to be re-sited when Earl William came to lay out his new fortress. The gabled roof of the central tower, the entire south transept, and the greater part of the church furnishings belong to the nineteenth-century restoration. However, good features include a handsome Norman west front (the oculus window is modern) and a very imposing large-scale nave of the same period, with typically high-set windows on the south wall only. Rare and interesting also are the two nave altars, one on either side of the west crossing arch: Norman to the north, Early English (very neatly contrived with its own piscina) to the south. The fine early rib-vault of the tower is worth noting, as is the internal wall passage, opening decoratively into the nave; to the east, an outsize statue niche (empty since the Reformation) breaks into the northernmost shafts of an ornate triple lancet, Early English like the south transept arch and the nave altar on that side, and of high quality. In the churchyard to the west, a fine modern monument draws the eye and the step. But be warned: its legend is hauntingly sad.

To the west again, a large parish cross, sturdily set on a heavy octagonal base, is an unusually complete fifteenth-century survival. To the east, the pretty brick Trinity Almshouses (for twelve poor women) are of the foundation of that learned but devious courtier and savant, Henry Howard, earl of Northampton (d. 1614), himself a Norfolk man.

Creake There is little left of Creake Abbey except the east end of its church, with other remains of the conventual buildings incorporated in Abbey House (private property) to the south. However, this is an important site for several reasons; it is also a very delightful and evocative spot, utterly peaceful and unspoilt. You can visit Creake at any time, for there is no guardian to worry you or take your tickets. What you need to know is that Creake was one of the lesser Augustinian houses, beginning life (as was not uncommon in this order) as a hospital, then converted to a priory in the 1220s and raised to abbey status in 1231 after a transfer of patronage to the Crown. Despite this promotion and Henry III's initial interest in the house, Creake was never a rich abbey. What remains of it today belongs chiefly to the earliest building period in the mid-thirteenth century, of which the Early English lancets in the surviving presbytery are an obvious reminder. In the fourteenth century, before 1350, a large north chapel (presumably a family chantry) was added to the north transept, and it is from this that the nicest vistas can be obtained, south-west through the arcades and the crossing. But from this period onwards, Creake's fortunes waned, to reach an especially low ebb towards the end of the fifteenth century, when a serious fire burnt out a large part of the church, leaving the canons without the means to reconstruct it. In the 1480s, following the fire, the nave was abandoned and its walls cut down to near foundation level. Parts of both transepts were also left ruined, and blocking walls were introduced to make a small church of the former crossing, presbytery, and north chapel. We do not know how the fire affected the conventual buildings to the south, but the community at Creake was much reduced by this date, to be wiped out entirely within a few years by one of those epidemics – perhaps, but not necessarily, another outbreak of the plague – that were the scourge of late-medieval England. On the abbot's death in 1506, there was nobody left at Creake to elect a successor, with the result that the abbey and its lands reverted by law to its 'founder' and current patron, the Crown. Almost immediately, they were transferred to the endowment of Margaret Beaufort's Christ's College (Cambridge), to which they still largely belong. Margaret, countess of Richmond and mother of Henry VII, was much given to the support of scholarly works, among her labours being the further endowment of divinity chairs at both Oxford and Cambridge and the planning of another Cambridge college (St John's). In the event, Creake Abbey went a better way than the majority of its fellows, suppressed within a generation of its collapse.

***Fincham** This church has its merits as a single-period Perpendicular building: it has a characteristically fine show-front towards the road on the south, both the hammer-beam roof and the rood screen are good specimens of their period, and the ancient brick floor is attractive. However, there would be little reason to make the short diversion necessary to get here were it not for Fincham's fine Norman font, removed to its present position from the neighbouring, demolished St Michael's.

This crudely carved but memorable piece is one of Norfolk's more touching survivals from the twelfth century. On its north face, Adam and Eve clutch their private parts while Eve plucks the apple; towards the east, the Three Magi (wearing crowns) hold their gifts aloft; to the south, there is a Nativity scene, with Mary, Joseph, and the Christ Child in the manger; to the west, Jesus is baptized by total immersion – the practice still in the larger fonts of Anglo-Norman England, but soon to be modified to the less drastic sprinkling of the infant usual in the later Middle Ages. One merit of re-siting such a font in a Perpendicular church is that the brilliant lighting does it full justice. Fincham's font is a gift to the photographers, even if the faith it recalls is both alien and remote from the sophistication of its present fifteenth-century setting.

Gedney There are some sorts of churchyard gardening that benefit a building, and Gedney's is certainly not one of them. However, nothing can spoil the impact of this finely placed Fenland church: a landmark for miles around. And the promise of the exterior is fully matched inside. At Gedney, the massive west tower is Early English, the north and south aisles are Decorated, and the remarkable clerestory is Perpendicular; the chancel, though lofty and spacious again, has been over-restored and is now the least memorable part of the building. Gedney, as a consequence of the (decently hidden) Victorianization of its chancel, is best seen from the west end looking east – most churches are better the other way round. And this, of course, is the first sight you will get of it as you enter the finely carved south door. Study this door before you go through it, for it is itself a remarkable example of fourteenth-century church carpentry, bearing a contemporary inscription which reads (in translation) 'The peace of Christ be on this house and all dwelling in it. Here is our rest.' On the wicket door, another inscription reads 'In hope', and there is an inset French ivory (a Crucifixion

scene) again dating to the fourteenth century. Once within, a fine stone floor sets off to perfection the lofty arcades carrying Gedney's best feature, the twelve-window clerestory on each side. This in turn lights a good Perpendicular tie-beam roof, patched but still largely original. A big Victorian rood screen, if not seen too closely, helps reinforce the division between the good part of the church and the bad, other features of this noble interior including most of an early-fourteenth-century Tree of Jesse window north of the screen (at the east end of the broad contemporary north aisle) and a good female brass (c. 1400) in the south aisle, once very splendid before it lost its elaborate surround. Gedney Church was one of the properties of the Benedictines of Crowland, an ancient and wealthy pre-Conquest foundation which undertook much reclamation in this part of the fens and which profited, as did the fenlanders themselves, from the rising value of the drained and newly cultivated lands. It was here in the fens that population had grown most rapidly in the thirteenth century, to peak in the early 1300s just when Gedney's church got the wide aisles we see here today. The building is a tribute to contemporary energy, being at its grandest west of the chancel arch, where the responsibility of the parishioners began.

Great Walsingham Due north of Little Walsingham and well to the west of its own village, Great Walsingham Church is a splendid building of the Decorated style, now missing its chancel (demolished in the sixteenth century) but nicely set and full of individual features of interest. Its present form is due to a total rebuilding which seems to have followed the formal appropriation of the church to Walsingham Priory in 1314. The south porch is Perpendicular and so are many of the church furnishings, including the magnificent fifteenth-century benches. However, the four-bay arcades, the lovely clerestory (circles with quatrefoils), the steep nave roof, and the aisle windows with their

95 Fifteenth-century benches, of which a complete set has survived, at the parish church at Great Walsingham

characteristic reticulated tracery, are all of the second quarter of the fourteenth century, while it is to this period also (most exceptionally) that the three church bells belong, cast at Lynn before 1350 and still ringing from the belfry for which they were made well over half a millennium ago. In the heads of the windows, particularly those of the north aisle, some good fourteenth-century glass has survived, and another nice feature is a late-sixteenth-century Memento Mori black-letter text on the north aisle wall, near the east end. But for most visitors to Great Walsingham, the supreme experience is its splendidly intact set of poppy-head pews, all of the fifteenth century though the work of several hands. Notice the way they retain their wall panels in both aisles (a rare survival); in the north aisle, the carved bench-ends (with apostle figures) are of especially good quality; in the south aisle, the angels hold shields bearing initials, presumably those of the medieval donors. A pleasantly irregular brick and tile floor, parts of which may well be original, sets off the whole interior to perfection

***King's Lynn If anybody needs convincing of the evils of wholesale pedestrianization, let him take a look at King's Lynn. What Nikolaus Pevsner, twenty years ago, found a 'delightful little town' scarcely disturbed by nineteenth- or twentieth-century development, is that no longer. After shopping hours, its centre is deserted and its heart is dead, life flickering only on the edges of the ring-road, beyond the car-parks that have done the rest of the damage. It is along the old water-front, between Tuesday Market Place on the north and the Millfleet on the south, that medieval King's Lynn still concentrates. Here there is much to see, with attractive vistas down Queen Street and Nelson Street, and with medieval lanes and passages feeding back to these streets from the quays. Look especially here at the Hanseatic Warehouse on St Margaret's Lane, west of the Saturday Market Place and St Margaret's Church. It is a fifteenth-century timber-framed building, designed to make the best use of a characteristically long urban plot, from the street-front on the east to the quay on the west. Again and again along these streets, behind the elegant disguise of a Georgian façade, you will find this same plot-shape repeated. Next to the Hanseatic Warehouse, immediately to the south, is the imposing courtyard dwelling (Hampton Court) that was one of the larger merchants' houses of King's Lynn. As at Thoresby College, on the corner of College Lane and Queen Street to the north, only a few traces are now visible here of the medieval buildings. But these grand courtyard houses and spacious urban plots can already tell us much, just from their scale, of this once prosperous mercantile community, specializing in trade to North Germany (the Hanseatic towns) and to the Low Countries. The men who treated themselves so well also put money into public buildings. Opposite Thoresby College and immediately north of the church is the gild-hall of the Holy Trinity Gild (1421): a nice chequered gable-end later extended west-wards in the sixteenth century with charac-teristic Elizabethan 'Renaissance' display. Of much the same period, the St George's Gildhall, at the north end of King Street near the Tuesday Market Place, has recently been restored and is now in use as an arts centre. Walk down the lane beside it; you will get a better impression of the hall than its front gable will give you, as well as appreciating the size and shape of the plot on which it is built.

Medieval King's Lynn was of three parts, with the bishop of Norwich's mid-twelfth-century extension (north of the Purfleet) soon coming to rival in importance the older centre (concentrated to the east of the priory church of St Margaret's), and with another settled area (having All Saints as its church) south of the Millfleet. Of the three churches, All Saints is the least interesting and can probably be missed. However, to its north (amongst characteristic urban waste) the fifteenth-century octagonal crossing-tower of the Franciscans of Lynn survives in a small public garden next to Greyfriars Road. It is an important frag-ment, not just for its architectural interest (Franciscan survivals are rare in England) but for its reminder of the role of the friars in the late-medieval urban church. All four major orders of friars, with the short-lived Friars of the Sack in addition, had settled in Lynn before the end of the thirteenth century. They did so because the Benedic-tines at St Margaret's, for all the size of their great church, were a weak dependency of Norwich, and because the town itself was growing so quickly. Elsewhere – at Dunst-able or Bury, for example – they had a much harder time getting established.

There are no more than fragments now of the Benedictine priory that might, had it been more powerful, have put up a better fight against the friars. These lie to the south of St Margaret's Church and include the arch of a great gate. Across a former cloister to the north, the present parish church is an impressive, complex, but ultimately unsympathetic building, much marred by the mid-eighteenth-century rebuilding of the nave and by a subsequent Victorian restoration. The chancel, as one would expect in a priory church, is especially impressive. It is good Early English work with a strange Perpendicular clerestory, and it preserves some interest-ing late-medieval church furnishings, including stalls with misericords, some par-ticularly good carved screens, and a brass eagle lectern. At the other end of the church, the mid-twelfth-century towers have had a chequered history, but the south-west tower is relatively complete and retains some nice Norman details at its base. Most important, however, at St Margaret's are the two great civilian brasses, mid-fourteenth-century and very badly worn, now re-set at the west end of the south chancel aisle. They are of Lynn notables, Adam de Walsoken (d. 1349) and Robert Braunche (d. 1364), and are probably of Flemish rather than English workmanship, appropriate for a port with Flanders trade links. Certainly, it was the prosperity brought to Lynn by its overseas trade that assisted the almost total rebuilding of the other great church (St Nicholas) in the extended town east of the Tuesday Market, completed in a single campaign in the 1410s. The best features of this church, still ranked as a 'chapel' of St Margaret's, are its especially handsome vaulted south porch, its fine clerestory and contemporary angel roof, two good bench-ends (the best are in the Victoria and Albert Museum, South Kensington, and are notable for their accurate depiction of fifteenth-century merchant ships), and the late-fifteenth-century eagle lectern. The tower alone survives from the earlier building, being Early English work surmounted by a Vic-torian spire.

Close to St Nicholas, towards the south-west down Chapel Street, the Lattice House is a fifteenth-century timber-framed build-ing (rare for Lynn) with a long street-front range and two contemporary much shorter cross-ranges set at right-angles to it. The recent conversion to pub and wine-bar has been done with considerable sympathy for the best features of the original structure, and has resulted in the opening up of the hall in the cross-range to the south (against Market Lane), now an attractive bar.

*** Little Walsingham The heart of Walsingham, and our major reason for coming here, is the Augustinian priory (now 'Walsingham Abbey') founded in c. 1169 for the custody of the Holy House (Santa Casa), already a centre of pilgrimage. Not a great deal survives of the priory, nor are the gardens in which it is sited open all that often. Nevertheless, this is a pretty little town, with Georgian and sixteenth-century timber-framed buildings attractively grouped round its two market squares (the Common Place and the Friday Market) and with many individual points of interest. First visit the Shire Hall Museum, one of the nicer buildings on the Common Place: there is a useful display, along with much folk bric-à-brac, explaining the Walsingham pilgrimage. Just down the High Street to the south, the priory gatehouse is a good, if battered, fifteenth-century building incorporating a carved head poking out of a quatrefoil, thought to be a representation of the canons' porter. Beyond it, in the grounds of Abbey House, the remains of the priory are fragmentary but nicely set. They include the very handsome late-fourteenth-century east end of the church (a nice example of expensive East Anglian flushwork in knapped flint and stone), with the south wall of the refectory (about a century earlier), and with the fourteenth-century vaulted undercroft of the canons' dormitory in the former east claustral range, south of the chapter-house. Following excavations in 1961 (the ninth centenary of the traditional, but probably erroneous, date of the first setting up of the Holy House), the site of the fifteenth-century chapel, built to enclose the shrine and its miracle-working image of Our Lady, has now been established immediately north of the priory church, from which it was entered by a door roughly central to the north aisle. It had certainly nothing to do with the dismally modern Anglican Shrine, east of the Common Place, once claimed unconvincingly as its location.

Well to the south, at the bottom of the High Street branching left, Little Walsingham's parish church comes as something of a shock (not wholly unpleasant), having been burnt out completely in 1961 and rebuilt within the original Perpendicular shell. A nice surviving west porch is one of its better features, and there is a good monument in rather antique style to Sir Henry (d. 1612) and Lady Sidney, successors to the post-Dissolution grantee of the priory site to the north. But much the happiest survival here is the exceptionally handsome Seven Sacrament font: a typically East Anglian piece of the best and most elaborate kind, although sadly deprived now of the charming Jacobean cover with which Lady Sidney (of the monument) had equipped it in 1625.

Branch right instead of left and you will come almost immediately to the boundary wall of the former Franciscan friary, on the road south to Fakenham, established at Walsingham in 1347-8 under the determined patronage of that great and pious lady, Elizabeth de Clare (d. 1360), sister of Eleanor (benefactress of Tewkesbury) and of the younger Gilbert, last of his line, who had been killed at the débâcle of Bannockburn. Most regrettably, for such complete sets of friary buildings are extremely rare, the site is private. However, what you can see from a convenient five-bar gate on the road is the southern arcade (three window openings and a door on either side) of the little cloister, with other buildings to the right (part of the dormitory and the chapter-house in the east range of the great cloister) and with the gable ends of a big building (probably the guest-house) rising beyond and to the west. The friary church lay in the usual position north of the great cloister (towards Little Walsingham); it is now almost wholly gone, but excavations in 1932 established its plan – big preaching nave to the west, with the 'walking-place' characteristic of Franciscan churches under a narrow central tower, and with a long choir or presbytery to the east. The situation of the Greyfriars on the main pilgrimage route from the south, together with the size of the Franciscans' guest-house and nave, are all significant, for they show how right the Augustinians at the priory were to object, as they did most eloquently to their 'very honourable and noble Lady of Clare', to an intrusion that threatened their own revenues. In point of fact, the Holy House and image of Our Lady continued to grow in public esteem, and there was money enough for both canons and friars to do well. But the competition was obvious and it could have been fatal if Walsingham, like some other noted shrines in late-medieval England, had experienced a falling-off of interest. That competition, of course, is still rather comically evident at Walsingham today as the Anglican Shrine and its Roman Catholic equivalent at the Slipper Chapel (Houghton St Giles) do battle for the hearts of the faithful. Astonishingly, each shrine is as hideous as the other. If God resides anywhere in Little Walsingham these days, my guess is that He will have chosen the parish church.

Long Sutton A nice small-town market street takes the visitor off the main road towards a great church already temptingly glimpsed to the south. The first thing to be seen is an Early English tower, originally free-standing at the south-west angle of the church, complete with turrets at the corners and with an early lead-covered spire. Like the even finer tower at West Walton, this one had open arches at ground level, subsequently blocked (and showing as such) when the tower was joined with the main body of the church. Extensions to do this, with other alterations including a drastic Victorian restoration, have disguised the original character of a church which, because of its documented building date, is one of the most interesting in England. It was in about 1180, we know, that William (lay owner of the church) gave it in perpetuity to the Cluniac monks of Castle Acre Priory to swell the endowment of their house. Together with the spiritualities of

Sutton, William made the further gift of 'three acres of land in Sutton, in the field called Heoldefen next to the road, to build a parish church there. And my wish is that the earlier wooden church of the same vill, in place of which the new church will be built, shall be taken away and the bodies buried in it shall be taken to the new church.' Here we can see the actual record of a process, no doubt common throughout England in the twelfth century, by which the transfer of ownership from lay hands to the Church was followed closely by a major rebuilding in stone. The monks' new church, to our great good fortune, has been preserved almost entire within the present building. Over the handsome Late Norman arcades, the original clerestory shows as single shafted windows, under a later fifteenth-century clerestory and piercing through to an expensive decorative external blind arcade, now sheltered by the roofs of the north and south aisles. In effect, the whole twelfth-century church, west of the chancel arch, has been protected from the elements by later rebuildings: we know exactly what William and the monks of Castle Acre first intended. In this otherwise over-restored building, three other features are worth attention. A polygonal vestry, with a vaulted lower chamber, projects unusually and very picturesquely at the north-east angle of the chancel; there is a good quantity of medieval glass, including complete figures, in the north aisle window-heads; the brass eagle lectern is Late Perpendicular – it would be exciting if found anywhere but in East Anglia, where such survivals are relatively common.

North Creake A particularly handsome fifteenth-century hammerbeam roof, with nice discreet colouring, full panoply of angels, and an unusually elaborate cornice or wall-plate, is the main reason for stopping at this otherwise rather gloomy church. An oddity here is the absence of a south aisle, which has resulted in a strange piling-up of nave and clerestory windows on this side, giving the nave a lopsided look. Nice quatrefoil openings decorate the pretty early-fourteenth-century south porch, and it is to this period also that the over-restored chancel belongs, the main features of which are a fine tomb-like Easter Sepulchre on the north wall (very splendid and characteristically ornate) and a similarly elaborate piscina and sedilia group south of the altar. Re-set centrally in the sanctuary floor, and now protected by a rug, a large tomb-slab preserves a good civilian brass of *c.* 1500. If this is the brass of Sir William Calthorpe (d. 1495), it is likely to have been moved here from Creake Abbey, immediately to the north, where the Calthorpes, until the early suppression of the abbey in 1506, traditionally lay buried. Certainly, the figure carries a church in his hands, and Sir William is known to have contributed substantially to a rebuilding of the abbey after the serious fire at Creake just a few years before his death.

***Oxborough** Very little of Oxburgh Hall, as we see it now, goes back to Sir Edmund Bedingfeld's original castellated manor-house of the 1480s. Yet Oxburgh, if anywhere, is reason for a suspension of disbelief. It was Georgian Bedingfelds who pulled down Sir Edmund's great hall, doing the greatest damage to Oxburgh's fabric. However, they then did some nice things inside. In contrast, Victorian Bedingfelds perpetrated much ghastliness internally, but decorated Oxburgh externally with the handsome bays and oriels, overhanging the moat, which are now among its principal ornaments. Oxburgh's approaches too, with their fine turreted garden walls, gigantic herbaceous borders, parterres and close-cropped lawns, are incongruous but eminently forgivable. Come here warned that what you are seeing is a fairy-tale concoction of different elements. The moat is genuine and so is the great gatehouse of the north front, which you can see very temptingly from the road. Almost everything else – not that this seems to matter a jot to the OAPs who crowd Oxburgh's tea-room – is an utterly delightful fraud.

Concentrate, then, especially on the north front of Oxburgh, which, in the gatehouse most of all, is a virtuoso performance in late-fifteenth-century brickwork. Notice the crenellations, the stepped Flemish-style gables, the deliberate repetition of the machicolation motif, false everywhere except over the great door. Gun-ports survive at the base of the turrets. However, Oxburgh's defences are about as convincing as those of Archdeacon Pykenham's contemporary brick gatehouse at Hadleigh, one of their closer parallels. At Oxburgh, as at Hadleigh, a statement was being made about the personal dignity of the builder. To be acceptable, it had to make use of the latest and most fashionable building material (brick) and of the prevailing architectural convention (crenellations in the military style). If these combined to make a secure private mansion, proof against thieves and casual marauders, so much the better for the wealthy patron who had plate and other rich furnishings to protect.

Externally, Oxburgh's astonishingly complex brickwork is its best feature. And this you will see again internally in the fireplaces, bays, and vaulted turret chambers of the King's Room and the Queen's Room, over the main gate, but most particularly in the fine rubbed-brick newel stair which links both apartments to the roof platform above and to the Armoury, next to the gate passage, at ground level. Not surprisingly, an affection for the new material – or at least for ceramics – stuck with the Bedingfelds of the next generation, so that their family chantry chapel, built against the south side of the chancel of the now largely ruined parish church, was to be decorated with two of the finest terracotta monuments ever erected in England – products of a short-lived Italian fashion which coincided with the first decades of the Northern Renaissance. Do not fail to pay your tribute to these astonishing objects, both of the 1520s and both crudely extravagant in their mingling of Renaissance motifs. If the chapel is locked (which it usually is), they are plainly visible through its clear-glass windows, one of them piercing through into the chancel next door which is all that

96 The northern show front of Oxburgh Hall: a masterpiece of late-fifteenth-century brickwork with only minimal defensive provision

survives of the parish church. At Oxborough Church also, there is a nice Perpendicular piscina and sedilia group, in the customary position on the south wall. The eagle lectern, furthermore, is a fine specimen, dating to *c.* 1500 and complete with its donor inscription calling on us to pray for the soul of Thomas Kipping.

Snettisham This exceptionally grand mid-fourteenth-century church, with its noble crossing tower and landmark of a spire (rebuilt in 1895), is a triumph of the Decorated style, the characteristic extravagance of which is here particularly obvious in the intricate tracery of the great west window, one of the most elaborate (for a parish church) of its kind. Under the window, a triple-arched Galilee porch is an unusual feature. However, Snettisham sadly has lost its chancel, with the result

that it now has a truncated look, most harmful internally where a mean little chancel has been improvised in the crossing and where the lofty nave arcade looks out of proportion without the balance of a compensating east end. Internally too, the interesting experimental Decorated clerestory – two-light windows alternating with round ones – seems less successful; nor has a fairly thorough Victorianization of the church furnishings helped this rather sombre interior. Points of interest, though, are the soaring arcades with their broad seats at the base (the only seats in the nave before pews were fitted), the exceptionally early thirteenth-century sanctus bell at the west end, the brass eagle lectern of *c.* 1500, and the pleasant pulpit (a tactful Victorian remodelling of its Perpendicular predecessor, incorporating earlier work). Take yourself round to the east end of the church where you can best appreciate both the former scale of the demolished chancel and the quality of the surviving tower. And do try the north door if the west door is locked. The best of Snettisham is visible outside, but it would be a pity to miss the arcades.

***South Creake

A lovely village setting and a marvellously light and spacious interior combine to make South Creake one of the most memorable churches in East Anglia. Notice how well the old brick-and-tile floor sets off the stone arcades and whitewashed walls, and how these in turn make the most of the surviving medieval woodwork. South Creake has lost its fifteenth-century pews, with the exception of a few bench-ends preserved in the chancel just east of the screen, but the screen itself is an exceptionally satisfying and delicate piece, and the little pulpit, although re-set now on a modern base, is a genuine Perpendicular feature. Protestant zealots have very thoroughly defaced the figures (saints and Latin Fathers) on both screen and pulpit, and they may also have had a go at the angels on the hammerbeams of the handsome nave roof, for the wings of these are now mostly replacements; similarly the Seven Sacrament font (once very fine) has been badly hacked about, as have the interesting piscina and sedilia (a Perpendicular set of a very unusual form) in the spacious late-thirteenth-century chancel. South Creake was one of the churches of the Cluniac monks of Castle Acre Priory, and they appear to have looked after it well. Certainly, they served it better than the lay rectors who succeeded them, for it was one of those who, after years of neglect, put in the unhappily cross-beamed chancel ceiling which provides the only jarring note in this fine interior. There is an interesting church chest (iron on wood and perhaps as early as the fourteenth century) under the west tower; the stone seats at the bottom of the nave piers are a comparatively rare feature; and there is much late-medieval glass, including several figures, in the north aisle and clerestory

windows. But what you will want to remember about this splendid church is the whole far more than its parts. It rarely happens that the elements come together so harmoniously.

**Swaffham

Often known in the past as 'Swaffham Market', it is the great market-place at Swaffham that remains the dominant feature of this pleasant, sprawling East Anglian town, with the church tucked away among trees to the north-east. As we see it now, Swaffham Church is almost entirely Perpendicular, being a rebuilding of the second half of the fifteenth century, the west tower (less its fanciful Gothick lantern) completed by 1510. The promise of the exterior – the stone tower and generously windowed brick clerestory are particularly effective – is not quite maintained by the spacious but rather dull interior. Sadly, too, the Victorian church furnishings are over-heavy. Nevertheless, Swaffham's fine double hammer-beam roof, richly decorated with angels, has a good claim to be the best of its kind in Norfolk, and the other roofs in the building, although plainer, are all of them also original. Amongst Swaffham's surviving monuments and fittings, two are especially important. In the chancel, north of the high altar, the tomb-chest and effigy (badly cramped under a re-set contemporary canopy) are of John Botright, rector of Swaffham (1435-74), who was chiefly responsible for the rebuilding of the church following an earlier collapse. Botright was a pluralist, being Master of Corpus Christi College (Cambridge) and Chaplain to Henry VI among other offices, but he seems to have taken the affairs of Swaffham very much to his heart, compiling in his own hand the so-called 'Black Book of Swaffham' as a permanent record (following years of mismanagement) of church property, furnishings, and benefactions. Listed with those who contributed most handsomely to the rebuilding were John Chapman and Catherine, his wife, who built the north aisle (with glazing, pews, and paving of 'marbyll') and who gave generously also towards the new tower. John Chapman, known as the 'Pedlar of Swaffham' and a wealthy local merchant in his day, is portrayed still (pack on back and dog at feet) on two of his own bench-ends, re-used to make a clergy stall on the south side of the chancel arch; opposite, the equivalent stall again re-uses bench-ends, perhaps family portraits, where the Pedlar in his shop has his wife above, both piously fingering their rosaries. Swaffham's parochial records, some of which remain (or have remained until quite recently) in the former priest's chamber over the vestry, are unusually complete. They include memoranda and accounts of one of the more important parish fraternities – the Gild of St John Baptist at Swaffham – covering (with many gaps) the years between 1475 and 1539. Like other local gilds, the Gild of St John would have maintained its own altar in Swaffham Church (the Holy Trinity Gild had its chapel in the north transept, the Corpus Christi Gild at the east end of the south aisle), although we have no record now of its placing.

***Walpole St Peter There is nothing especially promising about the approaches to Walpole St Peter. 'Queen of the Marshlands' is how the church has been described, and marshes are not to everybody's taste. When you get there, however, all changes. Although not remarkable, the immediate setting of the church is most pleasant; the building itself is magnificent. Take it slowly, for Walpole St Peter will be your most cherished recollection of the Fens. Look first at the splendid south porch. It was the last part of the church to be built, and dates to the second quarter of the fifteenth century, carrying the arms of Sir John Goddard (d. 1435), who was among those who contributed to the work. Particularly fine are the carved bosses of the vaulted entrance passage; they include a Last Judgement and an Assumption, with many religious emblems and other pious devices. Modern doors protect the original Perpendicular doors, and then you are inside what has good claims to be the

loveliest church in the country. Immediately appealing is the fine stone floor of this much cherished and beautifully maintained building. But especially nice too is the way that the Jacobean west screen, east of the main entrance, has left unencumbered space at this end of the church, from which its general proportions can be admired. The lofty nave and its aisles are of the second half of the fourteenth century; they were added to a west tower of c. 1300 which was the only part of the original church to survive the flood and collapse of 1337; early in the fifteenth century, a spacious chancel was added at the east end, rising over a curious vaulted passage which is thought to have been put there to give processional space and which handsomely elevates the high altar. It is the chancel, with its canopied stalls and decorative stattue niches, that is the undoubted showpiece of the church; it would be hard to find another to equal it at this period, representing a highly unusual investment on the part of the rector, the then bishop of Ely, at precisely the time when most rectors (like almost every other contemporary landowner) were more given to economy and retrenchment. The base of the fifteenth-century chancel screen survives, with twelve rather crudely painted saints, and there is a nice parclose screen of similar date in the south aisle; the benches in both aisles are late-medieval, as is the graceful brass eagle lectern and contemporary font (dated 1532). Otherwise, the nave furnishings are largely Jacobean (1600-1630), and are none the worse for that, being an exceptionally complete set, with good pews (boxed and taller at the west), a grand solidly-spired font cover, a nice pulpit complete with its tester, a tower gallery, west screen, and poor box (dated 1639). The great brass chandelier, nicely complemented by the smaller modern chandeliers in the chancel, is of 1701.

**Walsoken It is hard to remain unaffected these days by the sad situation of this church, placed as it is in a shabby eastern suburb of Wisbech. But persevere; it is

worth seeking out, even if you have to circle the suburbs to find it. Externally, Walsoken looks Perpendicular. However, the handsome west tower, with its ornate west door and double-tiered blind arcading round the base, is Early English work of high quality, and this gives some clue already to what we should expect of the interior. Even so, it comes as a surprise. The chancel arch is Early English, with odd shaft-rings surviving on the south. But the nave arcades are of the most ornate Late Norman: as well preserved a pair as you will see anywhere in England, and exceptionally handsome of their kind. Take yourself at once to the chancel in front of the high altar, and look back under the splendidly Gothic point of the chancel arch towards the tower arch, similarly pointed, at the west end of the building, with Romanesque arcades (very neat and symmetrical) on either side. Above all this, a good Perpendicular timber roof is supported by a nice light clerestory of the same period, and there is a well-placed Seven Sacrament font (the west face of the octagon given over to a Crucifixion) at the far end of the nave, carrying this inscription on its base: 'Remember the soul of S. Honiter and Margaret his wife and John Beford Chaplain 1544'. Other features of the church include another Late Perpendicular roof (very fine) in the south chapel, with some stalls and bench-ends of the same period, and with a particularly nice, delicately carved two-storey screen separating south chapel and aisle. Over the chancel and tower arches are two curiosities: crudely carved figures of David (with harp) and Solomon (in judgement), formerly accompanied by paintings on either side and dating no earlier than the seventeenth century.

*** **West Walton** Do make a point of visiting this church and of collecting its key if locked. Certainly, many of its best features (including the great detached bell tower and remarkable contemporary south porch) are external. They may be appreciated whether you get into the church or not. But

98 The handsome Late Norman arcades, with Perpendicular clerestory and roof, at Walsoken Church

the quality of the tower, the porch, the west façade, the north door, and the clerestory blank arcading (all Early English and dating to c. 1230-40) is fully maintained in the work within. Broad aisles to north and south flank a magnificent six-bay arcade with decoratively shafted piers and multiple-moulded arches. Beautiful stiff-leaf capitals are a feature of the arcade, which is then finished off with a splendid contemporary clerestory, retaining the original painted hangings in its blank arches – chequered backgrounds with fleurs-de-lis and roses, griffins and doves, medallions, crosses, and quatrefoils. In this spacious, rather crumbling but utterly delightful interior, later additions have

◀ 97 Walpole St Peter from the altar steps, looking back through the chancel arch into the nave usually been tactful, the worst being an early-nineteenth-century east window, the best a handsome Perpendicular roof, with a contemporary fifteenth-century font (good, like the nave roof, but again not of the highest quality) nicely set on a three-step base near the west end. This is a church to linger over, both inside and out. But what you are most likely to remember of West Walton, fixed especially in the mind by its odd placing, is the massive tower, cathedral-like in quality and scale. Apart from its Perpendicular parapet and pinnacles, this is a one-period building, establishing without question the unmatched decorative perfection of Early Gothic. In the porch, the mason's touch is fine but less sure (the sixteenth-century brick gable, of course, is no help); in the tower, he has got it right every time.

**Whaplode   At first the setting of this church seems unpromising, but a broad green churchyard opens out to reveal a fine building at its centre and your interest will immediately be aroused. On the south side, in an unusual position, a handsome Early English tower of four stages (with the characteristic blind arcading on each of them below the bell stage) rises in place of a south transept. Under the nave roof, a twelfth-century clerestory (intact on the north) is again decoratively treated externally with a blind arcade, increasing in elaboration towards the west end of the building, where it has been extended in the latter years of the same century. Internally, the change is marked by an alteration in floor level and by the lighter emphasis of the three final bays, each of them very broad with early stiff-leaf capitals, making this west end (with its lovely irregular stone paving) exceptionally spacious and uncluttered. The chancel arch, low and powerful, is good Norman zigzag. However, the chancel beyond is austere and dull, reflecting a cut-price rebuilding at Whaplode which has generally done much damage to the church's fabric, dating to the seventeenth century. It may be to this period too that the nice but rather flimsy-

looking hammer-beam roof of the nave belongs. But the seventeenth century's most welcome legacy at Whaplode is the grand monument, west of the south door, to Sir Anthony Irby (d. 1610) and to Alice his wife (d. 1625), the pure classicism of its ten posts and canopy somewhat spoilt by the baroque vigour of the crowning heraldic achievement. On one side of the tomb-chest, an infant daughter (Elizabeth) carries the skull that tells us of her early death; the surrounding rail is original; circling the canopy, a bold inscription survives to remind the reader of Irby family dignities and pure blood. What a contrast this makes with the foliated cross slab, now on the floor of the north aisle, which was held to be adequate in the thirteenth century to cover a priest burial of that period! They stand at either end of a funereal tradition at its most extravagant in the later Middle Ages.

**Wiggenhall St Mary   Poor, sad, neglected Wiggenhall St Mary! Its early-sixteenth-century carved bench-ends are among the most elaborate and complete in a county already rich in such survivals. But the church looks abandoned and has been given over to the bats. Come here quickly while you still can. Wiggenhall St Mary has been protected from vandals by its approach through a private yard; it may not always enjoy such immunity. Give most of your time to Wiggenhall's benches: they have fine pierced backs, very splendid poppy-heads, undamaged saints' figures in canopied niches, and other figures and animals on the shoulders. The church deserves rescue for these alone; they will never look as satisfying in a museum. However, Wiggenhall has other good features also, including a fine brass eagle lectern (dated 1518), the painted dado of the rood-screen (with eight saints), and some fifteenth-century glass in the window-heads. The best of the Jacobean furnishings is a nice font cover, surmounted by a bold Pelican in her Piety. But there is also a contemporary pulpit with its hourglass stand still in place, and the monument in the

99 The Early English nave (*c*. 1230-40) at West Walton, seen through the graceful contemporary chancel arch

south aisle to Sir Henry Kervil (d. 1625) and his wife, with much heraldry and a chrysom child (died in infancy) on the tomb-chest, is a handsome piece of its kind, although rather old-fashioned in taste. Please be sure to visit this church. Unlike its sisters in the area, it is at least kept open; and it is in desperate need of your interest and your help.

Wisbech Real prosperity came to Wisbech only in the eighteenth and early nineteenth centuries. Consequently, the town is memorable now principally for its Georgian buildings, of which the most remarkable are concentrated on North Brink, next to the River Nene, with the opposing South Brink only a degree less handsome. Curious and notable too in a market town of this size and character is the elegant early-nineteenth-century crescent, immediately west of the parish church and on the site of the former Wisbech Castle: you could fancy yourself in Cheltenham here, much more readily than in the Cambridgeshire fens. In this setting, a medieval church sits uneasily. But take note of its placing, adjoining the castle and with the market-place (Wisbech's 'New Market' as against the still-used 'Old Market' on the other side of the river) immediately to the north-west. Then admire the north tower, incorporating a porch, which is the building's last medieval feature, and its best. Finished as late as the 1530s, it carries the arms of Thomas Goodrich, bishop of Ely (1534-54), along with much other heraldry and with reli-

gious devices, among them the emblems of St Peter and St Paul (to whom the church is dedicated), the wheel of St Catherine, a chalice and a monstrance (for carrying and exposing the host). Nothing of this elaboration of religious imagery would have been permitted following the Reformation, only a few years away. Inside, the church is distinctly odd. In part this is due to the collapse of a Late Norman or Transitional west tower, causing the north tower as we now see it to be built. However, a major enlargement of the church had already been undertaken in the early fourteenth century, and it is to this that Wisbech owes its most individual feature, the nearly unique double nave. Frozen picturesquely in this rebuilding process is the classically inspired Late Norman north arcade; its equivalent on the south was lost in the collapse of the west tower. This alone would make entering the church worthwhile. But look also at the handsome and unusually large military brass (under the carpet at the west end of the chancel) to Thomas de Braunstone (d. 1401), constable of Wisbech Castle. And pause for the vestry, south of the high altar. Built in the early sixteenth century, it was probably intended as a new chantry or gild chapel for the powerful Holy Trinity Gild (ancestor of Wisbech's later-sixteenth-century Corporation, granted its charter in 1549 in the same year that the gild was suppressed); on the parapet outside are the monogram and rebus, several times repeated, of Thomas Burwell, then prominent in the business of the gild.

HOTELS AND ITINERARIES

Neither King's Lynn nor its once delightful hotel, the **Duke's Head** on Tuesday Market Place, are the attractions they used to be. The one has been spoilt by insensitive town-planners; the other by over-much development and by professional decorators unable to leave well alone. To be sure, the rooms at the Duke's Head are comfortable enough, and the hotel boasts of its food. But how can one justify a 'Victorian' restaurant in perhaps the finest of East Anglia's late-seventeenth-century town-houses? The food

was not as good in the old Duke's Head, but at least the decor did nothing
to interfere with it.

Stay at King's Lynn, for there is much to see and there is no better centre
for your tour. But a night is all you will want to give it. If you are coming
in from the north, the same chain (Trusthouse Forte) runs a more modest
but much pleasanter hotel at the **White Hart**, in Spalding's Market Place;
if from the south, the **Bell** at Thetford, although very much extended to
provide extra rooms, still retains original features of great charm. Going
further afield, the **Angel and Royal** (another Trusthouse), at Grantham,
is a genuine late-medieval inn with a famous fifteenth-century façade. But
you might prefer to save that for another tour.

Comparatively modest hotels which you might consider, all of them having good features, are the **George** at Swaffham, the **Rose and Crown** at
Wisbech, or the charmingly situated **Black Lion** at Little Walsingham,
medieval behind its Georgian façade. Curiously, this is not good territory
for the middle-class restaurant, run by the redundant executive and his
wife, which has recently become such a feature of other touring areas in
the country. You will be lucky if you eat at all well on this tour, for you
will almost certainly have to settle for whatever you can get at the hotel.

*   *   *

The landscape of the Fens is of limited appeal to the outsider, and although
its churches individually are some of the best in the country, you may
not want to linger here too long. **Whaplode**, **Gedney**, and **Long Sutton**
provide a good introduction, but it is the great church at **Walpole St Peter**
that you will particularly want to see, with its interesting near-neighbours,
West Walton and **Walsoken**; nor should you miss, as you head out eastwards on the road (A47) from **Wisbech** to **King's Lynn**, the melancholy
charms of **Wiggenhall St Mary** (the Virgin). Little in the countryside will
have attracted you so far; you may also have had a surfeit of parish
churches. Accordingly, there might be something to be said for by-passing
King's Lynn, heading either south to **Oxburgh Hall** (open in the summer
months from 2–6 p.m. only) and then back to King's Lynn by way of **Swaffham**, or north to **Castle Rising** and perhaps to **Snettisham**.

Castle Acre, with its three important monuments, is not somewhere to
be hurried. So it will be worth striking out in that direction again after
giving what you need of the morning to **King's Lynn**, and (if the weather
is right) taking a picnic for the priory site or castle. A long but fast drive
will then take you north to the very pretty country of the Creakes and
the Walsinghams. There, it is **South Creake** you must see and **Little Walsingham** that will take you most time. **Creake Abbey** may be visited at

100 The great church at Walpole St Peter, so-called 'Queen of the Marshlands'; note the fine south porch, datable to the second quarter of the fifteenth century and one of the best of its kind

any hour, so you could very well save it for the last call of the evening, which would anyway suit the site well.

High priority are Castle Acre and Castle Rising, King's Lynn, Little Walsingham, Oxborough (the Bedingfeld monuments in the church as well as the Hall), South Creake, Walpole St Peter, and West Walton. Creake Abbey, in the second group, is well worth seeing, as are the churches (in particular) at Gedney and Great Walsingham, Swaffham, Walsoken, and Whaplode. Your visit to Wiggenhall St Mary, as well as being instructive, could be chalked up as a charitable deed.

Appendix 1

Opening times

Opening times may vary from year to year. The details given below are intended only as guide-lines. Winter opening times are especially vulnerable to cuts, and should be checked wherever possible against the information published in the annual guides available at most good bookshops.

At present, the standard opening times of Ancient Monuments in the care of the Historic Buildings and Monuments Commission are as follows:

mid-October to mid-March   weekdays 9.30–4   Sundays 2–4
mid-March to mid-October   weekdays 9.30–6.30   Sundays 2–6.30

A shortage of custodians has led to the closing of some monuments on one or two days a week, usually including Mondays; others may be closed over the lunch hour. A few of the smaller monuments are open access, and may be visited at any reasonable time.

Alfriston Clergy House	April–October: daily 11–6
Battle Abbey	Ancient Monument standard hours
Bayham Abbey	Ancient Monument standard hours
Bodiam Castle	November–March: Mondays to Saturdays 10–sunset; April–October: daily 10–6
Bolton Castle	daily in summer months
Burghley House	April–September: weekdays 11–5; Sundays 2–5
Byland Abbey	Ancient Monument standard hours
Castle Acre	Ancient Monument standard hours
Castle Hedingham	May–October: daily 10–5
Castle Rising	Ancient Monument standard hours
Clare	*Castle*: open access to country park
	Priory: private property but grounds open at all reasonable times
Creake Abbey	open access
Easby Abbey	Ancient Monument standard hours
Fotheringhay Castle	open access
Fountains Abbey	Ancient Monument standard hours
Glastonbury	*Abbey*: daily 9.30–sunset (June, July and August 9–7.30)
	Tribunal: Ancient Monument standard hours
	Barn (Somerset Rural Life Museum): daily throughout the year
Goodrich Castle	Ancient Monument standard hours

Great Dixter	April–mid-October: daily (except Mondays) 2–5.30
Grosmont Castle	open access
Hailes Abbey	Ancient Monument standard hours
Helmsley Castle	Ancient Monument standard hours
Herstmonceux Castle	Easter–September: Mondays to Fridays 2–5.30; Saturdays and Sundays 10.30–5.30
Jervaulx Abbey	daily until dusk
Kirby Hall	Ancient Monument standard hours
Kirkham Priory	Ancient Monument standard hours
Little Walsingham	*Abbey*: April, Wednesdays 2–5; August, daily (except Tuesdays and Thursdays) 2–5; May, June, July and September, Wednesdays, Saturdays and Sundays 2–5
	Friary: private property but visible from the road
Longthorpe Tower	Ancient Monument standard hours
Lyddington Bede House	Ancient Monument standard hours (April–September)
Lytes Cary	March–October: Wednesdays and Saturdays 2–6
Michelham Priory	mid-April–mid-October: daily 11–5.30
Middleham Castle	Ancient Monument standard hours
Montacute House	April–October: daily (except Tuesdays) 12.30–6
Mount Grace Priory	Ancient Monument standard hours
Muchelney Abbey	Ancient Monument standard hours
Nunney Castle	open access
Oakham Castle	Tuesdays to Saturdays 10–1, 2–5.30; Sundays and Mondays 2–5.30; closes at 4 in winter months
Oxburgh Hall	April–mid-October: daily (except Thursdays and Fridays) 2–6
Pevensey Castle	Ancient Monument standard hours
Pickering Castle	Ancient Monument standard hours
Purse Caundle	Late April–October: Thursdays, Sundays and Bank Holidays 2–5
Richmond Castle	Ancient Monument standard hours
Rievaulx Abbey	Ancient Monument standard hours
Rockingham Castle	Easter–September: Sundays and Thursdays (Tuesdays during August) 2–6
Scotney Castle	April–October: Wednesdays to Fridays 11–6; Saturdays and Sundays 2–6
Sherborne	*Old Castle*: Ancient Monument standard hours
	New Castle: Easter–September, Thursdays, Saturdays, Sundays and Bank Holidays 2–6
Sheriff Hutton	private property but footpath adjoins
Sissinghurst Castle	April–mid-October: Tuesdays–Fridays 1–6.30; Saturdays and Sundays 10–6.30
Skenfrith Castle	open access
Sudeley Castle	April–October: daily 12–5.30 (grounds from 11)

Appendix 2

A complete list of recommended hotels

Alfriston

Star Inn
High Street
Alfriston
East Sussex
(0323) 870495

George Inn
High Street
Alfriston
East Sussex
(0323) 870319

Bibury

Bibury Court Hotel
Bibury
nr. Cirencester
Gloucestershire
(028 574) 337

Broadway

The Lygon Arms
High Street
Broadway
Worcestershire
(0386) 852255

Broadway Hotel
The Green
Broadway
Worcestershire
(0386) 852401

Burford

Bay Tree Hotel
Sheep Street
Burford
Oxfordshire
(099 382) 3137

Castle Cary

George Hotel
Market Place
Castle Cary
Somerset
(0963) 50761

Chipping Campden

Noel Arms Hotel
High Street
Chipping Campden
Gloucestershire
(0386) 840317

Clare	Bell Hotel Clare Suffolk (0787) 7741	
Fairford	Bull Hotel Market Place Fairford Gloucestershire (0285) 712535	
Glastonbury	George & Pilgrims Hotel High Street Glastonbury Somerset (0458) 31146	
Grantham	Angel & Royal Hotel High Street Grantham Lincolnshire (0476) 5816	
Helmsley	Black Swan Hotel Market Place Helmsley North Yorkshire (0439) 70466	Crown Hotel Market Place Helmsley North Yorkshire (0439) 70297
Jervaulx	Jervaulx Hall Hotel nr. Masham North Yorkshire (0677) 60235	
King's Lynn	Duke's Head Hotel Tuesday Market Place King's Lynn Norfolk (0553) 4996	
Lastingham	Lastingham Grange Hotel Lastingham North Yorkshire (075 15) 345	
Lavenham	Swan Hotel High Street Lavenham Suffolk (0787) 247477	
Ledbury	Feathers Hotel High Street Ledbury Herefordshire (0531) 2600	

Little Walsingham	Black Lion Hotel Friday Market Place Little Walsingham Norfolk (032 872) 235	
Long Melford	Bull Hotel Long Melford Sudbury Suffolk (0787) 78494	
Montacute	King's Arms Inn Montacute Somerset (0935) 822513	
Oundle	Talbot Hotel New Street Oundle Northamptonshire (0832) 3621	
Richmond	King's Head Hotel Market Place Richmond North Yorkshire (0748) 2311	
Ross-on-Wye	Royal Hotel Palace Pound Ross-on-Wye Herefordshire (0989) 65105	
Rye	Mermaid Inn Mermaid Street Rye East Sussex (079 73) 3065	George Hotel High Street Rye East Sussex (079 73) 2114
	Hope Anchor Hotel Watchbell Street Rye East Sussex (079 73) 2216	
Sherborne	Eastbury Hotel Long Street Sherborne Dorset (093 581) 3387	

Somerton	Red Lion Hotel Broad Street Somerton Somerset (0458) 72339
Spalding	White Hart Hotel Market Place Spalding Lincolnshire (0775) 5668
Stamford	George Hotel St Martin's High Street Stamford Lincolnshire (0780) 2101
Sudbury	Mill Hotel Walnut Tree Lane Sudbury Suffolk (0787) 75544
Swaffham	George Hotel Station Street Swaffham Norfolk (0760) 21238
Tewkesbury	Royal Hop Pole Hotel Church Street Tewkesbury Gloucestershire (0684) 293236
Thetford	Bell Hotel King Street Thetford Norfolk (0842) 4455
Thirsk	Golden Fleece Hotel Market Place Thirsk North Yorkshire (0845) 23108
Uppingham	Falcon Hotel High Street Uppingham Leicestershire (057 282) 3535

Wansford

Haycock Inn
Wansford
Cambridgeshire
(0780) 782223

Wisbech

Rose & Crown Hotel
Market Place
Wisbech
Cambridgeshire
(0945) 3187

Acknowledgements

For the plates published in this book, I am indebted to Anthony Kersting for Figs. 4, 5, 9, 13, 14, 16, 17, 19, 21, 22, 24, 26, 27, 30, 32-6, 39, 40, 41, 47, 49, 50, 52–6, 58, 61, 63, 64, 66, 67, 69, 70, 72–4, 76, 78, 79, 81–3, 85, 87–9, 94, 96, and 100; to Olive Smith, widow of the late Edwin Smith, for Figs. 1-3, 6-8, 10-12, 15, 18, 20, 25, 28, 29, 31, 37, 38, 42–6, 48, 57, 60, 62, 65, 75, 77, 80, 84, 86, 90, 92, 93, 95, 97-9; and to Hallam Ashley for Figs. 23, 51, 59, 68, 71, and 91.

Index